The
Principles and Practice
of Political Compromise
A Case Study of the United States Senate

BARRY JAY SELTSER

Studies in American Religion
Volume 12

The Edwin Mellen Press
New York and Toronto

Library of Congress Cataloging In Publication Data

Seltser, Barry Jay.
    The principles and practice of political
compromise.

    Bibliography: p.
    Includes index.
    1. United States. Congress. Senate--Ethics.
2. Compromise (Ethics)   I. Title.
JK1274.S44 1984   328.73'.071   84-14838
ISBN 0-88946-657-2

Studies in American Religion
Series ISBN 0-88946-992-X

The Edwin Mellen Press
P.O. Box 450
Lewiston, New York 14092

Printed in the United States of America

Every book has its intended audience. This one is for that mysterious and humble soul in all of us, the "average American"--confused by the nature of politics, struggling with the inevitable compromises in daily life, and willing to read and to be challenged. This book is for you.

TABLE OF CONTENTS

ACKNOWLEDGMENTS

Books, like other compromises, depend on other people. This one emerges only with the help of many persons, who gave support, time, and encouragement beyond all expectations.

First, I should thank the many writers who went before me into the complicated world of political compromise. In particular, the contributors to the recent volume on <u>Compromise in Ethics, Law, and Politics</u> (edited by J. Roland Pennock and John W. Chapman) have provided a set of insights and ideas upon which I have built in this essay. My other intellectual debts will become clear in the course of the book.

The Aspen Institute provided space, funding, and assistance during an exciting year in its Washington office. In particular, Colin Williams and Steven Strickland helped to make the year possible and worthwhile.

Many intellectual and personal colleagues have read and reacted to this manuscript in various forms. Two sets of seminars at Indiana University--a Poynter Center Interdisciplinary Faculty Seminar and a Humanities Seminar of visiting scholars in the Department of Religious Studies--provided opportunities for much criticism, and I am very grateful to all participants for taking this project so seriously in its formative stages. Three good friends--Dan Chambliss, Kent Guy, and Steve Willett-- read and criticized the manuscript, and will doubtless be surprised to find it in print after all this time. Dan Lowenstein made many helpful comments, and led me in some interesting directions. Herbert Richardson read the book, and (miracle of miracles) liked it. In addition, Henry Clark, Jack Crossley, Ron Garet, Bill May, and Don Miller at the University of Southern California, and Steve Stein and Luke Johnson at Indiana University, have been supportive colleagues and friends at various stages. Their continued confidence in my ability to complete and publish a worthwhile book is a tribute to their generosity, if not to their insight.

Three other colleagues must be mentioned with special gratitude. David H. Smith of Indiana University provided extremely helpful advice (which I have not always followed, of course), and gave me the encouragement and time to continue working on this project while I attempted to follow in his footsteps as a teacher. At Yale, Kai T. Erikson never ceased to believe in this project, and helped me in the search for publishers and readers. And Jim Dittes, as always, was a supportive and close friend of both the manuscript and its author.

Finally, special thanks to the "subjects" of this study: thirty-four United States Senators, twenty staff members, and many other Washington reporters, lobbyists, and researchers. In particular, Senator Jack Danforth was ever ready to help provide the needed resources; the study would not have been possible without his support and effort. His staff assistants provided friendly assistance during a year where I continually harassed them for information, insights, and interviews. I hope they will see the book as an effort to take their lives seriously.

Barry Jay Seltser
Los Angeles, California

The
Principles and Practice
of Political Compromise

INTRODUCTION

Consider the following true stories from the world of American politics:

(1) A United States Senate committee is discussing a proposed reform of the nation's criminal code. The bill is an agreement between the leading liberal and the leading conservative in the Senate: Edward Kennedy (Democrat of Massachusetts, the Chairman of the Committee) and Strom Thurmond (Republican of South Carolina, the ranking minority member). In an effort to hold the coalition together, Kennedy reluctantly beats back each amendment proposed by his liberal colleagues. One such amendment would write into law recent court rulings establishing corporate liability, an issue close to Kennedy's heart. He opposes the amendment, yet he says: "I prefer to have codified it myself....If it was up to me I would like to etch it in concrete." Later, when Senator Howard Metzenbaum (another liberal) demands a stronger consumer fraud protection section, Kennedy replies: "Well, Howard...my heart is with you...but I am afraid my vote isn't." The amendment is then defeated, 8-7, as Kennedy's vote provides the difference when he sides with the more conservative Republicans.[1]

(2) A conference committee of the House and Senate meets to consider two versions of the bill to create a Department of Education. The House version explicitly prohibits ratios and quotas in educational policy, in an effort to forbid most affirmative action policies; the Senate bill does not have such a provision. Both

---

[1] Senate Judiciary Committee, markup of S1722, November 20, November 28, 1979.

sides insist that their chambers feel very strongly about their respective positions on this question, and that to back away would be to undercut the will of their colleagues. Yet, a proposed compromise is eventually accepted, which reads: "There is a continuing need to ensure equal access for all Americans to educational opportunities of a high quality, and such educational opportunities should not be denied because of race, creed, color, national origin or sex." Although the sentence does not explicitly forbid quotas or ratios, it is ambiguous enough to permit the House conferees to agree to this new language.[2]

(3) A moderate Republican Senator decides to vote against a gun control bill, citing organized opposition in his state by a powerful group. In speaking about the issue, he admits that he personally favors such legislation, but that he may not be re-elected unless he "compromises." He argues that he can do more good by remaining in the Senate and fighting for other issues than he could by taking a "hopeless" stand on gun control and being forced to leave office.

Such situations are the lifeblood of American politics. Legislators are called upon to yield on important issues, for the sake of what they perceive as a greater good. We are not surprised that such actions take place. But we are often ambivalent in our reactions to such activities. How do we feel when a senator votes against an amendment which she believes is important? Should elected representatives resolve difficult questions by rewriting sentences to leave the intent of the legislation in

---

[2]House-Senate Conference on S210, September 13, 1979.

doubt? Are we comfortable when a group of legislators, acting on behalf of colleagues, agrees to a proposal which was overwhelmingly defeated on the floor? Can a politician be allowed to change his vote by citing the need for re-election?

Such questions concern the appropriate role of compromise in politics. This book addresses the question in two closely related ways. First, we want to understand why compromise plays the role it does in our law-making organizations. Second, we want to ask how appropriate, or how correct, compromise is in such settings. In other words, are there, and should there be, any limits to the process of compromise?

The subject of compromise occupies an odd place in the writings on American politics. On the one hand, almost any book or article provides numerous examples and descriptions of compromises made in the political process; descriptive summaries of political organizations, case studies of particular bills, or anecdotal accounts by participants all provide rich material in this regard. But there are few studies or discussions of compromise itself--what it is, what it means, why it is so important. Indeed, these apparently conflicting findings are mutually reinforcing: because compromise is so prevalent, it has been taken for granted in politics,

by observers and participants alike.[3]   I have attempted
to look more directly and systematically at the nature
of compromise itself.

     I propose to discuss the two related questions
of the prevalence and appropriateness of compromise
in the United States Senate by moving back and forth
between descriptive and normative analysis. The descriptive
task is to ask: What is happening? I shall draw upon
my interviews (in 1979-1980) with thirty-four senators
and twenty staff members, supplementing the discussion
with examples drawn from personal observation of the
Senate, transcripts of committee meetings, the Congressional
Record, and other writings.   (See the Appendix for
a detailed discussion of the interview procedure, the
sample, and related research questions.)

     The other aspect of the discussion raises questions
about the compromise process. Such questioning will
be interwoven throughout the book, although I shall
try to be explicit about the nature of such discussions.
I hope to leave the reader with a better understanding
of the actual role of compromise, and with some questions
about the appropriateness of compromise itself. The
issues upon which our politicians are called to compromise

---

[3]Among the few exceptions are the following: J. Roland
Pennock and John W. Chapman (eds.), Compromise in Ethics,
Law, and Politics, Nomos XXI (New York University Press,
1979); R. M. MacIver (ed.), Integrity and Compromise
(New York: Harper and Brothers, 1957); John Morley,
On Compromise (London: Chapman and Hall, 1874); T. V. Smith,
The Ethics of Compromise and the Art of Containment
(Boston: Starr King Press, 1956); Helmut Thielicke,
Theological Ethics, Volume I (ed. by William H. Lazareth)
(London: Adam and Charles Black, 1968 [1951]), esp. Part
III, "Man's Relation to the World."

are seldom neutral ones, and the question of whether they should compromise is an important one for our attention as citizens.

Let me indicate briefly what this book is not. First, I am not presenting an academic treatise on the organization of the Congress. We need to understand the important features of political life, but only as this knowledge helps us understand the importance of compromise. Therefore, many aspects of Senate life will be ignored here. Second, this book is not primarily concerned with compromise in general; because action always occurs within a particular setting, I will focus (in the central sections of the book) upon the United States Senate in 1979-1980. Many of the findings and arguments are relevant for other political settings, but this book seeks to fathom what is happening in this one context. Finally, this book is not a case study of a particular piece of legislation. Because I want to provide a rich sense of how decisions are made, I will use examples drawn from a wide range of legislative proposals. I hope thereby to capture the complexity of Senate policy-making and compromise.

The book is divided into three sections. The first two chapters raise the question of compromise, asking about its relevance to American politics. We need to know what people do when they compromise, and why they seem to do so much of it in political life. We will discuss briefly the nature of politics, and the norms which can be applied to political decision-making.

Chapters 3-5 look in detail at compromise in the Senate. We will first describe the rules, actions, and structures of Senate life, with an eye toward explaining why compromise is so important there. We will then ask about the types of compromise which occur in the

Senate, and about the language used to identify and justify these compromises. The emphasis on institutional factors reveals a sociological eye, although few persons concerned with personal ethics are likely to deny the crucial importance of such matters.[4]

Chapters 6-7 ask about the limits which may be set to the compromise process. We look at the responses given to this question by the senators themselves, and then examine in some detail the most common view that one should not compromise on matters of principle. This position will be evaluated in chapter 6. Finally, chapter 7 looks more broadly at some ethical criteria we might apply to questions of compromise in politics.

---

[4]Even a 1951 Senate report on "Ethical Standards in Government," which focused almost exclusively on questions of personal morality, recognized the importance of such organizational features:

> No thorough study of ethics can be limited to the study of ideas alone. Basic ideas and beliefs make social institutions operate, but it is also the function of institutions to encourage and reward behavior which is up to standard and to discourage and punish behavior which is below standard....[It will be necessary] to examine the institutional arrangements which have the function of making it easier for men in public life to do right and more difficult for them to do wrong.

Subcommittee of the Committee on Labor and Public Welfare, United States Senate, Ethical Standards in Government (Washington: Government Printing Office, 1951), p.8..

CHAPTER 1. THE NATURE OF COMPROMISE

What do we do when we compromise? The question is hard to answer, partly because we so frequently find ourselves in situations which seem to cry out for compromise. But what characterizes such situations?

We may be faced with a choice between something I want and something you want; unable to achieve our goals, we consider a compromise, whereby we find some middle ground. Or, I may have an idea about "the perfect woman" with whom I wish to spend my life, an idea which conflicts with the all-too-human frailty or imperfections of existing women (to say nothing, of course, of any frailties or imperfections I may possess); I can hold out for my ideal, or I can compromise by accepting a person with some but not all of my desired traits. (Whether the other person will compromise by accepting me is a more troublesome question.) Or, I may believe that I deserve an advance of $50,000 for this book, but the publisher offers me $500; if neither of us is willing to surrender but we both want to see the book in print, we may arrive at a compromise figure. Or, I may believe that no one should ever participate in violence against another person, but I find myself (or my country) confronted with an apparently implacable foe bent on destruction; I may compromise my pacifist ideal for the sake of self-preservation.

What makes compromise either possible or necessary in such situations? The most important factor is the existence of a conflict--a tension, or a struggle, between two persons, ideals, or alternative courses of action. Now, there are numerous ways in which such conflicts can be resolved. I can try to use coercion or force, I can appeal to an outside authority, I can try to educate or persuade, or I can unilaterally concede. Another option is to compromise--to seek some alternative path, third solution, middle ground position, or mutual concession. In so doing, the parties to the conflict give up their insistence on their original demands, and alter what they are willing to accept.

If we focus on the individual who is confronted with the possibility of compromise, there are two closely related ways in which such conflicts can be viewed. First, we can see the conflict as one between a desired outcome--an "ideal"--and the real world. I cannot achieve what I want because I am opposed by something outside of my self--another person , another group, or simply the world itself--which I cannot change. Whether we are speaking of a conflict between two groups over a piece of land, between one person's request and someone else's refusal, or between my ideal and the apparently rock-hard situation into which I am thrown, such cases involve a discrepancy between what I want and what some aspect of the world wants. I have an ideal, a principle, a vision, a demand--and reality, the "facts of the case," simply will not fall into line.

Alternatively, such conflicts can be seen as arising from the conflicts between two of my ideals.[1] I want to visit a depressed friend, and I want to prepare for my next lecture. Both desires stem from values, from ideals which affect (or, at least, should affect) the way I act. If I cannot realize both of them, I may choose to compromise between them. It is harder here to speak as if an ideal confronts the world, for the conflict is rather between two ideals.

In an important sense, all such conflicts can be understood in this second way. After all, why should

---

[1] I am indebted to David H. Smith for forcing me to consider this aspect more seriously.

I pay any attention to the demands of the world, unless I value my continued ability to live in it? Even when one alternative seems more "realistic" than the other, we are not drawn to this alternative unless we can see the value of being realistic in the first place.[2] This ethical demand expressed by the world may be stated in different ways: as a recognition of the rights of other persons, as an awareness of our own limited perspective, as a need to achieve harmony, or as a valued capacity to "go along to get along." In any case, we compromise with the world largely because we value our ability to live in it.[3]

These comments about the complex nature of conflicting ideals suggest an important corollary. To call a choice a compromise is to admit that the actor is confronted

---

[2]These two interlaced meanings of the compromise process are reflected in Helmut Thielicke's discussion of natural ethics:

> The moment our capability comes up against a demonstrable and fundamental limit, such as the wall imposed by the autonomous world of means, the imperative must necessarily be reduced to whatever sphere of action is thereby staked out. For in addition to the imperative itself, the objective world within which the imperative is to be realized is also a normative component of the ethical. Compromise is thus the final conclusion of ethical wisdom.

(Thielicke, Theological Ethics, p. 485.)
Note that Thielicke argues that Christian ethics is not bound by this willingness to compromise with the world, however.
[3]For related discussions, see especially three articles in the Pennock and Chapman volume on compromise: Theodore M. Benditt, "Compromising Interests and Principles," esp. pp. 31-36; Martin P. Golding, "The Nature of Compromise: A Preliminary Inquiry," esp. pp. 16-19; Joseph H. Carens, "Compromise in Politics," pp. 129-134. See also T. V. Smith, The Ethics of Compromise and the Art of Containment, p.45.

with a choice between two valued alternatives. As observers, we must be willing to recognize that it is at least plausible that both options are somehow valuable. For example, if a politician votes against a bill in order to gain support for a more important bill, we might call this a compromise, even if we disagreed with the choice. However, if the same politician votes against the bill in order to receive money to buy a new car, we would not merely call it a bad compromise--it is not a compromise at all, for the choice to receive a new car as payment for a vote is (in our political system, at least) not a "realistic" option but an inherently disvalued one. Thus, to accept someone's claim that a decision is a compromise, we must be able to accept the value of the conflicting choices. Note that we need not believe that they are equally valuable; indeed, what we usually call bad compromises are precisely those decisions where the sacrifice is made of the greater value for the sake of the lesser one. But bad compromises are still compromises.

I think this is an important point, for it helps us limit somewhat the range of decisions involved. The complexity of understanding and assessing compromises stems largely from this ambiguity concerning the nature of the situation. If we try to solve the problem by finding all value on one side of the decision, then we have removed the problem from the realm of compromise entirely. It is only when we have such ambiguous situations that the opportunity of compromise arises.

Let us pause here for a few qualifying remarks.

First, I am using the following terms rather broadly: "ideals," "visions," "values." The common meaning is that something is desired, or valued, or imagined, by an actor; we can use many words here, partly because there are so many ways in which we value or desire things. The precise nature of the object is less important than the fact that it is valued.

Second, in such a conflict, the observer need not believe that the ideal is desirable. All that matters is that the actor (that is, the person confronted with the possibility of compromise) plausibly perceives a discrepancy between this ideal and the situation, or between this ideal and another one. People hold all sorts of ideals, and we define reality in many different ways; the option of compromise depends only upon the actor's perception of the gap between wanting to realize ideals and the practical impossibility of doing so. But the term "plausibly" suggests that simply any claim by the actor will not suffice. To refer to our earlier example, an American politician who said that taking a bribe was a valued act is not thereby engaging in a compromise.

Third, I am not distinguishing here between conflicts of interest and conflicts of principle. We often speak of interests as particular needs or wants, and of principles as broader ideals or values. Although we shall consider this distinction in chapter 6, it is wise not to begin by placing much weight upon it. We cannot decide how to classify someone's demand for a particular amount of money or status, for example, unless we adopt a categorical rule such as: "When persons want money, their belief counts as an interest, not as a principle." But there are situations where the demand for a particular sum of money does seem to become a matter of principle, as in the call for a living wage. Furthermore, as we shall discover, most discussions of compromise involve attempts by each side to define (reduce?) the concerns of the opponent to "mere questions of interest," while

seeing one's own concerns as "matters of principle."
We shall consider a desired ideal simply as such, without
prejudging whether it is an interest or a principle.

Fourth, it might be objected that, if someone
really does have such an ideal, then how could one
ever consider compromising? After all, if an ideal
is an ideal, then why would we ever act otherwise than
according to its dictates? We are confronted with a
difficult problem here: if I act contrary to my ideal
(or, to put it somewhat differently, if I am willing
to water down or compromise my ideal), then is it still
my ideal at all? If "actions speak louder than words,"
doesn't my willingness to compromise an ideal simply
indicate that I no longer really hold it?

There is no simple answer to such a question. But
it is important to realize that we hold our ideals
or visions in different ways. Some ideals function
as specific dictates, directing particular responses
in situations; others function as general guidelines,
directing our attention but not necessarily our every
response; still others serve as long-range goals, inspiring
but neither guiding nor directing. There are some important
differences between our ideals, and the ways in which
they function for us. I may claim to be a religious
person, and still have moments of doubt; I may claim
to be honest, and still tell lies. Such ideals may
be held (and may be said to retain their hold on us)
even in our weaknesses and our lapses. But it is quite
another matter to claim that one is a pacifist when
one is willing to fight on particular occasions. To
be a pacifist, and to hold the ideal of pacifism, is
to react to all situations of potential violence out
of a firm refusal to take human life. The measure of
our commitment to this ideal is precisely the extent

to which we will not compromise, in spite of the barriers
which the world may place in the way of a pacifist
life-style.

I am suggesting that the way in which we hold
our ideals depends largely upon the nature of these
ideals. The failure to recognize this fact accounts
for much of the confusion generated in discussions
of compromise. For example, compromise is often seen
as a central identifying characteristic of democracy. One
argument here holds that persons in a democracy must
be willing to have ideals without forcing them upon
others. T. V. Smith writes:

> Democracy is a society of democratic men,
> and democratic men are men who will compromise
> with one another as regards all things which
> must be shared in order to go along together
> each merrily thinking his own thoughts....
> To be this kind of man one must be able to
> compromise issues without feeling himself
> compromised....Whoever cannot have ideals
> without perpetrating them is a fanatic...[4]

Smith uses the example of religious tolerance as his
central case. Certainly, if religious beliefs provide
our model of human ideals, then compromise seems to
be necessary; to speak about imposing one's religious
beliefs upon someone else is, in our society, to intrude
an essentially private matter into the public arena.

------

[4]T. V. Smith, The Promise of American Politics, 2nd
ed. (University of Chicago Press, 1936), p. 175. We
will return to this theme in chapters 2 and 7.
There is a similar tradition which sees the willingness
to compromise as an essential feature of the American
character. See, for example: W. W. Rostow, "The National
Style," in Elting E. Morison (ed.), The American Style
(N.Y.:Harper and Brothers, 1958), pp. 248-313; Benjamin
R. Barber, "The Compromised Republic: Public Purposelessness
in America," in Robert H. Horwitz (ed.), The Moral
Foundations of the American Republic, 2nd edition (University Press of Virginia, 1979), pp. 19-38.

But this example obscures the equally important (and politically more relevant) cases of ideals which are, by their very nature, social. (Indeed, in many societies, and in many understandings of its social function, religion is a highly public and interpersonal matter.) When we are considering ideals of justice, equality, or human rights, to speak of imposing these values, or of "perpetrating" them upon others, is a bit odd. Indeed, it would seem strange to speak of holding such ideals, and not wanting to impose them if necessary upon one's fellow citizens.

Therefore, we have to make distinctions between the different ways in which we can hold, or be held by, our ideals. Some of these will be overriding visions, which cannot be ignored without being undermined or destroyed; others may be compromised in various ways, depending upon our willingness to adopt them (and ourselves) to the requirements imposed by the world. In either case, the question of compromise arises in that moment when the ideal confronts either the real world or another ideal, and when we ask ourselves whether we shall yield. The call to compromise speaks to us in these terms: "Are you willing to renegotiate, redefine, or temporarily suspend your ideal, in the face of the situation?"

One more comment before we return to the mainstream of the discussion. It may be very important to consider whether, even when we are willing to compromise an ideal, we can retain that ideal at all. Perhaps the major danger of compromise lies not in the failure to apply our ideal in a given situation, but in the broader loss of the ideal as a functioning part of our lives. Our ideals are as susceptible to reinforcement and habituation as are our other beliefs; indeed, as a matter of character, their strength may be judged in precisely this way. Even if we allow an ideal to be overridden in a particular case, we might take from that encounter, not a disillusioned or cynical sense of the futility of the ideal but rather a heightened resolve to find ways to apply and live it out in the next encounter. Thus, in asking about our willingness to compromise, we should try to look beyond the particular decision, recognizing that we can compromise an ideal without losing it, but also realizing that we cannot do so repeatedly without seriously undermining its very status as an ideal.

We have been considering the conflict situation whereby an ideal confronts an obstacle. I have suggested so far that our ideals constitute alternative visions, and that they often conflict with the apparent "givenness" of our situations. Indeed, one indication that we are being asked to compromise is the posing of the demand: "Be realistic." In deciding whether or not to compromise (or, alternatively, in assessing whether someone else was correct in doing so), we are forced to decide which vision of the world we will act on. Shall I hold fast to my vision of the perfect woman, refusing to accept "second best"? Shall I insist on my asking price, refusing a lesser offer, and risk the loss of the bargain completely?

The call to compromise is based ultimately on the demand for realism, for accepting the world's options, for not being stubborn. Realism is a "loaded" term, of course--who, after all, would want to be unrealistic? In calling for a compromise, the realist claims that ideals must yield to reality. But notice that there is something highly manipulative about this argument, because the ability to define what is real is a powerful weapon for one person or group to wield over another. In Peter Berger's words: "...the fundamental coerciveness of

society lies not in its machineries of social control,
but in its power to constitute and to impose itself
as reality."[5]

But the opponent's claim to the more realistic
definition of the situation can be questioned. The
claim may be met in various ways. I can deny that my
preferred ideal is unrealistic; I can deny that the
compromise solution is realistic; I can attack the
acceptance of realism, arguing that what is realistic
depends largely on what people are willing to struggle
for. In any case, I can insist that the extent to which
an alternative vision can be "realized" depends largely
upon my willingness to accept the argument to be realistic. If I continue to insist on my vision, you may
reject it, ridicule it, or define me as crazy. But
you are forced to look at it, to listen to it, to take
it into account. And I may hope that, eventually, it
may look a bit less crazy, a bit less "unrealistic,"
than it first appeared. The situation may alter, or
your sensitivity may change, or you may fall in love
with it, as I have. In any event, we should be wary
of accepting the demand to compromise when based on
an alternative vision of "the real world." The history
of human activity is too full of examples of unrealistic

---

[5]Berger, The Sacred Canopy (N.Y.: Doubleday and Co.,
1967), p. 12.

ideals which have caught on. The line between the visionary and the fanatic is a thin one indeed.[6]

Our evaluation of compromise depends upon the specific facts of each situation. We approve of some compromises, and disapprove of others. But we also adopt general orientations toward the entire enterprise. We know people we would describe as uncompromising, and others who might be called compromising. Can we, or should we, adopt such an overall attitude toward compromise?

The choice is largely a temperamental one, which might be revealed by asking ourselves what we fear most about a potentially compromising situation. On one hand, many people fear especially the refusal to compromise; they would rather be accused of being "wishy washy" than of being "rigid." They tend to look for opportunities to be accommodating, to blend their views with others, to redefine their positions to fit in with their opponents. Such persons need not be unprincipled or weak; all that is at stake is a tendency to approach decisions with an eye toward avoiding impasse and isola-

---

[6]We might consider the example of the idealistic call of the pacifist for unilateral nuclear disarmament. The "realist's" counterargument is familiar, and is based on several aspects of "reality": the menace of opposing forces, the need to maintain all options, the inability to prevent nuclear proliferation. But the pacifist can respond that, in an age of nuclear warfare, with several countries possessing missiles capable of such devastation, the truly unrealistic course of action--indeed, the truly insane course of action--is not to disarm. We see here one way in which the proponent of the alternative vision may claim to be more, rather than less, realistic; to refuse to compromise might thus be seen as more realistic, in terms of the consequences whch would result. But such a line of reasoning can only be adopted by questioning the underlying definition of the situation presented as the argument for compromise.

tion. For such persons, the opposite of compromise is rigidity, and the person who compromises is viewed primarily as patient, accommodating, and cooperative.

Alternatively, there are those who prefer the charge of rigidity to that of compromising. They fear situations where ideals will be sacrificed and threatened, and are more likely to retrench and defend their own ideals in the face of such dangers. For such persons, the opposite of compromise is not rigidity but integrity, and the person who compromises is viewed more as naive, unprincipled, or as selling out.

Let us look at this last term: <u>selling out</u>. This phrase is crucial in understanding our ambivalence toward compromise. The term has a derogatory tone in our culture, but we might ask why this is so. After all, the idea of selling something is not condemned, and we could view a willingness to sell out as a positive sign of strength in divesting oneself of unnecessary baggage. If I am involved in a business, and I decide that my true interests or inclinations lie elsewhere, I may sell out to someone else. Indeed, such a willingness to divest oneself should appeal precisely to those who prize integrity and forthrightness. Why, then, does the notion of selling out seem to refer to the <u>loss</u> of integrity?

The answer, I think, lies in our propensity to view our underlying commitments as definitive of who we are. When we speak of a person selling out, we are referring to the self-divestiture of some underlying values or beliefs, not of some superficial element of one's life. The radical student who sells out by joining a Wall Street advertising agency is not simply trading his Levis for a business suit, or his long hair for a trim. He is seen as trading a set of values for a world of security and high income. It is precisely in perceiving the action in this way that we are apt to condemn such a decision as not merely a compromise, but as a sell out.

We might suggest three ways in which the charge of selling out gains its particular negative force here. First, the actor is accused, not of making a purely financial bargain, but of selling underlying principles for a more tangible reward. To sell out is to yield something of one's inner self for the sake of rewards which are seen as more superficial or material.

Second, the accusation of selling out may be a claim that a bad deal has been made. The sell out is equated here with the bad compromise, in which the actor has received a "raw deal" by trading away more than has been received. This need not involve the objection raised in the previous paragraph, where a deeper value has been sacrificed for the sake of material rewards. For example, one could be accused of selling out by not holding out for a high enough price. The accuser might be quite willing to allow some compromise; the sell out occurs only when the outcome of the compromise is too detrimental to my interests. Although these two meanings are often found together, they are significantly different: the first refuses to allow compromise at all, while the second demands a particular result in order to prevent the compromise from being defined as a sell out.[7]

  And third, there is often an important assumption in the notion of selling out: namely, that one should not change one's underlying principles or visions. When the radical student joins Wall Street, we can view his action as selling out the radical vision of life. But we might also believe that the student's visions have simply changed, and that he has traded one vision for another. Our choice of metaphor depends largely upon which side we are on. If I still retain that radical vision, then I am more likely to view the new decision as selling out for some ulterior motive. However, it is possible to place a higher value on personal change-- one's consciousness can be raised, and personal growth often involves exchanging one set of ideals for another. Such a change could be seen as the actions of a new person, or at least of a person with new and improved values. But the sell out interpretation stems largely from an underlying view that certain values are either less susceptible to such change, or are not supposed to be changed at all. In either case, what is central about the interpretation of compromise as a sell out is the belief that this underlying vision is still that of the actor. It is in that period when the vision is still held, but another vision (of security,

---

[7]This distinction is helpful in understanding the common reactions of group members to compromises made in their behalf. A representative who bargains away the constituents' prize possessions may have sold out "in good faith," by not demanding a higher price for the constituents. One can sell out the interests of one's group without thereby selling out one's right to be bargaining on their behalf, as long as the motive was to get as much as possible for them (rather than for oneself).

acceptance by others, or financial independence, for example) is offered in its place, that the temptation to compromise is most acute, and it is precisely at this point that the charge of selling out is most likely to be made.

Thus, the image of selling out involves a stance of loyalty to a vision of the world. One cannot sell out if one has not first bought in. We seldom bother to accuse our opponents of selling out their principles, unless we believe that they once shared ours. There is a feeling of betrayal in the view of compromise as a sell out, for the actor is seen as having led us on, of having turned against us.

I am suggesting that we may adopt two broad approaches to the question of compromise. Most of us waver between these two extremes, but there is an important distinction concerning where the burden of proof lies in such situations. Do we view compromise as the norm, and ask for justifications for the refusal to compromise? Or do we view the refusal to compromise as the norm, suspecting that most compromises are really sell outs?

Because our stance affects the way in which the discussion proceeds, let me indicate that I tend to distrust compromise, and to demand justifications for compromises. But this does not mean that I am opposed to compromise in all situations, nor that I refuse to discriminate between good and bad compromises. Rather, I place the burden of proof upon the "realistic" call to compromise, rather than upon the person who tries to hold out.

Yet, in those situations where the conflict is more clearly between two ideals, there may be no alternative to compromise. As we shall see in our consideration of political life, the willingness to compromise has many benefits. If the peacemakers are indeed blessed, then compromise serves an important purpose. Values may have to be sacrificed for the sake of other values; we must always ask, however, whether the greater value has won out. Compromise is morally problematic not because it settles for the worse, but because, in adopting a compromising mentality, we may forget to ask what is the better.

We have been discussing the central feature of compromise situations: namely, the conflict between valued visions of the world. Let us turn now to several other important elements of compromise situations.

Our second important factor is the existence (or, more importantly, the perception) of some middle ground to serve as a compromise outcome. In cases of financial disagreement, there seems to be no problem here. Four million dollars is better than three million, and not as good as five million. But persons may not always agree that something is better than nothing. There may be a minimum amount required to accomplish the desired goal, and the supporter may feel that anything short of this minimum is worse than no amount at all. Or, there may be a tactical advantage in refusing to accept a partial figure, in hopes of eventually gaining all of what one wants. We shall return to these tactical questions in chapter 4; note here simply that compromise is impossible unless both sides are willing to recognize a middle ground position.[8]

Notice what is, and what is not, ruled out here. The actor can still decide to compromise for tactical reasons, or simply to avoid the worst of two evils. But what seems to undercut any possibility of compromise is a posture of purity, in which the person refuses to consider any relative examples of the desired value or goal. Indeed, we can speak about a person being uncompromising in two ways. The individual may refuse to see a conflict of values, holding that the particular ideal being defended is not merely the most important but the only valuable alternative under consideration. But we can also speak of an uncompromising person as one who, while recognizing the conflict of values, refuses to yield to achieve a solution. This second actor is uncompromising but at least sees the conflict; it is the first person who would be the true hindrance to any effort to compromise. Some degree of flexibility is required, and the first step toward such flexibility is the recognition that there are other competing values involved.[9]

---

[8]For example, the following comment was made by a lobbyist for the Sierra Club in Washington, D.C.: "Pressing for the whole thing is the only way you get anything done in this town. I'd rather lose the whole thing than get these incremental bits. Have you ever seen any real change take place incrementally?" (Quoted in Bernard Asbell, The Senate Nobody Knows [N.Y.: Doubleday and Co., 1978], p. 356.)

[9]But the requirement of flexibility has its own problems. We tend to distrust people who compromise out of an overly flexible set of ideals, just as we may view with disdain those who refuse to compromise out of an overly rigid set.

Third, compromise can occur only when the persons have some <u>freedom</u> to determine how they will act. We are always free to choose in some respects, but there are different levels of free activity, and the ability to compromise depends upon a significant degree of freedom. We do not say that someone has compromised when she has a gun pointed at her. Similarly, I think we would not look at an elected official whose life was being threatened, or who was being blackmailed, and say that she compromised by going along with the demands. We might say that she should not have done it, or that she had no right to do it, but not that she had compromised in doing so. To speak of compromise implies a choice, a decision, made without explicit threat of force.[10]

Of course, there are many sorts of threats or penalties which are highly relevant to compromises in politics. A senator may risk losing a job by a particular vote, or may endanger future campaign support by not holding firm on a spending proposal. But the official can do something else for a living, and the tension between one's beliefs and the views of one's constituents is an inescapable one in American politics. (See chapter 2 and chapter 3 for a fuller discussion of this issue.) We want to be careful about using the argument that "he had no choice"--the decision to compromise, at least in our political system, is made freely.

One sign of this freedom is seen in the way we use the term compromise in our discourse. To compromise is to act in a way which calls forth an explanation

---

[10]Theodore Benditt makes this point in his excellent article, "Compromising Interests and Principles," pp. 26-37.

of some sort. This is connected up with the public
nature of political activity. In the political arena,
choices are public in two important ways: they are
open and susceptible to scrutiny, and they concern
the lives of the general public. As a result, we are
likely to ask for explanations for the decisions of
our representatives, particularly when those decisions
fall short of our expectations and desires. Therefore,
we ask our politicians for reasons. To call a decision
a compromise is to say something about how the action
is to be understood--namely, that it is a concession
of something important, and that it is a free and responsible decision for which we can ask for reasons. The
response, "But I had to compromise," is simply inadequate
in this setting. The compromise might be justified
by appealing to a greater good, or to limits of the
situation, or to another conflicting ideal. In all
cases, however, some such reason can and must be given,
reflecting the actor's freedom to have decided differently.[11]

Two other factors are particularly important in
politics. Compromises often are possible only when
the parties must reach a solution to the problem. If
one can leave the field and go home, compromise is
less likely. The United States Senate is a good example
of a field which cannot be left. Although the member
can resign, or refuse to have any part in the deliberations,
both alternatives deprive the constituents of their
representation. In addition, settings such as the

[11]This discussion follows C. Wright Mills' "Situated
Actions and Vocabularies of Motive," American Sociological
Review 5 (December, 1940), pp. 904-913. We shall return
to this approach to compromise in chapter 5.

Senate are "organizations of last resort" in our society; if we are going to provide legislation in a particular area, the Senate must pass it. There is no option of saying, "I just don't like the way this is going, so let's forget it." To do so is to vote against the legislation. Such a situation creates a form of pragmatic decision making, and puts a premium on passing a bill and solving a problem, rather than upon standing firm or maintaining one's purity.

Finally, compromise often depends upon the belief that I have had some <u>input</u> into the decision. Even if I agree with a decision, it is difficult to accept less than I want in the form of a dictated result. It is easier to point to a section of a bill as my particular contribution. This is related to the public nature of political decisions--the need to save face is always present in politics, and the elected official may need a way out in order to do what is necessary. Indeed, as we shall see, complex compromises stand a much better chance of success if they can incorporate items of concern to a large and disparate number of groups. This may be why so much of our social legislation resembles a hodge-podge of apparently conflicting interests and goals. Without such an approach, however, compromise becomes a dirty word, and the legislative task in a diverse society may grind to a halt.[12]

We are beginning to understand the ambiguous nature of compromise. To compromise is to be accommodating, to be flexible, to yield to the other's views, to weigh and adjust one's priorities, and to seek a required

---

[12]Senators often cite the proverbial comment that a politician is in favor of any compromise of which he is a part.

solution. Yet to compromise is also to be wishy-washy,
to refuse to stand anywhere, to sell out one's values,
to play the game, to accept second best rather than
fighting for one's beliefs. We do not have to choose
between these two extremes; indeed, we cannot choose
between them, for they are both ways in which we speak
about compromise in American society. The term is used
both to commend and to condemn, particularly in politics.

One way to understand the positive and negative
senses of compromise is to notice that the former refers
primarily to an other-regarding approach, while the
latter refers mainly to a self-regarding one. Especially
in politics, what is commended about compromise is
that it allows persons to work together, to smooth
out difficult decisions, to agree to disagree, and
to avoid the pitfalls of self-righteousness. If politics
is indeed "the art of compromise," it is because it
is a cooperative activity, requiring the merger of
conflicting interests into a concerted whole. This
approach to compromise is reflected in the following
comments made on the floor of the Senate at the beginning
of debate on the complicated windfall profits tax bill
in 1979, as reported out of the Senate Finance Committee:

> Senator Nelson: I think we came out with
> a compromise, where those who represent parts
> of the country that do not have the same
> problem...as the North does make compromises....
> I think we struck a compromise in a
> parliamentary body which will work and which
> we can pass, and I think if we go beyond
> that in either direction...I do not think
> we can have a bill unless we strike something
> closer to the middle.[13]
>
> Senator Long: When we try to put some
> formula together, none of us will be completely

[13]Congressional Record, November 14, 1979, S16608.

fair to everybody. None of us have the wisdom
to put together a formula that is completely
fair as applied to everybody....
    When we put these formulas together
and try to work something out, we usually
try to see that everybody gets something,
will just get a little something, as little
as it may be.[14]

Compromise is a good thing, because it enables persons
to work with one another and to solve problems.

But the person is also representing a set of interests,
values, and priorities which are not shared by other
senators. If we ask about compromise from the standpoint
of these values, we are apt to take a somewhat dimmer
view of the process. Compare the usage of the term
"compromise" to the term "accommodation," for example. We
can talk about accommodating ourselves or our positions
to those of someone else, but this involves a process
of taking the views and needs of others into account. We
do not talk about compromising to someone else's views;
rather, we compromise our own positions, in order to
reach an agreement. Thus, compromise seems to reveal
the complex interaction between our sense of who we
are, and the social context in which we must act and
decide. To compromise is to be willing to give up,
or perhaps simply to redefine, our own sense of what
we are and what we will accept from the world. It is
something in us, of us, about us, that is changed,
altered, or lost.

I am not suggesting that compromise is by definition
a bad thing. But there is something problematic about
compromise. Because it involves a concession, we (as
both observers and participants) should consider carefully

---

[14]Ibid., S16609.

what is being lost. Compromise not only allows an explanation, but demands one.

This requirement for an explanation is particularly important in American politics. In representative government, the people have the right to demand to see the arguments behind compromises, and politicians should be prepared to provide them. It is not enough to say: "But you have to compromise in politics to get anything done." We want to know what is being done, and why the compromise, implying as it does a sacrifice of something important, is the appropriate way to do it.

CHAPTER 2. COMPROMISE AND POLITICS

Why is compromise relevant to politics, and particularly to American politics? This chapter addresses these questions, preparing the way for the application (in chapters 3-5) to the context of the United States Senate.

What are the distinguishing features of politics which make compromise so prevalent? Perhaps more than other roles and occupations, politics is an activity. The politician is called upon to act, to decide, to make up her mind, to "come down" somewhere.[1] There is seldom any escape from such action; to be a politician is to saddle oneself with the obligation to act. The expression "the buck stops here" applies in many political contexts, extending far beyond the Oval Office; even where the buck is passable, the decision to pass it constitutes an important decision.

Joseph Carens has suggested that there are three aspects of political action which lead to the tendency to compromise. The first is the uncertainty underlying political action:

> [T]heoretical inquiries permit us to suspend judgment until we are satisfied that we have reached the truth. In such inquiries compromise is neither necessary nor appropriate. By contrast, in practical affairs we are often forced to act in the face of uncertainty before we are confident that we have reached the truth. Under such conditions, compromise may offer the best solution.

Second, conflicting goals may force the actor to compromise to achieve the best solution. And third, the collective

---

[1]On this point, see: Hannah Arendt, The Human Condition (University of Chicago Press, 1958), and her "Truth and Politics," in Between Past and Future (N.Y.: Penguin, 1954), pp. 227-264; Joseph Carens, "Compromise in Politics," op. cit..

nature of politics increases both the degree of uncertainty and the conflicts between goals, thereby creating an even greater incentive for compromise.[2] But what is the connection between uncertainty, conflicting goals, and collective action, on the one hand, and compromise, on the other? Let us try to sort this out.

Uncertainty itself does not lead to compromise. One could as well argue that, because we are uncertain concerning the truth of our views, we should stand fast and act on whatever knowledge or intuition we do possess. Indeed, a probabilistic notion of decision making would suggest precisely such an approach. Since we may have only a five per cent chance of knowing what is right, if we stand firm and act on this assumption we have a similar five per cent chance of acting correctly. But if we compromise and either water down our action or agree to someone else's notion of the truth, we have no idea of our chances of being correct. Unless we have reason to trust someone else, we must go with our own views; if we do trust someone else, then we are correspondingly less uncertain about the truth.[3]

Such an argument disposes of any intrinsic connection between uncertainty in political action and the need to compromise. The politician is no more uncertain of the truth, or of cause and effect, than is any other actor; we act on the information we have, and hope for the best.

But there is a way to suggest that compromise flows from uncertainty. This is what may be called

---

[2]Carens, "Compromise in Politics," op. cit., pp. 124-126.
[3]The everyday example here is the stopped clock, which is at least correct twice a day.

the "compromise from humility" argument. Because I am not certain of the truth, I may respect your different opinions, and may be more willing to compromise on my side to reach some middle ground. Such reasoning is the basis for the common argument that compromise and democracy are closely intertwined; only the fanatic would refuse to accept such limitations on personal knowledge, and such figures are notoriously out of place in democratic political institutions.[4]

Such an argument has some force when we are considering the style of life one should adopt within a political setting. But it has little relevance when we ask whether compromise should be adopted as the general mode of decision making. For it could be argued that humility should extend only to the manner in which we put forth our own notions of truth, not to the content of the actions we are willing and prepared to accept. The politician might be convinced that a refusal to discuss or listen to opposing views is undemocratic but this is quite different from feeling obliged to yield something of one's own views in order to preserve democratic institutions. The mere fact of uncertainty, even when combined with humility, cannot explain the prevalence or advisability of compromise in politics.

---

[4]See esp. Golding, "The Nature of Compromise," and Carens, "Compromise in Politics." For a fascinating discussion of the connection between democracy and compromise, see also Peter Singer, Democracy and Disobedience (Oxford: Clarendon Press, 1973), esp. pp. 30-41.

Yet there are some strong arguments behind this type of position. Let us discuss several features of politics which do seem to create a bias toward compromise.[5]

The Decisional Bias

First, political life requires us to make decisions. To say that the politician has to act does not simply mean that she cannot know all the facts before acting; we seldom know all the facts about anything. In his discussion of compromise in politics, Carens contrasts the active world of politics with the theoretical world of science, suggesting that the latter world does not require compromise. His example here involves two scientists with conflicting theories about the causes of cancer. But to believe that such questions are resolved entirely without compromise is a misunderstanding. Scientists compromise continually with questions of limited funds, available technology, conflicting models of explanation, and the desire to arrive first at a sound result. The scientist does not compromise only as long as she can still investigate; whether the theory is true or false, it can be tested and re-tested.

But the politician, and the scientist in the guise of a scientific actor, cannot afford this luxury, simply because a decision must be made. In this sense, all of us function both as contemplators and as actors in each of our social roles. What distinguishes the politician is merely the centrality and visibility

---

[5]The term "bias" is used in a neutral sense here. A bias is a tendency to lean in one direction, to favor one result over another. By identifying the built-in biases of politics, we can understand the prevalence of compromise in such a world.

of the decisional dimension of the action required
by that role. Scientists investigate, students learn,
lawyers advocate, writers argue--and politicians decide.[6]

As we might expect, the importance of deciding
is not an accidental aspect of politics. Indeed, we
choose persons to serve us precisely in order to make
decisions. Such an understanding of politics is not
restricted to democratic representative systems, however. A
dictator can be said to take over major decision-making
responsibilities for a society, or a community meeting
may refuse to delegate such powers to anyone. But what
we mean by politics is that arena of social life in
which policy decisions are expected to be made.

What does all of this have to do with compromise? Because politicians have to decide, they must learn to
make use of decision skills and opportunities. The
person who can sit back and think about an issue, without
needing to make a decision, can adopt a range of strategies: reading, reflecting, reconsidering, speculating,
arguing, researching. The politician has access to
all of these strategies, of course, but they can be
employed only up to the decision point. Once the thinking
and reconsidering are completed, a decision must be
made. This does not involve writing a paper setting
forth the pros and cons, nor does it mean recommending
a course of action with a set of caveats, amendments,
or qualifications attached. It means to take a stand
that this particular version of this particular piece

[6]Lord Atlee put it all too clearly: "If a politician
makes an ass of himself, he loses his seat; but a professor
who makes an ass of himself is never going to lose
his chair."
(Quoted in Maurice Cranston, Politics and Ethics [Lon-
don: Weidenfeld and Nicolson, 1972], p.5.)

of legislation is going to be voted for or against on the next roll call. Such an action is qualitatively different from the preceding reflection and weighing, for it involves putting oneself on the line both publicly and eternally. If I favor a policy stance in a paper, I can hedge my support in various ways; if a politician votes for that position, the vote is there, reified forever, available for a generation of potential opponents to point to. It can be hedged in a speech, but the vote remains king.[7]

Politicians are all too aware of the difference between thinking about an issue and deciding upon it. Indeed, a wide range of parliamentary maneuvers has been developed to minimize the effect of having to vote. But such attempts are usually doomed, for the act is too visible: the pairing of votes with an opponent's is still recorded as such, and recurrent failure to vote has a high political cost of its own. Hence, the actor seeks strategies to provide some aid and comfort for the ever-recurring problem of deciding, and compromise is always near at hand.

Compromise is not a strategy of thinking, weighing, or arguing; it is a way of deciding. The politician takes a view, combines it with another, and ends up with a compromise which can then be justified by appealing to both of the competing values or visions which undergird it. It is a way of trying to hedge bets in a game where

---

[7]It is often difficult to force people to adopt such a decisional mentality. In courses I have taught on public policy, students continually attempt to escape from hard choices by trying to find ways out of deciding. "They should study the matter further," "There must be another alternative," or "What if the situation were different?" are common escape routes, available to the student but not to the actor.

bets cannot be hedged. It is a way of broadening support
in a situation where every action, every vote, every
decision alienates persons who would have voted the
other way. Compromise does not provide an escape from
the dilemmas of deciding, but it does often minimize
the damage of such decisions.[8]

Thus, the need for the politician to move from
the realm of considering to the realm of deciding provides
a strong impetus for utilizing techniques of compromise. To
refuse to compromise in such a context would often
undercut the ability to act at all. The politician
confronted with a vote on a funding measure may prefer
to lower the amount of money being appropriated; such
a stance may represent considered judgment, careful
reflection, and perhaps even factual knowledge (although
the role of this last factor is greatly overestimated
in most discussions of policy making). But when the
roll is called up yonder, the choice is usually between
a particular sum of money, and no money at all. A failure
to consider compromise is often to leave the politician
unable to choose.

Such decisions are at the heart of political decision
making. It is not simply because we do not know what
is the right course of action, or because we cannot
coerce others to adopt our views, that compromise is
so crucial. Rather, it is first because we must decide,
and we are not often given the luxury of a purely desirable

---

[8]Senator Jacob Javits once observed that "we lose votes
no matter what we do, and no matter how we vote." (Congressional Record, December 6, 1979, S17942-3.) For
an intriguing discussion of the politician's need to
avoid alienating the constituency, and the mediocrity
which then characterizes so many of our political figures,
see Garry Wills, The Confessions of a Conservative
(N.Y.: Doubleday and Co., 1979), chapter 15.

option. When we are, then indeed compromise is irrelevant. But such situations arise more often in the
world of reflection and hypothetical reasoning than
they do in the world of actors and decisions.

The Pressure Bias

A second and closely related aspect of political
life is the time factor. Not only are politicians required
to make decisions, but they usually have severe time
constraints placed upon them. Some contexts allow more
time than others, and the amount of time available
varies according to the nature of the decision. But
less time is available than is desired, and often these
time limitations play major roles in the actual outcomes
of political decisions.

The type and amount of consideration which is
possible depends largely upon time. Recent theories
of decision making insist upon revising the traditional
rationalist model, which called for arraying and comparing
all of the alternatives and then picking the one with
the most favorable consequences. Because of time pressures,
such an approach is usually impossible in politics. The
politician must quickly narrow down the alternatives
to a small set of likely options, and then do the weighing
within limited time constraints. The result is the
creation of an _ad_ _hoc_ mode of decision making, where

the actor decides on the basis of very limited information and even more limited reflection.[9]

Such time constraints in politics are not accidental features of this realm of social life. The social world is complex and changeable, as social scientists regularly discover to their chagrin. Quick decisions are called for, not only because of the number of decisions to be made but also because of the nature of attempting to intervene in social processes. To wait very long before making a decision is to be confronted with an entirely different decision, due to new facts and configurations in the problem one was addressing. I may be unsure of the effects of a decision taken today, but I am likely to be even more unsure about the effects of a decision made tomorrow. Not only do conditions change, but we simply do not understand in what ways the changes will occur. Thus, the politician who refuses to abide by such constraints for quick decision making is caught on Alice's treadmill, running faster and faster simply to stay in the same place.

In addition, there is a version of Parkinson's Law in the political arena: information expands to fit the time allotted to gather it in. If a policy maker gives a staff member a month, rather than a week,

---

[9]Two particularly important examples of the challenge to the rationalist model are Amitai Etzioni's "mixed scanning" and Charles Lindblom's "disjointed incrementalism." See: Etzioni, The Active Society (N.Y.: The Free Press, 1968); Lindblom, The Policy-Making Process (N.J.: Prentice-Hall, 1968); David Braybrooke and C. Lindblom, A Strategy of Decision (N.Y.: Free Press of Glencoe, 1963). For a classic statement of the more rationalist model, see Herbert Simon, Administrative Behavior, 2nd edition (N.Y.: The Free Press, 1957).See also George C. Edwards III and Ira Sharkansky, The Policy Predicament (San Francisco: W. H. Freeman and Co., 1978).

to provide information about a problem, the resulting report will be four times as long, four times as complex, and one fourth as readable. Ironically, this provides an argument _for_ limited time. Decisions are easier to make if the actor is less besieged by endless reams of data, arguments, and opinions. The fact that more information can always be garnered, given sufficient time, is a background factor in the decision-making process. One always knows that information is limited, that you could know more, and that, as a result, a decision must be made before it is "ready."

There are differences here depending upon the kind of action involved. Some policy problems are enormously complex in terms of facts and figures, while others pose difficult ethical choices between conflicting principles or goals. But the time factor is always present. Whether time limits the ability to gather data or to weigh conflicting social values, the context of politics requires decisions to be made quickly and prematurely.

Such a situation has implications for the value of compromise. The politician is confronted with the need to make a decision, and is aware that all the facts are not in; such an awareness increases both the willingness to listen to one's opponents, and to reconsider whether one really wants to stand firm. It is here that we see most clearly the strength of the humility argument for democracy. It is not the uncertainty about the truth of one's position which is central here, as much as the limited information available. I may be certain that I am right in refusing to vote for a bill supporting capital punishment; but the fact that sufficient time is not available for reflection and deliberation can lead even the staunchest person to reconsider, not the truth of the stance but the wisdom of refusing to compromise. In situations where much time is given to airing views, we might expect compromise to be less significant, because the actor can maintain that she remains unconvinced by the arguments of the opposition. But limited time provides the politician with a convenient "out". The actor can say that there was simply not enough time to consider all the aspects of the decision, and that therefore a more makeshift strategy had to be adopted for arriving at a decision.

I am not suggesting that limited time for making decisions somehow justifies the prevalence of compromise. Rather, conditions of time pressure, combined with insufficiency of information, result--psychologically, not logically--in an almost exasperated willingness to "compromise and be done with it." As we shall see in our discussion of the Senate, such pressures play a significant role in determining both when compromise occurs and who is willing to do the compromising.

The Pluralistic Bias

Third, the realm of politics is a balancer's world. Social resources, individual and group interests, human needs, and value commitments all exert simultaneous and often contradictory pulls upon the political actor. The pluralistic bias of politics is particularly acute in highly technological and diverse societies such as ours. Let us look briefly at the nature of this pluralism.

Whether we consider competing claims as values or as interests, social claims such as opportunity, wealth, and power compete for the politician's attention in two ways. (1) They compete against one another at the level of values or interests. The need for a balanced budget conflicts with the need to provide adequate health care; freedom of opportunity conflicts with equality. (2) They compete independently across different social groups. One group's interest in attaining opportunity conflicts with a second group's desire for the same resource. As a result of both sorts of conflicts, the political world is essentially a distributional one, confronted with the task of sorting out claims, maintaining an aura of fairness, and providing reasons for the selected apportionment of such resources.[10]

To argue that this pluralism places a burden upon the political world is based on a model of scarcity of the goods being discussed. It is possible to deny such scarcity, but it is not very plausible. Certain freedoms may be distributed equally across a population, without thereby limiting other freedoms or values. But there are far too many examples where this is not the case. My freedom of speech is limited by your freedom to be safe from physical danger; your freedom of opportunity is limited by my freedom to move into your field of action. Similarly, each social good is scarce with reference to the population. While we may wish to make equality of educational opportunity available to all, the more educated the society becomes, the less practical value a year of education may have. In the words of W. S. Gilbert: "When everyone is somebody, then no one's anybody."

I would suggest that such a model applies to almost all social goods. As a result, political decisions

---

[10]This situation is exacerbated by the existence in American society of what is often called "value pluralism." In many respects, there is little common agreement concerning not only who should receive resources, but also which values are most important.

seldom involve deciding whether a group deserves to be favored with a particular resource. Rather, the decision usually involves balancing the desert of one group with the deserts of all other groups, or the desert of one group for resource A with the desert of that group for resource B.

Such balancing is common in politics, and the politician is called upon to attend less to the arguments in favor of a particular distribution, than to the arguments concerning why this distribution is preferable to all the others. As we might expect, one of the most useful strategies in both the manufacturing and the explanation of such balancing solutions is that of compromise. This is true in two important ways. First, compromise as a style allows the politician to justify the result by pointing to a necessary quality of the decision itself: "I wanted to get you more, but I had to balance it against something else." Regardless of the precise nature of the result, the fact that decisions in politics are seen as compromises absolves the politician of some of the responsibility of attaining all of what any person or group may want. Second, compromise as an outcome can be used to follow up the apology with a claim of success: "Yes, I did not get you everything you wanted, but I did force the other side to give up something they wanted as well, and look how much you ended up with." The plurality of values and interests is thus used by the politician to explain the compromises which were made necessary by precisely these same plural values and interests.

If social goods did not have to be distributed, and if they did not compete both with one another and independently across different social groups, the mere existence of plurality would not lead to compromise. But we would not recognize such a world as a political one. We expect politicians to confront such hard choices, where some must be deprived in order to benefit others, or where a certain value must be abridged for the furtherance of another. Whether such decisions are made by an authoritarian leader, a representative organization, or a local community meeting, they remain inevitable tasks for the political world.

I am arguing here for a relatively mild statement of such hard choices. Other writers have suggested that the realm of politics is pockmarked not merely with difficult choices but with tragic ones.[11] But the argument here is not dependent upon recognizing the possibility of such tragic choices. I am claiming merely that politics cannot escape the dilemma of trading off social goods, or of weighing and distributing the same goods to different groups, without ceasing to be politics at all. It is therefore not surprising that compromise--both as style and as outcome--appears as a necessary element of such a world.

The Representative Bias

A fourth feature of the political world is that the politician acts in someone else's behalf, or at least is expected to do so. There are numerous ways in which political figures may be said to represent others, and numerous political systems which range from a fairly explicit system of electing persons to

---

[11]The most interesting recent discussion of this question appears in Michael Walzer's brilliant essay, "Political Action: The Problem of Dirty Hands," Philosophy and Public Affairs (Winter, 1973) (reprinted in Donald Jones [ed.], Private and Public Ethics [N.Y.: Edwin Mellen Press, 1978], pp. 96-124). See below, chapter 6.

serve as representatives to systems of either paternalistic or tyrannizing authority. (See chapter 3 for a fuller discussion of this issue of representation.) But in all cases, the politician makes decisions which not only affect a large number of other persons but which are intended to do so.

Of course, it might be suggested that the action of any person has consequences for others' lives. If I decide to spend less of my money on food, that decision affects the livelihood of the local grocers. But I do not directly decide to make the grocers richer or poorer. The politician does make such decisions directly, decisions which can be said to be the politician's only in the sense that she makes them, not in the sense that they are primarily decisions about her life.

Politicians are not the only figures who represent others in this way. But they are the major ones in any society, with the possible exception of parents. It is in the very nature of political action to be deciding for others, to act in their behalf and on their lives, to make decisions about how other persons will behave toward one another. Political action is therefore a type of activity which is judged less by the standards of the actor than by the standards or outcomes of the persons or groups for whom the politician acts.[12]

We can see once again the importance of compromise, although in a somewhat different way. Many writers have suggested that this feature of politics prevents the application of any hard and fast principles or absolutes. Such an argument might be made in two ways.

---

[12]Some particularly intriguing discussions of this issue can be found in Stuart Hampshire (ed.), Public and Private Morality (Cambridge University Press, 1978).

First, there is the question of maintaining the purity of one's own position as a moral actor. To act as a politician is to give up the luxury of deciding to maintain moral standards of one's own, apart from the needs of the people one is representing. Second, one's actions in politics are assessed in terms of the effects upon other persons, in a much more direct sense than is usually the case. The politician is not simply another bystander who can choose between becoming the Pharisee or the Good Samaritan. The politician is always involved, not by virtue of being another person but by the more stringent criterion of being expected to act in behalf of, and as the agent for, other persons.

Such a view does not commit us to a thoroughgoing consequentialist viewpoint, however. Certain sorts of decisions may be forbidden to the politician, regardless of their apparent justification in a particular case. But what is ruled out is any approach which places more attention upon the character of the politician than upon the nature of the decisions and the effects of these decisions upon other people. Because the politician is not simply one more actor on the stage, but is both an actor and a director, the quality of the entire play should be more important than the playing out of a particular role. I do not want to minimize the importance of having decent persons as politicians, but I would insist that it is more relevant to look at the decisions they make than at the personal qualities they possess.[13]

---

[13]This point has been made frequently in the philosophical literature. For a particularly strong case, see Robert E. Goodin, Political Theory and Public Policy (University of California Press, 1982). We shall return to this point in chapters 6-7.

We might examine Max Weber's famous argument on this point. In his essay "Politics as a Vocation" (delivered as a speech in 1918), Weber is concerned with the appropriate personal stance which can be adopted by a sincere and honest person in politics. Weber's starting point is his claim that the essential defining feature of the political world is force: "...a state is a human community that (successfully) claims the monopoly of the legitimate use of physical force within a given territory."[14] For our purposes, what is crucial about this definition is that it leads us to see the politician as a wielder of power. Violence is merely one form of power, and politicians are confronted with the demand to use power in its myriad incarnations. We must thus be concerned about the proper standards to be applied to such activities, as Weber recognized: "It is the specific means of legitimate violence as such in the hand of human associations which determines the peculiarity of all ethical problems of politics."[15]

Power is found in all human relationships, and force is not limited to the political world (note the term "legitimate" in Weber's earlier quote). But no one else wields power so directly and for others as the politician is called upon to do. We need not point only to examples of military might or capital punishment; nations use their power to collect people's money, to stop persons from running into each other, to force children to be educated, and to decide who receives the benefits of economic growth and suffers the deprivation of economic stagnation. The politician is confronted

---

[14]Weber, "Politics as a Vocation," in H. H. Gerth and C. Wright Mills (eds.), From Max Weber (N.Y.: Oxford University Press, 1946), p. 78.
[15]Ibid., p. 124.

with the need to use power over precisely those persons
she is called upon to represent.

In a realm characterized by power, what ethical
standards make sense? It is here that Weber introduces
his distinction between two types of ethics--an ethic
of responsibility and an ethic of ultimate ends. The
former asks about the "foreseeable results of one's
action," while the latter asks only about the purity
of intentions. Weber's objection to the ethic of ultimate
ends is finally a purely descriptive one. Given the
nature of human action, and particularly of the irration-
ality of human history, "in numerous instances the
attainment of 'good' ends is bound to the fact that
one must be willing to pay the price of using morally
dubious means or at least dangerous ones--and facing
the possibility or even the probability of evil ramifications."16   Since "the decisive means for politics is
violence," it is simply impossible to adopt a stance
which ignores the immersion of the actor in such violence. Weber is convinced that <u>no</u> pure ethic can solve
this problem, and that the ethic of ultimate ends is
either wholly irresponsible (by failing to take account
of the realities of political action) or wholly irrelevant
(by removing the actor from the political world entirely).

16Ibid., p. 121.

> Whosoever contracts with violent means for whatever ends--and every politician does--is exposed to its specific consequences....
>
> Whoever wants to engage in politics at all...must know that he is responsible for what may become of himself under the impact of these paradoxes....He who seeks the salvation of the soul, of his own and of others, should not seek it along the avenue of politics, for the quite different tasks of politics can only be solved by violence.... Everything that is striven for through political action operating with violent means and following an ethic of responsibility endangers the 'salvation of the soul.' If, however, one chases after the ultimate good in a war of beliefs, following a pure ethic of absolute ends, then the goals may be damaged and discredited for generations, because responsibility for <u>consequences</u> is lacking...[17]

There is a short passage where Weber suggests that the two ethics can supplement each other. But the context makes it clear that he is referring only to the rare mature person who may take a "Here I stand" stance from within the ethic of responsibility.   There is little doubt where Weber's sympathies lie.

What can we appropriate from this discussion? It is clear that Weber is not drawing a distinction between good and bad politicians, or between ethical and unethical action. Rather, he insists that the very nature of politics undercuts the usefulness of a particular form of ethical reasoning: namely, the "absolutist" approach, which attempts to reason directly from principles to political action. Weber asserts that we simply know too much about human nature--about the linkage between violence and politics, about the re-emergence of routinized organizational processes in the wake of utopian or revolutionary change, about the unanticipated consequences

---

[17]<u>Ibid</u>., pp. 124-126.

of all social action--for us to believe that politics is possible without a radically attuned awareness of such consequences. This is not to say that the politician should ignore ideals, or that the political world has no place for idealists. It is only to note that politicians can ill afford to be unwilling to compromise, to pay more attention to their own fulfillment of moral duties than to the consequences of their actions.[18]

Weber's emphasis on the use of force in politics calls attention as well to the second aspect of our discussion of the representative nature of politics. Not only does the politician act for others, but the nature of social conflicts places the politician in a different situation. Because the option of the bystander is simply not available, a different type of justification is required for political action. This point might be clarified by referring briefly to a common line of argument in Christian social ethics, in defense of both the relevance and the distinctiveness of the ethical injunctions of the Sermon on the Mount. These injunctions (such as the command to turn the other cheek and to refrain from resisting evil) are often used as models for ethical principles which stand over against the political world. Weber himself refers to them, in fact, as the "ideal-typical" examples of absolutist ethics. The Christian may ask whether such injunctions are relevant at all in politics. Paul Ramsey's approach here is to draw a sharp distinction between a person being attacked, and a person witnessing an attack on someone else. The ethical injunctions are said to apply to the former situation, not to the latter:

---

[18]See chapters 6-7 for a further discussion of this issue.

...Jesus deals only with the simplest moral
situation in which blows may be struck, the
case of one person in relation to but one
other. He does not here undertake to say
how men, who themselves ought not to resist
at all or by any means whatever when they
themselves alone receive the blows, ought
to act in more complex cases where non-resistance
would in practice mean turning another person's
face to the blows of an oppressor. We are
not at all uncertain what Jesus' ethic was
in bilateral, two-party situations.[19]

However convincing this may be, this line of reasoning
sums up many features of politics we have been discussing. The realm of political action, requiring decisions
in a pressurized setting where the politician acts
for and on behalf of others, leads to a different set
of ethical standards, and a greater appreciation for,
and reliance upon, compromise. We do not want to prejudge
the case by viewing this political perspective as a
lesser ethic, nor as a somehow "compromised" mentality
or way of acting. But such observations do suggest
that the place of compromise in politics is related
to the most centrally defining elements of the political
world.

---

[19]Paul Ramsey, Basic Christian Ethics (N.Y.: Charles
Scribner's Sons, 1950), p. 167.

CHAPTER 3. COMPROMISE AND SENATE ORGANIZATION

Let us turn now to a particular context of political activity: the United States Senate in 1979-1980. We want to examine the factors of organizational life which influence the occurrence of compromise on the part of the members.[1] We shall discuss a series of organizational features of Senate life:

1. The Role of the Senator
2. The Loyalties of the Senator
3. Conditions of Finitude
4. Conditions of Powerlessness of the Senator
5. Conditions of Powerlessness of the Senate

It is noteworthy that the Senate itself has often been understood as a product of the compromises at the Constitutional Convention. The nature of the organization, its role in the new government, and the process by which the delegates arrived at its creation all attest to this aspect of its history. The following quotation (from one of the major sources on the Senate's history) gives a rich sense of this connection between the Senate and political compromise:

> In almost every phrase relating to the Senate there is reflected the delegates' anxious compromising. The result was a legislative body unique in its basis of representation, in its relation to the Executive and to the other branch of Congress, in its procedure, and in its weighty non-legislative powers. It was designed to be a small body, associated with the President somewhat as an executive council, acting as judge in the trial of all impeachments, serving as a check upon 'the changeableness, precipitation, and excesses

[1] The discussion is based primarily upon the interview study conducted by the author. (See the Appendix for a further discussion of the study design.) This will be supplemented by material drawn from observations, transcripts of Senate committee and floor discussions, and other written documents.

of the first branch,' especially as the guardian
of the small states against aggression on
the part of the large states, and as the
protector of all the states against encroachment
by the new 'centralized power.' And it was
to be the people's defender against 'the
turbulency of democracy.'[2]

<u>1. The Role of the Senator</u>

We begin by asking about the nature of the task
which Senators are expected to perform. This means
we ask about their roles: what are the sets of ordered
expectations which define what it means to be a United
States Senator?

Although the role is highly complex, we can begin
(and, in a sense, end) with the observation that the
Senator is a <u>representative</u>. All of our comments in
chapter 2 about the representative bias of politics
are relevant here. But what precisely does it mean
to be a representative?[3]

First, we should note that the notion of a representative government, in the sense in which we use the

[2]George H. Haynes, <u>The Senate of the United States: Its
History and Practice</u> (Boston: Houghton Mifflin Co.,
1938), Volume II, p. 1037.
[3]I can merely point to some central aspects of this
complex topic here. The literature on this subject
is enormous. See, in particular: Hanna Pitkin, <u>The
Concept of Representation</u> (University of California
Press, 1967); J. Roland Pennock and J. W. Chapman (eds.),
<u>Representation</u> (N.Y.: Atherton Press, 1968); Roger
Davidson, <u>The Role of the Congressman</u> (N.Y.: Pegasus,
1969); Lewis Dexter, "The Representative and His District,"
<u>Human Organization</u> 16 (Spring, 1957), pp. 2-13; Congres-
sional Quarterly, <u>Guide to Congress</u>, 2nd edition (Washington: Congressional Quarterly, 1976), pp. 581-596.
    Six brief but helpful essays on this problem can
also be found in Norman E. Bowie (ed.), <u>Ethical Issues
in Government</u> (Phila.: Temple University Press, 1981).

term, is a peculiarly modern and western one.[4] Our representatives are distinctive in two ways: they are elected by a large number of persons, all of whom can claim to be represented by them; and they are reponsible to (although not necessarily responsive to) a diverse group of individuals, rather than to a particular economic or social grouping.

But what does it mean to speak of representing persons? Consider the complex nature of the connection between the representative and the represented. A common distinction is drawn between three models of the process. The delegate is expected to obey the wishes of the persons (the constituency) who have elected her; as a delegate, the representative is not allowed to use judgment in deciding how to vote or act, once those wishes have been ascertained. By contrast, the trustee is expected to use more judgment, taking into account the views of the constituents but not being bound by them. The broker is an intermediate type, using some independent judgment but trying always to blend conflicting interests and to follow the needs or desire

---

[4]Only a society structured around different interests attached to autonomous individuals can be concerned with the question of how to represent persons in a political process. For example, in societies where estates or classes are the central units, there will not be persons assigned the task of representing a group of individuals as individuals. For an interesting historical discussion, see Charles Beard and John Lewis, "Representative Government in Evolution," American Political Science Review 26 (April, 1932), pp. 223-240 (reprinted in Neal Riemer [ed.], The Representative [Boston: D. C. Heath and Co., 1967], pp. 96-107).

of the constituency.[5]

The selection of a model is very important for our purposes. If we accept the delegate model, questions of compromise arise only within the context of trying to follow the desires of the constituency. Alternatively, if we begin with the trustee model, then we cannot justify compromises which allow constituent opinion to override other considerations. We must therefore try to come to terms with this problem.

First, note that the choice between models is not a very clearcut one in practice. The desire to be re-elected prevents any Senator from ignoring, or consistently opposing, the views of the constituency. Similarly, the desire to be seen as "statesmanlike" prevents any Senator from following these views without question. Of the thirty-four Senators interviewed, thirty-one stated that they either had or would be willing to vote counter to the views of their constituents. Given the perceived value of being an independent person, it is perhaps surprising that even three Senators admitted that they would never do so. But there are some problems here (aside from the obvious one of whether to trust these responses at all). For example, how does one

---

[5]See the references in footnote 1. This distinction has "caught on" in the literature, although I shall suggest some problems with its usage. The distinction between delegate and trustee, in particular, has become an accepted part of the culture of American politics.

The meaning of representation is culturally bound in many respects. For example, Gordon Tullock has suggested that American political scientists tend to use the term as a synonym for being elected from a district, while European scholars often say that representing someone means taking that person's views into account. (Tullock, Toward a Mathematics of Politics [University of Michigan Press, 1967], pp. 144-145.)

know the wishes of the constituency? How does one decide when to override those views?

Before beginning to answer these questions, we should note that most Senators seem to find the question of such models fairly irrelevant to actual Senate life. The conflict between personal judgment and constituency views has been overemphasized in much of the literature, for it seldom arises in the lives of most Senators. Members are elected by, and have usually been long-time residents of, a particular state, and they are likely to be similar in judgment and taste to their constituents. One Senator reported that "if I get two critical letters a day out of 15,000 letters, it's a bad day." Furthermore, most states are heterogeneous enough to allow the Senator to find strong support for most positions; as one Senator noted, "you can almost always find majority support for your position if you look hard enough." Alternatively, very small and homogeneous states are more likely to send representatives who share the views of the people on most issues.[6]

In addition, both because of the length of the Senate term and the number of issues considered during any term, senators see themselves as relatively immune. Only in the case of a very "hot" issue, or of a consistent pattern of voting against constituency sentiment, does a senator lose much support in diverging from such sentiment. Such freedom decreases as one nears the next election, however, and is related not merely to the time but also to the difficulty of the next campaign. One of the most "trustee-like" Senators admitted

---

[6]It is interesting to find that, of the three Senators who claimed to adopt a pure delegate stance, two were from small, homogeneous states.

that he tends to pay more attention to constituent sentiment in the year before a campaign, an admission he made with a great deal of evident discomfort.

So the occurrence of a direct conflict between constituent views and one's own judgment is a rare event. But what happens in the event of a conflict? I would argue that a delegate stance is the more appropriate model simply because the very notion of representation seems to disappear at the other end of the continuum. Hanna Pitkin argues that representation also disappears at the delegate end, because to represent something is always to act "at one remove" from the entity being represented.[7] I think this is a far weaker case, however, since a delegate may be needed to represent a constituency which is simply too large to be physically present in the halls of decision. But if the trustee loses interest in the wishes of the represented, it is odd to speak of representation at all.

However, to accept the delegate model as the starting point is not to accept its application in all cases. Indeed, much of the disdain senators feel about this entire question revolves around their claim that the delegate stance, if taken to extremes, would commit the senator to polling the voters on every issue. As one Senator said: "If they wanted that, they could have hired a computer. I am sent here to think." Many senators referred to Edmund Burke's speech to the Electors of Bristol as justification for their independence:

> Certainly, Gentlemen, it ought to be the happiness and glory of a representative to live in the strictest union, the closest correspondence, and the most unreserved commu-

---

[7]Pitkin, The Concept of Representation, esp. chapter 7.

nication with his constituents. Their wishes
ought to have great weight with him; their
opinions high respect; their business unremitted
attention. It is his duty to sacrifice his
repose, his pleasure, his satisfactions,
to theirs--and above all, ever, and in all
cases, to prefer their interest to his own.
    But his unbiased opinion, his mature
judgment, his enlightened conscience, he
ought not to sacrifice to you, to any man,
or to any set of men living. These he does
not derive from your pleasure--no, nor from
the law and the Constitution. They are a
trust from Providence, for the abuse of which
he is deeply answerable. Your representative
owes you, not his industry only, but his
judgment; and he betrays, instead of serving
you, if he sacrifices it to your opinion.[8]

Notice several points about this often quoted
passage. First, Burke is careful to stress the importance
of constituency opinion and representative responsiveness,
just as he insists that these factors alone cannot
determine his vote. Second, Burke does not seem to
be saying that the representative should ever vote
against the interests of the constituents, but merely
that he may vote against their sentiments or opinions
if his conscience tells him to do so. And third, remember
that Burke withdrew from a later election when he realized
that he would lose, a fact which may make modern-day
politicians pause before endorsing his position.[9]
    Let us begin by accepting the delegate stance

[8]Burke, "Speech to the Electors of Bristol," November 3,
1774; in The Works of the Right Honourable Edmund Burke,
4th edition (Boston: Little, Brown, and Company, 1871),
Volume II, p. 95.
[9]On this last point, see Ernest Barker, "Burke and His
Bristol Constituency, 1774-1780," in his Essays in
Government (N. J.: Oxford University Press, 1945);
quoted in Heinz Eulau, "Changing Views of Representation,"
in Ithiel de Sola Pool (ed.), Contemporary Political
Science (N. Y.: McGraw-Hill, 1967), pp. 53-85.

as a starting point, and ask under what conditions a representative might be led away from such a stance. I would suggest the following seven potentially overriding considerations which might lead us toward the trustee end of the continuum.

  1. The representative may <u>not be able to determine the views</u> of the constituency. One's vote may then be based on what one believed to be the views of that group, however. This argument has much less relevance in an age of technological innovations and mass polling techniques, of course. But even if we cannot poll the constituency, we can try to represent them by figuring out what they would want if they could tell us. If this is the way the decision is made, then the representative remains true to the spirit and intent of the delegate model.

  2. The representative may perceive a <u>lack of consensus</u> among the constituency, or even a lack of majority support for any one position. Such a situation is quite frequent. But the senator could still make a decision according to a plurality of opinion, or according to the strengths of the views of the different groups. We are still not led very far afield here from the delegate stance.

  3. The decision may call for a <u>highly technical degree of knowledge</u>, which is not possessed by the constituency for reasons of understanding or interest. Here, we begin to allow the representative to override the expressed views of the constituency. If people do not care enough to study and learn the facts, it might be argued, then they have forfeited their right to determine policy. But such reasoning is inappropriate in situations where the public has formed any opinions at all. Because the representative has access to more

information than anyone else (by virtue of positioning
in the corridors of power), this argument may undermine
the obligation to take the constituency's views seriously
at all. The more common case is that of highly technical
legislation, where the public has no clearly articulated
(or even clearly felt) position at all, and such examples
fall under our earlier two categories. A decision
to override for reasons of technical knowledge is appropriate only when the public has misinterpreted or misapplied
the knowledge it does have. Otherwise, the legislator
would be able to ignore public opinion on the basis
of her superior knowledge in almost all instances.

4. A closely related argument involves cases where
the decision is based upon information of a classified
nature which cannot be shared. Questions of national
security or foreign treaties are the most relevant
examples here. Indeed, many senators distinguish between
domestic and foreign policy issues, allowing themselves
more room for judgment on the latter. The senator may
move toward the trustee model on such questions, and
the self-understanding of the Senate as a central institution in the determination of foreign policy provides
further support for such exceptions to the delegate
model. But, even here, the argument is usually made
that the representative will vote according to how
the constituents would feel if they did have access
to the information. Once again, the views (potential,
not actual) of the public remain determinative.

5. The constituents may not recognize what is
in their own best interests. As a result, the representative
may vote against their opinions in order to protect
their real interests. Such an argument can degenerate
into an unacceptable paternalism, but it need not do
so. We generally believe that individuals are the best

judges of their own interests; but there are exceptions, and this argument need only claim that, in those instances, the representative should attend to interests rather to opinions. Brian Barry has suggested that my "interests" are those policies which increase my opportunities to receive what I want; we are dealing here with situations where I am simply mistaken about what will provide me with what I want.[10] We can think of numerous examples: the effects of foreign treaties, energy policies, or the use of potentially dangerous products such as tobacco. It is not paternalistic, at least not in the pejorative sense, to recognize that persons sometimes cannot judge what is in their best interests, particularly in instances of complex social policy.

If this is true, then there is a strong argument for allowing the representative to vote against the wishes of the constituency. But note that this involves a very limited move. Just as a legal trustee is expected to act on behalf of the best interests of the client, so the representative here maintains primary concern for the interests of the represented. It would be inappropriate here to vote against constituency interests for any other reason, such as one's own moral views or one's allegiance to another social group. Indeed, this is one of the major problems with the trustee analogy in the political comparison, for it forces

---

[10]Barry, "The Public Interest" (1964), reprinted in J. Charles King and James A. McGilvray (eds.), <u>Political and Social Philosophy</u> (N. Y.: McGraw-Hill, 1973), pp. 279-288.

us to stop here.[11] To go any further would destroy the legal analogy. But we can go further, and many discussions which use the term "trustee" seem to include these other examples as well.

6. The issue under consideration <u>may not affect the constituency</u> directly, or at least not as it affects other social groups. For example, another region of the country may be threatened by a policy decision, and the senator's constituents may oppose the decision to help them. Can the senator, as a representative, attend to the needs of persons other than the immediate constituency? Or, the issue may involve a foreign policy question affecting few citizens in the nation. In such cases the senator may decide that the interests of the constituency are not relevant to the decision. Such an argument moves us further along the road toward a more independent model of the senator's role.

7. Finally, the representative may recognize <u>a higher constituency</u> for the sake of which even the important interests of the electing group may be overridden. This higher constituency might be the United States, an ideal, or some understanding of conscience or personal integrity. We have here a direct confrontation between the two notions of representation. To

---

[11]Burke might be interpreted as stopping here, in spite of the common view. But his views are more complex, since he does often speak of the representative as no longer being tied in any special way to the interests of the electing district.

See, in addition to the "Speech to the Electors of Bristol," Burke's "Speech at his Arrival at Bristol" (October 13, 1774) (in <u>Works</u>, Volume II, pp. 81-88); "Speech at Bristol Previous to the Election" (Sept. 6, 1780) (in <u>Works</u>, Volume II, pp. 365-424); and "Speech at Bristol on Declining the Poll" (Sept. 9, 1780) (in <u>Works</u>, Volume II, pp. 425-429).

decide to override the interests of a constituency is to move decisively away from viewing oneself as their delegate--and, perhaps, as their representative as well.

In our society, what alternative constituencies are appropriate for the legislator to use in overriding constituency interests? We would probably object to a legislator using family or financial interests as an alternative constituency; indeed, most conflict of interest legislation is designed to eliminate the use of such factors. But consider the case of religious belief or affiliation. In American politics, one's religion is usually not seen as an appropriate higher constituency when it is defined as a distinct organizational entity. We might remember John Kennedy's need to distance himself from his Catholicism in 1960. The concern then was not over his religious beliefs, but over the perceived organizational effects of the Catholic hierarchy in relation to one of its adherents. At the same time, the politician is not expected, or perhaps even allowed, to appear totally unaffected by the broader convictions of a religious faith. Indeed, for Kennedy to have suggested that his Catholicism was totally irrelevant might have led the public to conclude that he was not really a "religious" person at all. In short, American society seems comfortable with the values of "the Judaeo-Christian tradition," but somewhat uncomfortable with loyalty to specific manifestations of that tradition.[12]

The other generally acceptable higher constituency is the nation as a whole. Senators often refer to the need to represent the entire country, rather than their state or region. As I noted above, foreign policy decisions often provide opportunities for political heroism here; the Panama Canal treaty ratification was cited by almost every senator as the best (and often as the only) example in the recent past of a direct conflict between personal judgment and constituency views. Senators who voted against the apparent wishes of the constituency used the broader interests of the United States as the explanation. Most senators believed that the people were informed about the treaty, able to assess their own interests, but not able or willing to adopt a national perspective to the problem. Thus, one can refer to one's role as a "United States Senator" as a justification for overriding such strong views.

Even here, however, the examples selected by the participants seldom describe a clear conflict between the interests of the constituency and those of another group. In the Panama Canal example, most senators believed that the long term interests of the country (and, therefore, of their constituents as well) were being protected

---

[12]The expectations of the American people that their leaders will be religious are best expressed in the famous statement by President Eisenhower that "Our government makes no sense unless it is founded in a deeply felt religious faith--and I don't care what it is." (The New York Times, December 23, 1952; quoted in Will Herberg, Protestant, Catholic, Jew [N.Y.: Anchor Books, 1960], p. 84.) See also John Murray Cuddihy, No Offense: Civil Religion and Protestant Taste (N.Y.: The Seabury Press, 1978).

The country recently elected its first divorced President; the reader might consider whether we are ready for our first avowedly atheist President.

by the new treaty. The choice of a higher constituency
is seldom used to explain action against constituency
interests. Rather, the more common line of reasoning
is to suggest that the higher interests are in harmony
with those of the constituents, if only the latter
would recognize that fact.

From this discussion, it is clear that the complexity
of the representative role requires most senators to
compromise between the two poles of delegate and trustee. The only way to avoid this dilemma is to opt for
one or the other pole in all cases. But we would probably
not want a polling procedure on every issue, nor would
we feel represented by a politician who refused to
be influenced by our opinions or interests. As a result,
senators must find arguments and reasons for placing
themselves along the continuum on each issue, and the
need to explain divergences to constituencies is likely
to lead to a compromising mentality. One is willing
to listen to the popular will in some cases, but not
in others; the actor gives in to popular sentiment
on one issue in order to fight harder against it on
the next vote.

There is no way out here, for the politician in
our system seems required to live in a world of grey
shadows. Hanna Pitkin makes this point well:

> Political questions are not likely to be
> as arbitrary as a choice between two foods;
> nor are they likely to be questions of knowledge
> to which an expert can supply the one correct
> answer. They are questions about action,
> about what should be done; consequently they
> involve both facts and value commitments,
> both ends and means. And, characteristically,
> the factual judgments, the value commitments,
> the ends and the means, are inextricably
> intertwined in political life....It is a

> field where rationality is no guarantee of
> agreement. Yet, at the same time, rational
> arguments are sometimes relevant, and agreement
> can sometimes be reached. Political life
> is not merely the making of arbitrary choices,
> nor merely the resultant of bargaining between
> separate, private wants. It is always a combin-
> ation of bargaining and compromise where
> there are irresolute and conflicting commitments,
> and common deliberation about public policy,
> to which facts and rational arguments are
> relevant.[13]

The very nature of politics requires structures of
representation to assure that we as citizens are both
protected and consulted, governed and governing, ordered
and freed. The representative is caught in the midst
of a complex set of choices concerning how and where
to draw the lines of popular and direct control over
policy-making decisions. The dilemma results not from
confusion about the role but from the role itself. To
seek to escape from the dilemma by maintaining complete
independence or rigid adherence to popular sentiment
is to undermine the very essence of what it means to
be a representative.

There are two ways to compromise in this situation. First, the politician can try to find a difference
between relevant examples, as in the cases of senators
who consider foreign policy issues within a trustee
framework, and domestic ones more frequently within
a delegate one. It might be asked whether such an approach
is a compromise at all, since the senator is apparently
simply applying different criteria to different cases. But
such a decision does reflect an attempt to deal with
two valued but conflicting definitions of the role
by finding a middle ground; this solution represents

---

[13]Pitkin, The Concept of Representation, p. 212.

an effort to avoid being charged with either ignoring or pandering to the constituency.

The more common strategy of compromise, however, is to redefine a single meaning of the role which falls between the two poles. The senator may decide to listen to opinion, take it seriously, inform people of the facts, and "stay close to the pulse" of the voters. But such attention need not determine one's votes. Such a strategy allows the senator to use any of our seven arguments as justifications for moving away from the strict delegate stance, because no commitment was ever made to the stance in the first place. Rather than weighing whether a particular issue should be decided as delegate or trustee, the senator tries here to adopt a generalized middle ground model, moving toward the delegate pole in certain situations (such as before a campaign) and toward the trustee pole in others (such as being confronted with a personal moral objection to a popular bill). This compromise strategy allows the senator to be a representative regardless of the particular vote on a given bill.[14]

Of course, one could adopt one or the other model at all times, and three Senators claim to do so. The fact that such an option is open reinforces the fact

---

[14]For comparative purposes, note Davidson's finding that members of the House of Representatives were more likely to adopt an intermediate "politico" style of representation than either the trustee or delegate models. Not surprisingly, Davidson also reports that members from safe districts tended to be on the trustee end of the continuum. (Davidson, The Role of the Congressman, esp. pp. 117-129.) By contrast, Eulau et al. found a predominance of the trustee style among state legislators in 1957. (Heinz Eulau, J. C. Wahlke, W. Buchanan, and L. Ferguson, "The Role of the Representative...," American Political Science Review 53 [September 1959], pp. 742-756.)

that the compromise is a decision made by the senator, rather than a necessary and defined aspect of the role. The need to struggle with the question is inevitable, but the solution adopted by the politician is not.

In addition, note that other aspects of compromise in the Senate derive from this central question of the nature of the role. This is apparent when we consider the changes which might result in the adoption of radically different models by most members of the organization. If most senators suddenly decided not to seek re-election (or, perhaps, if Senate votes were not recorded), much jockeying for position would cease. There would still be compromises, but senators might be much less sensitive to the needs of their states. Alternatively, if the cultural acceptance of the use of independent judgment was undermined, the delegate pole might be chosen much more frequently, with a resulting increase in the bartering between regions and interest groups. Thus, as we turn to our other organizational features, we will continue to ask about the effect of the representative role.

Finally, it is interesting to discover that the delicacy of the choice of representative model is clearly understood by the actors themselves. Indeed, an important norm of Senate life is that one does not place a colleague in a position of having to vote against constituency sentiment. It might be said that one's own adherence to the delegate stance helps determine one's protectiveness towards colleagues. Senator Daniel Moynihan, one of the strongest proponents (in both word and deed) of a slightly modified delegate stance, once gave the following argument in a committee session during consideration of an amendment which appeared to have benefitted his own state:

> Senator Moynihan: ...I've got to tell you
> why I'm not going to vote for Senator Danforth's
> bill, although everything he said is right
> in my view. Everything he said is right. I'm
> not going to vote for it because it would
> cause severe difficulties for Senators around
> this table who represent communities which
> would be [adversely] affected. They would
> be thought not to have protected the interests
> of their states, and a Senator is sent here
> to do that.[15]

Moynihan then proceeds to castigate other senators
for failing to pay sufficient attention to the needs
of his state. But his comment does reflect a particular
understanding of what "a Senator is sent here to do,"
an understanding which, in its capacity for projection,
creates an underlying sympathy for those who must struggle
with the difficult role of being a representative.[16]

2. The Loyalties of the Senator

Our argument concerning the higher constituencies
to which the senator can appeal raises a broader question: To whom is the senator loyal? Although this issue
is related to the representative role, the senator
may be required to step outside of the senatorial role
in making certain decisions. We are concerned here
only with actions taken in the policy-making process,
however; the private life of the senator is not our
primary concern.

But even within the public arena, there may be
situations which cannot be explained solely by reference

---

[15]Senate Finance Committee, markup of HR3919, October 10,
1979.
[16]I would not want the reader to shed any tears for the
legislator's predicament, however. The rewards of office
are obviously high, and people seldom have to be convinced
to run for political office.

to the internal dynamics of the senatorial role. As with all social roles, that of a senator may require the actor to balance other roles at the same time, and one's loyalties to other definitions of self impinge constantly upon the acting out of the primary role. The result is often referred to as role conflict.[17]

Such conflicts may arise in different ways. There may be tensions between one's duties as a representative of Nevada, and one's personal views about gambling; a senator may be caught between the demands of being a Christian minister and a legislator voting for military preparedness. Note that all such conflicts do not arise from differing definitions of what one must do to fulfill the representative role. Rather, they pose contrasts between the obligations of the representative, and other sets of obligations one has as a person with a religion, a family, or a conscience. The examples raised in section 1 concerned differing ways of acting as a representative; our problems here concern differing ways of acting as a person who is both a representative and something else.

Once again, we can solve such problems by choosing one side or the other. The senator can decide that, once the role of senator is adopted, the obligations inherent in that role will be overriding in all cases. One will then echo the Senator who said to me, in explaining why he voted against his "conscience" in several cases: "I wasn't sent here to vote my own conscience; I was sent here to represent my constituency." In fact, this Senator adopts a fairly independent style of representation. But

---

[17]The reader is referred to the large body of literature in sociology and social psychology concerned with these issues.

he never allows himself to use his own judgment against his perception of the interests of those who elected him. The more commonly stated position, however, is a somewhat modified version of this stance, whereby the senator does pay attention to other non-role factors in some cases.

One way to arrive at such a solution is to build into the nature of the representative role the expectation to "act as one's own person." We stumbled across this argument earlier, and suggested that it simply puts off the reckoning concerning when one does so. In what sense am I representing my constituents if I am loyal to something or someone apart from their interests? Perhaps I thereby provide an example of an upright person, or perhaps I am giving them the benefit of my better judgment. We might expect voters to be pleased by seeing such an example, but it would be hard to imagine them feeling that they were being represented by such activities. Of course, the senator can claim that this is indeed a proper kind of representation, but we would do better to see this as the choice of another loyalty which overrides the obligation to the constituents in this instance. To accept the attempted redefinition of the representative role is to say that anything an elected official does is representative, a view which seems to contradict the common meaning of the term. After all, we can (and often do) accuse a "representative" of failing to represent us.

On the other hand, the senator can opt for the other end of the continuum, claiming that she is ultimately loyal to something else, and that the interests of the constituency always take second place. Now, some senators seem to believe that certain other members of the Senate take such a position, although it is worth noting that only one senator actually used this description about himself. The most common higher loyalty referred to is either conscience or religious beliefs. It seems to be accepted that one may vote as one's conscience or religious beliefs dictate, regardless of conflicts with one's representative role. But senators generally refuse to describe their own actions in this way, while holding an almost grudging respect for those who are perceived as doing so.

As we suggested earlier, it may be a luxury for an elected official to use such non-role criteria. But however admirable it may be, it is also suspect within the organization of the Senate. And for good reason, I think: the senator who operates from a higher loyalty is continually calling into question the apparently more "mundane" and "political" allegiances of her colleagues. After all, this person is also a representative, and the other senators also have consciences. How, then, can one deal with a person who seems to be judging (by actions, if not by words) the more earthbound activities of others?

For our purposes here, note that such a solution to the loyalty problem is both possible and extremely rare. When it does occur, it is usually tolerated by the other senators only if lived out with a humble style, and tolerated by the voters only if the more mundane constituent issues are also served. A Senator who is viewed as particularly loyal to non-Senatorial role definitions spent much of his interview explaining in great detail how attentive he is to the wishes and needs of his constituents. The willingness to override representative role obligations often depends upon a greater degree of attentiveness to offset the perception of too much independence.

We would not expect many senators to adopt such a stance; indeed, if our earlier discussion of the representative role is correct, we would probably not want them to do so. If we want to be represented, we expect not only a full-bodied substantive notion of representation, but also the willingness to use this notion. A parent who often said to a child, "I know I should spend more time with you, but I have to go bowling," would not be said to be redefining the role of parent--she would be said to be failing to act as a parent. Similarly, the representative who adopts a strong delegate notion of the role but continually allows it to be overridden by other role obligations, is somehow missing the point of what it means to act as a representative in the first place. Roles are sets of expectations, and we expect representatives to act in certain ways, not merely to ask what a representative would do and weigh that against other role obligations. To occupy a role means precisely that: to occupy it, to fill or possess a social space, to sit in it and act out of it.

The dilemma here is an important one. I can decide to represent you by always upholding whatever I should do as your representative; but if I do this, I am forced to ignore all my other roles. I can decide to represent you by being true to other roles when they conflict with my political responsibilities, but then I may not be representing you at all. Or I may try to use my judgment to choose those cases where I will act out of each role. But this solution should make you uneasy, for I have not told you whether this stance of judgment is defined inside of the representative

role itself. If it is not, then the representative
role is likely to lose out.

So we come back to the difficult choice. I can
compromise by trying to redefine the representative
role to incorporate within it some room for maneuvering.
This solution is the one most commonly adopted in the
Senate, I believe. The redefinition proceeds as follows: It
is mistaken to believe that a representative is really
different from anyone else; all persons have many loyalties,
many of which conflict with one another; the obligations
of a representative are therefore limited by other
loyalties in some situations; but it is in fact in
the constituents' interests to be represented by a
person who can recognize such conflicts and choose
alternative role obligations, because only such a person
is truly conscientious and loyal. The argument usually
ends with an attempt, therefore, to redefine the senatorial
role as a representative, not by claiming that a representative should so act, but that a person acting as
a representative should do so.

The argument is self-serving, of course. But if
we allow such an objection to forestall possible solutions
in politics, we are doomed to navel-gazing. At least
there is a certain plausibility in the position. No
attempt is made to argue that one must act this way,
nor is it said that one has an independent stance from
which to decide when to override the representative
role obligations. The actor simply admits that she
is like everyone else in the society: caught between
conflicting loyalties, and forced, from within the
bounds of all such loyalties, to make hard decisions. Sometimes one's duty to represent will win out; sometimes
one's religious views may be more powerful; sometimes
conscience will be determinative. But the decision

must be made in full awareness that the override does destroy something of value: namely, the very real obligation to act in each of these roles. To decide to override the obligations of the representative does not mean that one no longer has those obligations; it simply means that one has chosen to act as the occupant of another role.

Surely there is a question of degree here, as most senators are quick to admit and comment upon. To be loyal to another role as a common occurrence would be seen as stepping outside of the role completely. But there is room for some maneuvering, and the result is a fairly well-agreed-upon compromise solution which enables the senator to return to the voters and say, in effect: "I have represented you well, and when I have not, it is because I must be true to something higher; is this not the highest tribute I can pay to your integrity as my constituents?"

Such compromises are seldom explicit. Indeed, the few senators who do have explicit philosophies here are often mentioned by others as exceptions, and they usually are persons who have worked out such issues before entering the Senate. But, consciously or not, senators adopt some blending of their conflicting roles, and they struggle (particularly during re-election campaigns and interviews) to dredge up reasons for acting the way they do. Indeed, the fact that such stances are not explicitly adopted lends even greater weight to their significance; the senator is always acting out of some such compromised model, and to become too aware of what that model is would undermine the ability to act, much as the bicycle rider wavers when thinking about balancing. Adopting such blendings and interweavings of role obligations is part of the senator's

life; the observer can call attention to them, even
if the actor is seldom aware of them as compromises
at all. It is easier to forget what pure action might
be in a context which mitigates against it.

3. Conditions of Finitude

We have already seen that conditions of finitude
affect the style of political action. In Senate life,
such conditions are most apparent on four levels: time,
information, predictability, and societal resources.

Finitude of Time. The severe time constraints
and immense workload of the Senate are noted by almost
every writer on the subject of the Senate, and most
members commented unfavorably on these conditions. One
of the most reflective senators ended the interview
by shrugging his shoulders and saying: "Don't get the
idea that I sit down on every issue and think through
what is the moral thing to do....I don't have time
to do such thinking on every issue." Another Senator
responded to my question about whether members had
time to arrive at reflective decisions by saying: "You're
half right--we don't have time to make any decisions."
And a Senator's secretary answered my request for a
thirty minute interview by stating flatly that "he
doesn't even give his wife thirty minutes."

Perhaps the best documentation of Senate time
pressures is found in a 1976 study, which found 11
hour working days, 500,000 pages of printed hearings
and reports, 2734 meetings, and 20 million pieces of
mail received in the Senate mailroom every year.[18]

---

[18]U. S. Commission on the Operation of the Senate, Toward
a Modern Senate (Washington: Government Printing Office,
1976).

Senators usually arrive early at the office, spend mornings at one or two committee sessions (often dashing back and forth between them), grab lunch with a constituent, run between office and the Senate floor several times in the afternoon between other appointments, and often stay late for floor votes or meetings with staff. Although this pace varies with different members, the overall impression is of people with minimal time to devote to any single activity.

The fact that senators report overwork might reflect laziness or impatience. After all, people often feel that they are expected to work too hard. But this response misses the point. The job of senator seems to require time for reflection to perform the work; the major complaint raised is not that senators do not have enough time for family or other activities, but that they don't have enough time to do the job itself.

The fact of limited time is largely hidden, however. Being a world of action, the Senate continues to function, regardless of the time available for such reflection. Bills are reported out, votes are taken, sessions end; unlike many office situations where work piles up when time is scarce, the output of the Senate is not particularly affected. Senators learn to accept the constraints; they may complain about them, but they live with them. It is a common observation to see a senator dashing down the hall to make a roll call vote, trailed by a staff member explaining what bill is being considered and how the senator is supposed to vote. But the vote will be taken, even though most senators may have only a few minutes to reflect on its merits.

There are some countervailing factors here. Most votes are somewhat routine, and a senator usually has taken a position on other bills which determine the vote on similar pieces of legislation. In addition, some members become seen as experts in certain areas, and a senator can often look to one or two colleagues to provide the lead on votes in their areas of expertise. One learns quickly which issues require special attention, and most senators select carefully those arenas to which they will devote time and attention. But, even with such specialization, each senator must vote on every bill which comes to the floor, and few bills can be carefully studied and digested by either staff or senator.

Such time constraints have two major effects on compromise. First, in terms of the legislation itself, senators are accustomed to weighing the pros and cons of each bill in a hasty fashion. A limited number of questions (including the key one, "how does this affect my state?") are thrown at the relevant staff member, or at the colleague sponsoring the bill, and a decision is made with little time for reflection. In such a context, senators are often less concerned about the merits of the bill than they are about establishing a pattern of voting, or being true to an already established pattern. A senator with a record of pro-labor votes, from a strongly unionized state, will require a very strong argument to vote against any pro-labor bill. As a result, the strategy of decision making is always a compromise between the desire to know enough about a bill to make an informed decision, and the often opposing desire to know little enough about it to be able comfortably to vote the way one wants to. In other words, there are costs of taking too much time on a bill; in realizing that there are two sides to the

question, I may be forced to depart from a previous
line of voting.

Now, such compromises result from the basic problem
of finitude of time, and they are not unique to the
Senate. But they have particularly crucial consequences
in an organization whose task is deliberation and decision
upon major policy questions affecting the lives of
an entire society. To make decisions on any basis other
than the merit of a bill is itself a compromise of
an essential aspect of one's job description. Admittedly,
to maintain a position of consistency across many bills
is commendable; but the time pressures create artificial
notions of how various bills fit together ideologically. A
bill becomes identified as pro-labor or pro-family,
and this label alone can determine the outcome of the
vote. It is largely for this reason that the sponsors
of a bill are so important; for a pro-labor liberal
senator to have his name on a bill may assure the support
of a number of other senators who do not have the time
to look more carefully into the content of the legislation.

Why is this a compromise, if the time constraints
are inevitable? The key point here is that the senator
does have alternatives. One could have more staff
concentrating on the relative merits of the legislation,
or demand more careful arguments from one's colleagues,
or refuse to accept a sponsor's definition of what
the bill will do. Admittedly, such alterations in behavior
are unlikely, without a decrease in the number of bills
introduced each session. But the time available might
be spent differently, and the choices are made freely.

The second aspect of the constraint of time concerns
the choice of ways to spend one's time. One Senator
commented that "we're always compromising. I should
be at a committee meeting right now, but I'm compromising

that to talk to you." They decide which meeting to attend, and which bill to slight; which constituent to see, and which to send off with a staff member; which bill to amend, and which to vote for unseen. Again, all of us make choices concerning our time and energies. The problem is simply compounded in the Senate, due to the extreme pressures and the expectation that a senator will take time to act knowledgeably.

We should view such decisions as compromises. Senators can choose where to place their limited energy and time. Such choices, therefore, as concessions of important values, must be justified over against the alternatives. For example, it is interesting that most senators manage to find the time and energy for the task of casework: answering the mail, doing favors for the constituency, and sending out literature reminding the voters that all these tasks are continuing. There are strong arguments for wanting senators to pay attention to such matters; we might wonder, however, whether some of this time and energy (especially on the part of the staff) might not be better spent on increased support of constituency needs through the legislative process itself, or through giving staff members more time to study complex bills. Whatever our answer, the decision to spend time on casework compromises the need to spend time elsewhere; conditions of finitude of time increase, rather than decrease, the need to explain and justify such decisions. It is only when we forget that these are compromises that we may forget to ask for an accounting of how that limited time is spent.

Finitude of Information and Complexity. Closely related to constraints of time are those of information and complexity. Human beings are limited in the amount and type of specialized knowledge they can incorporate, synthesize, and use; senators may be intelligent but they are still human. The outsider cannot grasp the amounts or complexity of information involved in most pieces of social legislation. However, one need only read the draft of a bill, or listen to a committee session, to gather an appreciation (and perhaps a fear) of such factors. And the amount and complexity of such information are increasing rapidly.[19]

There are major consequences of this problem. The Senate is beginning to develop a more specialized division of labor, whereby certain members are perceived as experts in particular areas. Although the Senate has not progressed as far in this direction as the House of Representatives, one still hears members referring to certain colleagues whose lead they will follow on certain types of legislation. What is particularly interesting about this process is that there is a correlation between areas of expertise and constituent need. As a result, certain regions or states are inordinately well-represented in terms of their effects on legislation. Of course, how "inordinate" this is depends upon our assessment of the appropriate connection between policy and local needs. For example, should

---

[19]This increase is due to a number of factors, including, according to one recent study: economic growth, expansion of substantive areas covered by Senate legislation, more sophisticated scientific and technical knowledge, increased size of government, and an increased desire to counter the growth in power and size of the executive branch. (Commission on the Operation of the Senate, Toward a Modern Senate.) It has been estimated that, although the number of bills passed per session has not increased, the number of pages and the number of titles per bill has risen substantially. (Fox and Hammond, Congressional Staffs: The Invisible Force in American Lawmaking [N.Y.: Free Press, 1977], p. 27.)

the existence of oil in one region give that area more weight in the determination of national energy policy?

The other result is that responsibility for handling and sorting out information falls upon the staff. Whether the increase in volume and complexity of legislation is a cause or an effect of increased numbers of staff, the correlation is a strong one. The following table indicates the rising number of staff positions on both personal and committee levels in the Senate:[20]

Date	Committee Staff	Personal Staff
1891	41	39
1930	163	280
1957	558	1115
1967	621	1751
1976	1534	3251

This increase has turned most Senate offices into small bureaucracies, with an average of thirty-one staff members on each personal staff and numerous other staffers on committees. Staff are increasingly significant in suggesting and implementing legislative proposals. But, while they provide the senator with welcome relief, they are one more burden, as the senator is besieged with demands from these people who are hired to provide relief from the burdens of work.

Such information and complexity provide additional stresses for compromise. Here, what is compromised is not an ideal of adequate time in which to decide, but rather the opportunity to sort through and collate information in a meaningful way. Once senators recognize these limits, they are forced to compromise by establishing standards of adequacy rather than standards of knowledge. The former standards allow a decision to be

[20]From Fox and Hammond, Congressional Staffs, p. 178.

made with the full realization that much more information is available. Indeed, the senator usually does not want to use more stringent standards, because the need to be protected from informational overload creates a desire to minimize information.

Again, we should not be either surprised or offended by such a situation. The sheer weight of information, and the incredible complexity of this information, require the actors to expect far less of themselves than we might wish. But although this result seems assured by the volume and scope of policy making, the resulting standard of adequacy must be defended. One always has access to more information.

The need to view this situation as a compromise stems from the fact that the senator considers many pieces of legislation at once. If this were not true, then the limitation we are referring to would be only one of personal memory or individual skill. If I can devote all of my time to the study of mathematics, I will still be limited, but primarily by my own abilities and experience. But if I am expected to learn about five or six subjects at once, another factor enters as a condition of finitude: namely, the need to choose where I will put these already limited energies and abilities.

Senators are clearly in this second situation. Thus, they are likely to insist upon more complete knowledge on one or two topics, and accept standards of adequacy for all others. And this is the compromise imposed by this condition; the problem is not that each person cannot attain or digest enough information, but that one must choose to put one's resources (time, staff, energy, intellect) into certain areas, and thus to slight others.

Most senators are both aware of, and perturbed by, this result. First term members seem to be more concerned by such compromises, as we might expect. One such Senator complained to me that he was avoiding attending a committee session on a particular bill, "because that damned piece of legislation is so complex, I can't tell what the hell is going on." Another first-term Senator reported: "Sins of omission are more troubling to me here; things just slip by, and there's not enough time to devote to anything. I often have trouble sleeping." It is not simply the pressure of time which is involved here; it is primarily the contrast between the amount of information required to make an intelligent decision, and the information which has been examined when the senator raises her hand for a vote. One can rue the choice of certain areas within which to amass the required information, or one can simply accept this as a necessary compromise. But the sheer volume of information cannot account for the selection process by which certain sorts of information are selected out for special atten-tion. Doubtless senators must make such selections, if they are not to become spread too thin (or go totally mad). But the choice of demanding anything more than a standard of adequacy on one bill leaves the actor forced to make compromises on other bills.

Such compromises are made, once again, in two ways. Senators can adopt an "all-or-nothing" strategy, which in this case involves specializing narrowly and following the lead of another senator (or of one's own past voting record) on all other matters. One thereby compromises by bargaining away one set of informational opportunities for another. Alternatively, the senator can adopt the intermediate strategy of becoming a generalist on all issues, thereby compromising by having only

minimally adequate information when a vote is cast. Both
of these strategies are chosen by members of the Senate. In
general, the first-term senators seem to adopt the
second strategy more often, and the more senior members
(having established voting records and having more
access to the power centers of the Senate) choose the
former.[21]

   Finitude of Predictability. The complexity of
policy decisions is caused partly by informational
overload. But there is also the difficulty of predicting
consequences of social policy decisions. We saw earlier
that the mere uncertainty of the rightness of one's
position need not lead to compromise. But what does
seem to lead to compromise is another form of limited
knowledge: not uncertainty but ignorance. When we
speak about uncertainty, we refer to limited knowledge,
to be sure. But ignorance suggests that we have no
solid ground at all on which to stand.

   Thus, uncertainty paralyzes us only in the sense
that we would prefer to act out of a surer sense of
where we stand. But ignorance leaves us without the
grounding to make any move at all. This is why uncertainty
does not lead to compromise, since we can (and usually

---

[21]Because I interviewed senators at one point in time,
however, I cannot determine whether senators move from
one strategy to another during their careers, or whether
the style of approaching the question has altered during
the last few years. My guess is that the former explanation
is more correct.
   In his study of Senate liberals, Foley suggests
that liberals are more likely to be generalists, and
that seniority seems to lead to an increased willingness
to compromise. See Michael Foley, The New Senate: Liberal
Influences on a Conservative Institution, 1959-1972
(Yale University Press, 1980), esp. pp. 136-160.

do) gamble with the best information we have. But if we are truly ignorant, how can we even begin to decide, unless we toss a coin?

This distinction may help us understand precisely in what way social policy decisions are unpredictable. Are politicians uncertain about the consequences, or are they ignorant about them? To believe the former is to recognize that "the best laid plans of mice and men gang aft aglay." But to believe the latter is to throw up one's hands in despair. For example, I may be able to identify a number of complex interactive social effects of a piece of legislation, all of which may influence the decision; but I may be uncertain about whether they will occur, or which ones will be more important. To be able to identify probable influences, weigh them, and come up with some probabilistic prediction, does not rule out uncertainty. But it does rule out ignorance, for we now have some basis from which to make a decision.

In which sense are we unable to predict the outcomes of policy decisions? It is a commonplace of the social sciences that it is more difficult to predict human action than to predict other behavior. One might cynically suggest that such an observation is less an empirical claim about the world than it is a defensive statement about the social sciences themselves; since our models of human action have failed to attain the levels achieved (or at least claimed) by the other sciences, we may find it more comforting to blame the measured rather than the measurers.

But there is a less cynical interpretation, one based on an important claim about human action. The interconnectedness and unanticipated consequences of social action make it unrealistic to expect to draw

"If A, then B" models. We simply cannot predict what will happen if we do A, because there are too many other variables which might change. But does this sort of unpredictability leave us uncertain or ignorant of the consequences of our policy choices?

I would suggest that, on most policy issues decided in the Senate, the actors operate in conditions of uncertainty but not of ignorance. There are several reasons for this assertion. First, it is unlikely that any issue lacking fairly well-developed arguments and information will come before the highest law-making bodies of the nation. The long hesitation in Congress concerning the adoption of a comprehensive energy bill in the late 1970's was due largely to a sense that the Congress was not simply uncertain about which programs would work, but that it and the experts were ignorant. Second, when issues do come before the Senate, the information and argument-generating sectors (staff, Library of Congress, lobbyists, constituent groups) all swing into action. Third, most questions come before the Senate precisely because someone has felt strongly enough to compile and present a sufficient body of facts and arguments to enough members of Congress to overcome the charge of ignorance about the proposal.

If these arguments are correct, then we are left with conditions of uncertainty, meaning that we can make informed guesses about the effects of public policy decisions. To the extent that this is true, a compromising mode is less appropriate than when the problem is one of true ignorance. Indeed, much discussion concerning the appropriateness of compromise centers around the question of whether the decision is made in ignorance. If I am convinced that I have no sound argument for my position, I may be more willing to compromise with

you. Note, however, that if I want to convince you
to compromise with me, then I might withdraw to this
stance, to try to convince you that neither of us really
knows anything about the decision, and that we should
therefore try to strike a deal.

This strategy occurs more often on matters of
financial appropriations. Many senators argue that
there is no way to connect up the desired outcome of
a social policy with a specific sum of money. If I
favor a program budgeted for four million dollars,
and you oppose it, then I may be willing to settle
for two million if I cannot present some sound arguments
for why the higher figure is required. But if you remain
adamant about your opposition, I may be willing to
settle for less even if I <u>am</u> convinced that the four
million figure is needed. "After all," I may say, "I
don't know if the program will work, but it might;
let's try it out at the lower figure, and see what
happens."

The crucial move in such compromises based on
recognition of the finitude of predictability is to
use a term such as "arbitrary" in selecting the figure
proposed. For example, in a session of the Senate Committee
on Energy and Natural Resources, Senator Domenici objected
to providing across-the-board federal grants for conversion
efforts from one energy source to another. His insistence
led to a compromise lowering such grants from fifty
percent to twenty-five percent. When Domenici continued
to object, the following interchange took place with
the chairman of the committee:

> <u>Senator Johnston</u>: Peter, your questions are
> very good and there is no answer. This approach
> is sort of a compromise approach and drawing
> some arbitrary lines....

Senator Domenici: Bennett, the Administration
bill, it's full of holes at this point...
Senator Johnston: You have to draw some arbitrary
lines somewhere and it seems to me the 25
percent line is twice as good as the Administration's 50 percent line.
Senator Domenici: Twice better than nothing
is still nothing, so that is not an argument. Two
times zero [is still zero].[22]

Note the strengths and weaknesses of this line of reasoning. Once we admit that the particular figure is arbitrary,
we are operating in the realm of ignorance. The advantage
is that we can claim to be flexible and humble; the
disadvantage is that, if we cannot give a good argument
for why twenty-five percent is worse than fifty percent,
then we are open to the counter-argument that twenty-
five percent is also no better than zero percent. In
this instance, Johnston's desired compromise won, because
other members wanted some grant program included. For
these senators, the arbitrariness of the middle figure
may have been a positive feature, since their need
to argue for a particular figure was thereby elimin-
ated. They could claim (both on the floor and back
in their states) that they voted for the figure as
a compromise made under conditions of ignorance, and
that they therefore avoided the twin evils of refusing
all aid and permitting too much. If the result was
ineffective, they could not be held accountable, for
the decision was arbitrary to begin with.

In short, defining a policy decision as being
made under conditions of ignorance is itself an important
step in the policy-making process. Certain issues are
not simply made objectively under conditions of ignorance
,or uncertainty; such terms are often labels we allow

---

[22]Senate Committee on Energy and Natural Resources, markup
of S2470, May 29, 1980.

to be applied to certain decisions. The decision maker may have access to more information than is admitted to.

We want to be clear when such compromises are tied to these constraints of predictability, and when they are due to other political or personal considerations. The sin of hubris is no more serious in politics than the sin of false humility. If there are arguments and evidence for policy decisions, we want them to be used.

Finitude of Societal Resources. The final form of finitude relates to our discussion of scarcity in chapter 2. In the Senate, as in all political institutions, choices must be made between various goods, or between the allocation of goods to different groups. The result is a continuous series of compromises on everything from land and water resources to federal aid to education.

The nature of such compromises depends largely upon the acceptance of the scarcity paradigm. Perhaps no area has generated more passionate debate in the Senate than the recent attempt to impose this paradigm on the budgetary decisions of Congress itself. The newly formed Senate Budget Committee is charged with the task of establishing and defending budget limits each year. As we might expect, the chairperson of the committee wages an endless battle on the Senate floor to prevent amendments covering additional projects from pushing the total budget figure over the ceiling figure. In such a situation, compromise depends upon agreement that there is a meaningful ceiling in the first place; if exceptions can be made for your pet bill, then they will be made for mine as well. Because any senator can find high-sounding arguments for making exceptions for a particular project, members will refrain from making such arguments only if they believe (or are constrained to act as if they believe) that there is a limit, a number, a total amount, which can be divided up in different ways, but which cannot be expanded.

The conflict is usually drawn between the Committee's insistence that such limits be adhered to, and the other senators' demand on the floor that their independence and equality cannot be threatened by something as arbitrary as a budget number. Listen to the following exchange between the Chairman of the Committee (Senator Muskie) and Senator Roth:

> Senator Muskie: ...nobody knows better than I the uncertainties that can face a budget maker and the changes that time and circumstances require. But I believed, and I thought the Senate believed, that the only way you could achieve discipline in this undisciplined body was to have a plan for doing so to which people of divergent views, philosophies, values, and priorities could make their fair contribution and then accept the results.
> The Senator [Roth] says he has been voting for things that he was against. Does he think I have not?
> I have from the beginning and I find myself standing almost alone in the process from time to time.
> That is what is required of each of us...
> This process is not going to work just because I vote against my convictions and against a popular proposal. There has to be a majority of this body voting in that way, exercising restraint, in the overall interests of a balanced budget, budgetary prudence, and public confidence in this body. And if each of us yields in response for a popular idea, whatever it costs, he can forget about the budget process....
> Senator Roth: ...I am surprised that I have not been accused of being responsible for the Three-Mile Island accident and the bubonic plague....

> ...those of us who are not on the [Budget] Committee have the right to attempt to influence the budgetary process and are not required merely to accept on the Senate floor the recommendations of that committee any more than we are required to accept those of the Finance Committee, or others...[23]

It is significant that Senator Roth is one of the strongest advocates of a balanced budget. The issue is not between favoring a budget or opposing it. Rather, the issue concerns the general problem of accepting a model of scarcity in policy-making settings. Demands for social programs continually expand, due to increases in population, pressures, and imagination. The willingness to compromise concerning which programs will be funded, however, seems to depend less upon the actual ratio of demand to available resources, than it does upon the perceived availability of such resources.

Thus, finitude of social resources can be denied. Perhaps the most interesting and difficult problems involve those instances where such finitude seems to reappear with frustrating insistence. It is hard to think of a single resource which is necessarily finite, in the sense that it could not be increased by some sort of policy decision. What seems more important are two observations.[24]

First, present conditions do place limits. We cannot have unlimited spending for social programs and military appropriations, although we may be able to increase both areas if we are willing to sacrifice something else. Similarly, access to certain consumer

---

[23]Congressional Record, December 5, 1979, S17837-8.

[24]For a fascinating discussion of these questions, see Guido Calabresi and Philip Bobbitt, Tragic Choices (N.Y.: W. W. Norton and Co., 1978).

goods may be limited for the foreseeable future. The access of Americans to decent health care, for example, is not a resource which needs to be finite, but which will remain so until conditions of both training and distribution of health personnel are radically altered.

Second, our perceptions of what is finite can change, and we can adopt policies depending upon those changed perceptions. It has generally been the policy in this country that access to education is not, and should not be, finite. Schools were allowed to expand, and higher education became not merely an accessible good but almost a requirement for social productivity and participation in many areas. But a resource such as education is finite in terms of the meaning of the resource. Once everyone has a college degree, the nature of that degree is undercut. Furthermore, it is possible to have a society of college educated persons, all of whom can function at an earlier defined level of competence. But this is not a likely result, and the more common effect is to water down the requirements of the degrees. This is not to suggest that we should restrict access to higher education. But it does mean that the use of education as a credential may be anachronistic. The distribution of education in a society, in terms of what it means to be educated, may be finite, in spite of our best efforts to alter the distribution.

A similar argument can be made concerning any social good which might be distributed across a wide range of the society. We can import or produce enough automobiles to provide one for every adult. But the consequences may be so detrimental to the society that questions of finitude arise after, rather than before, the redistribution has taken place. The ability to provide a resource, in other words, need not imply that the society can tolerate its unlimited supply or usage. The argument concerning energy is analogous; whether we can find and develop sufficient resources to meet increasing consumer needs, the costs of waste and use may be so high that the question of production is irrelevant.

Again, there are many ways to decide whether a resource is finite. Societies often ignore such questions until they are forced to confront them. But the need to make such decisions, and to adopt a stance toward questions of scarcity, remains a fundamental one in the policy-making realm. Our willingness to compromise on what we want depends upon our recognition of how much we can get, which in turn depends upon how much we think there is. There is no easy way to make such decisions. But we want to notice how our political leaders make such decisions, because their willingness to compromise with our perceived needs and desires is affected by their views of scarcity.

4. Conditions of Powerlessness of the Senator

We turn now to the question of the arrangement of power and authority in the Senate. We will look briefly at both formal and informal structures and norms affecting the frequency of compromise.[25]

As an organization, the Senate can be seen as an assortment of mechanisms for ordering social activity. Sociologists focus particularly upon the nature of the authority structure and the social control systems

---

[25]Perhaps the most useful study from this perspective remains Donald Matthews' U. S. Senators and Their World (University of North Carolina Press, 1960). His discussion of Senate folkways is a classic treatment, to which we will be referring.

which operate to order and sustain activity. Once we understand how these operate, we can ask about the norms which govern organizational life.

What can we say briefly about these structures in the Senate? The most important observation is that, compared to most other organizations, the Senate is characterized by its relative absence of such structures. There are rules and procedures, of course: committee assignments are made according to certain standards, votes are taken in certain predetermined patterns, and members can be disciplined for stepping outside of established lines of conduct. But we learn more about the Senate by recognizing the functional irrelevance of such structures. Each member of the Senate is basically powerless in relation to every other member--which, taken from the other side, means that each member is absolutely powerful and almost immune from control. This image of independence and equality is embedded in the self-understanding and traditions of the institution, as represented by the famous statement of Daniel Webster in 1830:

> This is a Senate of equals, of men of individual honor and personal character, and of absolute independence. We know no masters; we acknowledge no dictators.[26]

We might begin by asking about the leaders of the Senate. As we have already seen, some senators do gain influence over others through knowledge or power of personality. But such senators do not really have power, in the sense of being able to force someone

[26]Webster's "Reply to Hayne," January 27, 1830; quoted in George H. Haynes, The Senate of the United States, Volume II, p. 1083.

to do something against his will.[27] The apparent power center of the Senate is the majority leader, who does indeed possess certain "powers" in the chamber. The majority leader can gain access to the floor over any other senator, manipulate the calendar, or refuse to recognize a senator's right to an informal hold on legislation (thereby ignoring a senator's preferences on the scheduling and time agreements for a bill).

But each of these powers is effectively controlled by the right of any other member to refuse to give consent to the numerous requests arising on any given day. Because unanimous consent is required for everything ranging from dispensing with the reading of the daily journal to the calling up of most bills, the majority leader cannot afford to be seen as exercising power over anyone. As one staff member reported: "The majority leader _can_ ignore the informal hold, but he will then have one irate member on his hands." Another senior staffer commented, with some sympathy for the plight of the majority leader: "Remember, these men have _very_ long memories."

---

[27]I am using these terms in a fairly standard way. Power is the ability to force people to do things they would not otherwise want to do; authority is the perception of such power as legitimate by the person being affected; and influence is a way of affecting others by using argument or personal skill. Thus, influence implies that the person ends up agreeing with the influencer; such is not the case with either power or authority.

In his Power in the Senate (N.Y.: St. Martin's Press, 1969), Randall Ripley suggests that the modern Senate is characterized by an "individualistic" style of power distribution. Many of his observations support the conclusions of this study, although the Senate may have progressed even further in this direction since 1969.

Consider the following exchange on the Senate floor between Majority Leader Byrd and Senator Weicker, during the debate on the Chrysler aid package in 1979:

> Senator Byrd: ...I feel that I do have a responsibility to do whatever I can to get this bill up and have the Senate act upon it one way or the other.
>
> Mr. President, I understand...that Mr. Weicker intends to filibuster the legislation, and that is his right, of course, to utilize the rules to whatever advantage he may seek....
>
> Senator Weicker: ...I do not think I have ever indicated that I would use a term that the distinguished majority leader uses, filibuster.
>
> I did make the statement that I felt that a 1.5 billion dollar matter was not going to be something that was rushed through the Senate under the threat of people not getting home for Christmas.
>
> This tactic is typical...of the M.O. [method of operation] of the distinguished majority leader....
>
> Senator Byrd: Mr. President, the majority leader does not have much power. This business about the power of the majority leader--I wish I had some power. I think I would know how to use it....[28]

The implied threats on both sides reflect the tenuous nature of power relationships in the Senate. Of course, the majority leader can make things very uncomfortable for a senator who consistently refuses to go along. But the reverse is true as well, and such powers are highly guarded and sparsely used.

The key element here is the equality of all members of the Senate. Each member is elected by constituents from the different states, and only the constituents

---

[28]Congressional Record, December 15, 1979, S18765.

can throw the member out.[29] In addition, each member has a single vote on every piece of legislation. Thus, unlike the situation in most organizations, the participants have little effective control over the actions of their fellow members. Although mechanisms for disciplining exist, they are seldom used. Several factors (such as shifting ideological alliances and decreasing levels of party discipline) mitigate against the effective use of any disciplinary action, and they make each member acutely aware of the danger of alienating, angering, or controlling other senators. Because discipline is short and memories are long, no one has much power.

One result is that the Senate runs largely on the more informal norm of reciprocity. As the tendency of people to exchange favors and benefits, reciprocity is the crucial underpinning of any social institution; without it, interaction would be undercut, people would be unable to depend upon one another, and any sense of fair play or rule-oriented behavior would be destroyed. But the Senate is an organization virtually ruled by this norm, both in its formal rules and in its actual daily operation. For example, in a family, a certain amount of reciprocity is required; unless the child (the "subordinate") is provided with a sense that her needs are being met, and that the parent is sacrificing something in return, family interaction turns into warfare. But the family has a structure of power, and the parent can rely on this structure if necessary to keep order and achieve goals. But the Senate, lacking such defined roles and power relationships,

---

[29]There are very limited exceptions to this statement. The Senate can deprive a member of most prerogatives and rights, but it is virtually forbidden from expelling a duly elected member.

depends much more emphatically upon the fact and the
appearance of reciprocity.

Underlying norms such as reciprocity take on particular
importance in an organization lacking any strong explicit
social control mechanisms or authority structures. They
replace such formal structures, and thus assure that
a group of one hundred equal individuals will be able
to work with one another in the face of an apparently
anomic, and at times chaotic, system of social organization. Matthews sums up this aspect of Senate life
when he writes:

> [Reciprocity is] a way of life in the Senate....
> Each of them has vast power under the chamber's
> rules. A single Senator, for example, can
> slow the Senate almost to a halt...A few,
> by exercising their right to filibuster,
> can block the passage of all bills. Or a
> single Senator could sneak almost any piece
> of legislation through the chamber by acting
> when floor attendance is sparse and by taking
> advantage of the looseness of the chamber
> rules....the amazing thing is that [these
> powers] are rarely utilized....If a Senator
> does push his formal powers to the limit,
> he has broken the implicit bargain and can
> expect, not cooperation from his colleagues,
> but only retaliation in kind.[30]

Consider the related senatorial norm of courtesy. A
central aspect of Senate debate, this norm is established
in the formal rules of the organization. Senate Rule 19
reads, in part: "No Senator in debate shall, directly
or indirectly, by any form of words impute to another
Senator or to other Senators any conduct or motive
unworthy or unbecoming a Senator." The functions of

---

[30]Matthews, U. S. Senators and their World, pp. 100-101. Foley
argues that, while most Senate norms were becoming
less rigid by the early 1970s, the norm of reciprocity
was even more crucial. (Foley, The New Senate, pp. 249-
250.)

courtesy are evident, as Matthews notes: "Courtesy, far from being a meaningless custom as some Senators seem to think it is, permits competitors to cooperate. The chaos which ensues when this folkway is ignored testifies to its vital function."[31]

It is interesting to notice the response given by the members of the organization to deviations from this norm. Listen to another stage of Senator Weicker's attack on the Majority Leader's style, an attack which seems to go beyond the bounds of senatorial courtesy:

> Senator Weicker: ...I have seen...a propensity on the part of the majority leader not to pull the U.S. Senate together but to make sure it stays at odds, and with petty motions and petty recriminations and petty threats fail consistently to achieve the large objective....
>   Now, a wheeler and a dealer does not a leader make, and that is exactly the nature of the problem here.[32]

Such comments are invariably met by spirited defenses of the offended senator, usually by members on both sides of the aisle, in an effort both to disassociate themselves from the sentiments and to defuse the conflict. Such disputes are usually resolved with a return to the jovial courtesy characteristic of most public interaction among senators:

> Senator Byrd: ...If this majority leader went around harboring grudges, I would never have any support in the effort to keep the legislative process moving....
>   If I have done the Senator any wrong, if I have ever been unkind to him, if I have ever said an unkind word to him on this floor, if I have ever attacked him here, I am ready to apologize....
>   I will come more than halfway across the aisle and shake the Senator's hand.

---

[31] Ibid., p. 99.
[32] Congressional Record, December 12, 1979, S18333.

Senator Weicker: I am delighted to shake
the Senator's hand. I am delighted to agree
with him on the sense of what is proper on
this floor.
Senator Byrd: I have never said a word of
harm to him, and tonight I am willing to
love him as I love every Member of this body.
Senator Weicker: Merry Christmas. [Laughter]
Senator Byrd: The same to you.[33]

Occasionally a senator will appeal directly to
the Senate rules to object to a violation of courtesy.
During a debate on Senator Danforth's proposal to tax
the royalties from oil on state-owned land, Senator
Tower of Texas makes the following comment on the floor:

Senator Tower: The Senator from Missouri
has offered an amendment that is most divisive,
that is doing the most to foment regional
ill-will and destruction of almost anything
I have seen in this body, and his suggestion
that this is going to create vast economic
dislocations is the biggest batch of balderdash
that I have heard, and we call it something
else in west Texas....
Senator Danforth: Mr. President, I make a
point of order that this kind of debate is
not in order.
Presiding Officer: Under rule 19, the Senator
is correct....[34]

Although violated occasionally, the norm of courtesy
is protected zealously by members. Indeed, the very
structure of the public record of Senate debates (the
Congressional Record) reinforces such a norm, as senators
have two opportunities to delete passages before it
is bound and published. Underground copies of transcripts
of speeches actually delivered on the floor (and later
deleted by the speaker) are circulated among the staff,
in cases where particularly offensive or insulting

---

[33]Congressional Record, December 15, 1979, S18767.
[34]Congressional Record, December 15, 1979, S18661.

remarks have been made.[35] The desire of members to maintain such tight control over their public interaction underscores the importance of norms such as courtesy.

The relationship of such norms to compromise is evident. The need to compromise increases with the relative powerlessness perceived by the actor. If I cannot force you to do what I want (or, more significantly, if I cannot be perceived as trying to force you to do what I want), I am likely to be more willing to compromise with you. Alternatively, if you remain adamant, I cannot adopt a harsher attitude, and thus I must turn to compromise if I am to achieve any solution at all.

5. Conditions of Powerlessness of the Senate

We have been discussing internal aspects of Senate organizational life. But organizations exist in broader settings; when senators compromise, they often must take into account such outside influences. Not only is each senator powerless in relation to colleagues, but the Senate as a whole is somewhat powerless due to its relation to other groups and institutions. Let us briefly examine a few of these outside influences.

We have already discussed the most important feature of the outside world: the constituency. Mail campaigns, personal appearances, speeches, newsletters, polls, campaigns--all provide opportunities (not always welcome) for interaction and mutual influence between senator and constituents. As Dexter has emphasized, the process here is a transactional one, in which each side both

---

[35]Having seen some of these transcripts, I can report that certain senators are quite adept at the art of personal innuendo, norms of courtesy notwithstanding.

affects the views of the other and continually redefines the nature of the relationship.[36] Senators choose which portions of the electorate to attend to, they educate and alter the nature of that electorate, and they refine and elaborate the style with which they communicate. As a result, few decisions are made without attention to public opinion, but just as few decisions are made simply by following a tabulation of popular sentiment.

We discussed some of the effects of the relationship between senator and constituency upon the compromise process. But there are other important influences from outside the Senate. First, the Senate is only one house in a bicameral legislature. All legislation (with the exception of treaties) must pass both houses of Congress, and this process is a complex and often hostile one. Each House is jealous of its prerogatives, and occasional deadlocks have held up the entire process while tempers cooled. The differences between the two houses intensify the likelihood of such problems; the longer terms, larger constituencies, smaller size, and looser rules of the "upper chamber" provide incentives for both arrogance and jealousy to intrude into the attempt of each chamber to pass its own version of a bill. Consider, for example, the following Senate floor debate over the Senate's less restrictive attempt to limit federal funding for abortions. Senator Magnuson supports the more liberal Senate position, while Senator Helms favors the more restrictive House version:

---

[36]Dexter, "The Representative and His District," pp. 6-8.

> Senator Magnuson: I just want to say that
> this is the thirty-fifth time the Senate
> has voted on this proposition, and the sixty-
> seventh time the House and Senate has voted
> on it. So I guess one more time is not going
> to make much difference.
> Senator Helms: The Senator is absolutely
> correct, Mr. President. And there would not
> have been so many of these votes if my friend
> from Washington had not repeatedly altered
> the House language. So he has encouraged
> these votes to some extent.
> He is the one who is dissatisfied with
> the language which has been repeatedly voted
> by the House. So, apparently, my friend from
> Washington enjoyed the rollcall votes on
> that, and I am perfectly willing to participate
> in another rollcall vote.
> Senator Magnuson: Well, that is an uncalled-
> for remark, that I am responsible for the
> vote. I and sixty-six other Senators.
> Senator Helms: I did not mean to be unfair,
> and the Senator knows that. But the facts
> are the facts.
> Senator Magnuson: And the Senator from North
> Carolina represents the House; he does not
> represent the Senate in this matter. He represents
> the House.
> Senator Helms: The Senator from North Carolina
> represents the Senator from North Carolina.
> Senator Magnuson: He represents the House. I
> represent the Senate.[37]

Later in the same discussion, Senator Exon introduces
what he calls a compromise, initiating the following
exchange:

> Senator Exon: I do not believe that the compromise
> I am offering is going to satisfy very many
> people...
> I do say, in all sincerity, that I believe
> the compromise I have offered is the only
> compromise we have a chance to pass, both
> in the Senate and in the House of Representatives,
> in a timely fashion...

---

[37]*Congressional Record*, November 15, 1979, S16705.

Senator Magnuson: Mr. President, the Senator
from Nebraska is talking about a compromise. Why
does he not let the conferees determine the
compromise? Why make the compromise on the
Senate floor? The House is just as adamant
about this as we are....[38]

Two points are worth noting here. First, notice
the insistence on representing the Senate. Even when
one agrees with the position taken by the other chamber,
senators stand in an adversary relationship with the
House. Second, there is a tension between paying too
much and paying too little attention to the House's
version of a bill. To err in the former direction jeo-
pardizes the autonomy of the Senate, but to err in
the latter direction risks destroying the possibility
of an eventual solution. The process of compromise
between the two chambers, therefore, is not restricted
to the conference committee process, but it infests
the debate in each house.

There are also complexities flowing from the conference
process itself. For example, the conference committee
is usually composed of the ranking members of the House
and Senate committees which reported out the legislation. These members may not be representative of
the broader views of their chambers, because the bill
may have been severely altered on the floor. There
is thus a continual fear on the part of other senators
that a hard floor fight on an amendment may be bartered
away in the conference. Consequently, much attention
is paid to receiving assurances from conference members
that one's interests will be protected later on. Although
each chamber has the opportunity to vote on the completed
conference bill, time constraints and the desire to

---

[38]Congressional Record, November 15, 1979, S16711.

avoid a reopening of the entire process are strong incentives to accept the conference version. Amendments lost in conference are unlikely to be reattached to the bill.[39]

The conference process also highlights a major incentive for compromise: however difficult it may be to put together an ideological coalition on the Senate floor, it is even more unlikely that such a coalition will be congruent with the legislation emerging from the other chamber. Such limits are useful in most cases, minimizing the damage done by extreme legislation and increasing the likelihood that the final product will reflect a broader spectrum of social interests. But there are examples (such as the debate over abortion funding) where the divergent concerns of the two chambers result in a compromise which represents simply a "least common denominator" position. Too much attention to the views of the other chamber can be as damaging to coherent legislation as too much protection of the wishes of one's own colleagues.

The power of the executive branch plays a major role as well. By introducing and lobbying for legislation, and by holding the threat of a veto over the Congress, the White House's views are always considered, and often are crucial in determining which compromises will be put forth and accepted by the senators. In addition, interest groups, lobbyists, the media, and state and local governments, are all highly relevant in the decision-making process of the Senate. We cannot

---

[39]For a good discussion of the conference process, see Stephen Horn, <u>Unused Power: The Work of the Senate Committee on Appropriations</u> (Washington, D.C.: The Brookings Institution, 1970), esp. pp. 147-163.

take the time here to detail these influences, except to note that, in most cases, the senator is so besieged by these outside influences that any particular one seldom has much weight for very long. Of course, there are exceptions on particular issues. But, in general, one of the most significant aspects of Senate life is the relative isolation of the senator from many of these influences. The large number of pressure groups decreases the effect of any one of them in most instances. Staff members often point to the overinflated sense of power of most Congressional lobbyists, for example; the five or ten minutes spent with the senator (or, more likely, the thirty minutes spent with the staff member) have little effect, in light of the ten or fifteen such meetings in a given day on a particular bill.[40]

But there are also some carefully designed aspects of Senate life which enhance the sense of isolation from the public. The perquisites available to senators, although often exaggerated, give them a highly distinctive life style. Furthermore, Congress usually exempts itself from much of the legislation it passes, such as the Clean Air Act, occupational health and safety laws, and most equal opportunity legislation. To the extent that such isolation hinders the ability of the Senate to represent the public, we might wonder about the effects on substantive legislation of such procedures. The compromises which result may be traced partially to the Senate's own ambivalence concerning the proper relationship between its internal institutional structure

---

[40]Jones and Woll even interpret such outside influences primarily as pawns in the internal power struggles in Congress. (Rochelle Jones and Peter Woll, The Private World of Congress [N. Y.: The Free Press, 1979].)

and the myriad forces in society to which it is expected to respond.

Conclusion

The preceding discussion has suggested some central ways in which the organizational context of the Senate creates the need and the climate for compromise. Caught between the desire to serve the constituency and the desire to be loyal to other values, the senator compromises; caught between the need to make informed decisions and the pressure of the world of action, the senator compromises; caught between the powerlessness of each individual and the need to take stronger stands, the senator compromises; caught between the power of the Senate and its dependence on outside influences, the senator compromises. In all such cases, we find compromise at the heart of the very definition of senatorial action.

By thus broadening our usual understanding of political compromise, I have emphasized the different ways in which Senate activity consists of repeated concessions and trade-offs of valued options or ways of acting. Many of them are built into the job description; many derive from organizational factors. But all of them are efforts--made freely but under pressure--to deal with conflicts between valued alternatives by finding an acceptable middle ground.

But compromises are not merely broad aspects of organizational life. They are also day-to-day actions, taken in haste or in urgency, adopted willingly or reluctantly, justified strenuously or in whispers. We turn in the next chapter to some specific types of compromises.

CHAPTER 4. A CATALOGUE OF SENATE COMPROMISES

How can we best describe the range of compromises which occur in the United States Senate? In discussing several types, we shall stay as close as possible to the daily decisions of Senate life. Each section will begin with an example drawn (whenever possible) from consideration of the windfall profits tax bill in 1979-1980. Further examples will then be provided.

1. The Glorious Middle: Splitting the Difference

Let us begin with two examples of the most common type of compromise. In a Senate Finance Committee session on the windfall profits tax bill, Senator Talmadge argues with a Treasury Department spokesperson about differences in their respective proposals for phasing out tax credits:

> Senator Talmadge: And [the Administration] would phase [credits] out at 100 percent at what level?
> Treasury: $27.56.
> Senator Talmadge: Mine would phase out 100 percent at what level?
> Treasury: $30.00.
> Senator Talmadge: Very little difference. Why do we not split the difference?[1]

Much later in the process, two versions of the bill reach a House-Senate conference committee to iron out the differences. The two bills are very far apart, with the total revenue figures differing by about one hundred billion dollars. In a very brief opening session, the House conferees suggest an even split of the difference, and the senators agree. Thus, with no discussion of the merits of the two figures, the final figure (of over two hundred billion dollars) is agreed upon. Senator Dole objects to the decision, arguing that the figure

---

[1]Senate Finance Committee, markup of HR3919, September 11, 1979.

is much too high and that it does not deal with how
the revenues are to be allocated. But the conferees
adopt this "splitting the difference" strategy, arguing
that only by doing so will the bill ever be dealt with
quickly and equitably.[2]

Such compromises are common, and they reflect
many of the organizational features we discussed earlier: time pressures, equality among members, complexity
of legislation, and tension between the Senate and
the House. This type of compromise can only occur,
however, when the dispute in question is reducible
to a numerical one. We can find a middle ground between
one billion dollars and two billion dollars, or between
twenty-five percent and fifty percent. Such compromises
do not depend upon monetary conflicts, however; any
numerical scale can be involved.

Such compromises are important when conflicting
groups demand their fair share of scarce resources. When
the organizational context is one of equality among
the bargainers, splitting the difference is likely
to be seen as the fairest possible distribution. Thomas
Schelling has suggested that this middle ground solution
is often both intuitively obvious and pragmatically
appealing to both sides:

> In bargains that involve numerical magnitudes,
> for example, there seems to be a strong magnetism
> in mathematical simplicity....The 'obvious'
> place to compromise frequently seems to win
> by some kind of default, as though there
> is simply no rationale for settling anywhere
> else....The outcome may not be so much conspi-
> cuously fair or conspicuously in balance
> with estimated bargaining powers as just
> plain 'conspicuous.'...

---

[2]House-Senate Conference on HR3919, December 20, 1979.

In fact, a focal point for agreement often owes its focal character to the fact that small concessions would be impossible, that small encroachments would lead to more and larger ones. One draws a line at some conspicuous boundary or rests his case on some conspicuous principle that is supported mainly by the rhetorical question, 'If not here, where?' The more it is clear that concession is collapse, the more convincing the focal point is.[3]

Schelling's analysis suggests that we examine carefully the character of this conspicuous middle point, however. Why is an even split seen as the fair or obvious solution? In the Senate, and in the House-Senate conference committees, there is a strong presumption of equality in the claims made by the various sides. The presumption can be overridden, of course, and it may be undercut by the power of a chairperson or the political needs of a region. But the presumption is critical; without it, there would be little opportunity for equal splits on such complex measures as the windfall profits tax bill. The willingness of each side to yield fifty billion dollars of its own version is explained only by this presumption.

Note also that such compromises do not involve disputes over the integrity or value of the programs themselves. One Senator told me, in a voice laden with frustration, that "all bills you are asked to vote for are good bills." Even if a senator does disapprove of a bill, the desire to be accommodating and courteous to the wishes of one's colleagues drives the process toward a common ground. When the dispute concerns numerically divisible questions, an even split allows each

---

[3]Schelling, The Strategy of Conflict (N.Y.: Oxford University Press, 1963), pp. 67-69, 111-112.

side to retain a sense of power and success. One need
not then make a case for why this particular number
was adopted, because the process itself serves as the
justification for the outcome.

This solution relies, therefore, upon a common
view of the general point of the legislation. The senator
who opposes any windfall profits tax will be unlikely
to want to agree to an even split; the senator who
is a pacifist will be unlikely to split the difference
between a fifty billion dollar military appropriations
bill and no bill at all. The even split is a conspicuous
solution when the dispute is not over whether a program
is good, but over how much money (or time, or energy)
is needed for the program. As many senators point out,
one cannot speak easily about a right amount of money
for a social program; such programs are commonly viewed
as matters of judgment rather than conscience, of economics
rather than principle. A legislative assistant for
a conservative Senator admitted that disputes over
questions such as disability benefits or progressive
income taxes are no longer matters of substantive disagreement; almost everyone in the Senate accepts the
values of such programs. The only remaining issue concerns
the level of funds to be provided, and such choices
are soluble through a quick and mutual agreement to
split the difference.

Before leaving this form of compromise, we might
note a problem with the ease with which most senators
and staff members accept this solution. Questions of
appropriations of funds, or of the length of time of
a social program, cannot be so easily divorced from
the relative value placed upon the programs. As several
senators admitted, the decision to compromise on a
spending bill depends finally upon one's evaluation

of the relative importance of the program, and of the
social needs it is designed to meet. Appropriations
affect human beings, and a reduction or increase of
funds affects human happiness or well-being. This is
an obvious point, but one which is often overlooked. It
is all too easy to lose sight of the significance of
a cut of one million dollars in a social program, or
of the effect of a cut of several months in payments
to citizens. Such compromises may be necessary, and
they help to keep the decision-making process moving
forward. But they also threaten to become so habitual
that senators are tempted to forget that the separation
between judgment on matters of money, and principle
on matters of human need, is a distinction of convenience,
not a distinction of substance. Once such compromises
are justified as "mere" numerical splits, they threaten
to obscure the values which are traded away.[4]

2. The Slippery Middle: Other Middle Numerical Grounds

One can split the difference only when the dispute
concerns numerical questions. But such disputes can
also be settled by a compromise which seeks another
middle ground, arriving at a final figure closer to
one side than to the other. Let us look at a rather
complex example.

One of the most difficult aspects of the Senate
Finance Committee's deliberations on the windfall profits
tax concerned the question of providing assistance
for those living in colder states. Such assistance
was designed to be tied to income levels, to assure
that the poor in the north would be able to pay their

_____

[4]We will return to the ethical dimensions of this problem
in chapter 7.

rising heating bills. (Note that this debate was taking place in October.) There was general agreement on two points: (1) poorer people should be given some assistance, and (2) some consideration should be given to the size of the energy bills in the various regions. But the original proposals were opposed by several southern senators. In particular, Senator Bentsen of Texas insisted that the warmer states had their own energy problems in the costs of air-conditioning during the summer. The effort to reach a compromise soon turned on the issue of degree days--a measure of how much heating oil was required in a particular state during the average year.

The Committee struggled for a week to define what percentage of the total assistance package should be provided on the basis of degree days. Obviously, the higher the percentage, the more money would be given to northern states. In addition, there were different ways in which the money could be given to the states, and different ways to determine who within the states would actually receive the money.

The major effort to arrive at an acceptable solution in the Committee was made by Senator Nelson of Wisconsin, who experimented with different formulae which might be accepted by Senator Bentsen (who by then was threatening to oppose the bill on the floor if a more satisfactory figure was not found). It is important to remember that Nelson was from a <u>northern</u> state, and thus could move in Bentsen's direction without thereby appearing to be acting in his own interests.

But Nelson's efforts met opposition from both sides. When part of the plan resulted in giving the same amount of money to social security recipients throughout the nation, Senator Chafee of Rhode Island complained:

> Senator Chafee: I think this is getting ridiculous. The purpose of our gathering at these long sessions is to take care of the situation that resulted from decontrol of oil and the increased costs of heating as a result. Just to spray out checks to SSI recipients whether they are in San Diego or in northern Wisconsin for the same amount, this is not what I thought we had been sitting around doing.[5]

When Senators Dole and Bentsen attempted to give a weighting of sixty-six percent to the degree day formula (in contrast to Bentsen's demand for less than fifty percent), the Texan retorted:

> Senator Bentsen: I have already moved down...I am trying to work this out, you may have the votes in this Committee but this obviously will be fought on the Floor if you were to prevail in this situation, and I am not so sure you have the votes there.[6]

Bentsen's insistence here met with the following responses from other northern Senators:

> Senator Moynihan: ...Some states in the northeast are heavily dependent on oil and disproportionately so and that is a reality. It is not something which I feel we have to apologize for. It is the way the Lord made the United States.
>   I just want to say that I understand perfectly well the Senator from Texas will do what he does. I think he characteristically understands why the Lord put all that oil and gas in Texas. That is something I have never been able to understand myself.
> ...
> Senator Ribicoff: ...We have been sitting here and voting billions and billions of dollars where the beneficiaries will be in a half a dozen [southern] states. Now we are talking about the poor in the states. We suddenly found this horrendous because the poor of one state get $10 or $20 more

---

[5] Senate Finance Committee, markup of HR3919, October 16, 1979.
[6] Ibid.

than the poor of another state....

...You are talking about people who are getting lots of money--in the billions of dollars--against people trying to determine whether they can stay warm and not freeze to death in the wintertime.

Bentsen replies:

> Senator Bentsen: I am sure I read the profits that Exxon has made and Continental has made. I dare say that there is more of that stock owned in the northeast than there is in Texas by far....[7]

The debate dragged on, prompting the Chairman to suggest that the states should perhaps just be allowed to choose for themselves which of the two formulae they preferred.

The compromise which was finally adopted was more to the liking of two crucial senior southern Democrats on the Committee. Although several northerners were perturbed, they accepted the final package, and the vote in the Committee was twelve to zero.

> Senator Moynihan: The War between the states is over. We are brothers again.
> Senator Wallop: The white flag has been raised.
> Senator Long: Statesmanship has prevailed, twelve to zero.[8]

Notice that this dispute might have been decided by splitting the difference. But such a solution was unlikely, because of the greater complexity and interaction of the various issues at stake (degree day formulae, income assistance procedures, means of allocation) and the intensity of feeling and regional animosities. No senators were able to consider or agree to an even split, without thereby feeling that the interests of

---

[7]Senate Finance Committee, markup of HR3919, October 24, 1979.
[8]Senate Finance Committee, markup of HR3919, October 25, 1979.

their regions were being trampled. The nature of the question allowed each side to play upon the emotional images of freezing northerners and scorched southerners. In addition, the fact that the Chairperson of the Committee was a southerner, and that the bill was expected to encounter strong opposition from southerners on the floor, gave the southern position even more weight.

It appears that splitting the different is the more common solution in the Senate. But the fact that other middle ground solutions are possible reminds us that an even split is not the only option. If there are reasons to put forward in favor of an _un_even split, we want the members to be able to do so, without thereby being accused of standing in the way of compromise. The other middle grounds may be less conspicuous than the even split, but the most conspicuous is not necessarily the most fair.

3. Muddling in the Middle: Other Middle Grounds

We can also compromise by searching for a middle ground when the dispute does not involve numbers, provided that there is a common ordinal scale of some sort upon which to rank alternatives. We must be able to recognize an option which falls in between the two positions, so that a compromise is possible.

Because of the nature of the windfall profits tax bill, there are few examples of such compromises in that process. Let us examine instead the Senate's efforts to arrive at a compromise on the question of federal funding for abortion. The Senate considered this question primarily as an amendment to a series of appropriations measures. Although introduced by Senator Helms, the effort to cut off federal funding stemmed originally from the Hyde amendment in the House. The

battle here between the two chambers reached alarming
proportions, at one point threatening to shut down
the government for lack of funds.

But what was at stake in the Senate? The battle
was seldom stated bluntly as one between pro-abortion
and anti-abortion forces, or between pro-life and pro-
choice sides. Instead, most senators sought a middle
ground between the two extreme stances of allowing
abortion funding on demand, and not allowing such funding
at all. This issue is clearly not a numerical one,
except in those instances where an estimate of the
number of women receiving abortions for certain reasons
can be found. But it is an ordinal one: from the standpoint
of the anti-abortion senator, allowing abortions in
some cases is better than allowing it in all cases
but worse than never allowing it. Thus, the question
involves a set of distinctions which can be ordered
and ranked by all the participants.

The two major figures in this battle were Senators
Magnuson (who fought against the Hyde amendments) and
Helms. But at one point in the debate, as we have already
seen, Senator Exon introduced an amendment allowing
funding in cases of abortion for the following reasons: danger to the mother's life, rape or incest if promptly
reported, and "severe and long-lasting physical health
damage" to the mother. This included more conditions
than Helms wanted, but not as many as Magnuson desired. Exon
defended his position in the following terms:

> Senator Exon: ...the amendment I have just
> offered returns to the compromise that has
> been struck time and time again....I was
> not offered, and could not have, a chance
> to vote what I have long held as my personal
> opinion on abortion. That simply is that

we should allow abortions only when the life
of the mother is being endangered or by promptly
reportable rape or incest.
    There are a lot of people that do not
agree with my position on that. I do not
hold any ill will whatsoever to those who
want even more restricted abortion language,
or those who propose we have more liberal
abortion language....

Senator Helms was able, somewhat reluctantly, to support
Exon's amendment:

Senator Helms: ...This Senator is going to
use every opportunity he can to stop the
practice of using taxpayers' money to encourage
or promote the deliberate termination of
innocent human life.
    The amendment of the Senator from Nebraska
is a movement toward a resolution of this
matter. Unless Senators want to tie up this
legislation in conference... they should
support the Senator from Nebraska, as I am.
    I will say frankly to the Senator that
his amendment does not satisfy me completely. He
knows that. But I am going to support it
because it is a perfecting amendment to the
pending amendment which he has offered in
good faith....[9]

Such a compromise on this particular issue is
fascinating, because, when senators were asked whether
there were certain issues on which compromise was virtually
impossible, the issue mentioned most frequently was
abortion. Even on such a question, fraught with moral
and political dangers, there are potential middle ground
solutions which can be found. One cannot simply add
up the number of exceptions and divide by two. But
one can agree that the conditions under which abortion
can be funded are ordered, and the actor can then find
a point at which to stand.

───────────────

[9]Congressional Record, November 15, 1979, S16710-11.

The ordering was remarkably consistent. Most senators favored federal funding in cases of danger to the woman's life; fewer wanted to include cases of rape and incest; fewer still suggested including danger to the woman's health; and even fewer wanted to include psychological danger to the woman. The conditions were usually placed in the same order and along the same continuum. In such a situation, a compromise solution is possible, as each side moves toward the middle.

Such compromises often turn on the precise language used. We saw one such example in the opening paragraphs of the book, when we referred to the House-Senate conference on the establishment of the Department of Education. The House bill disallowed all ratios and quotas, while the Senate version did not include such a provision. The two sides locked horns in the conference, each insisting that its respective chamber was adamant:

> Rep. Brooks [the chair]: ...We in the House were pretty determined in our position, the House passed it and instructed the conferees to do that. I regret we are so adamant at it....
>
> Rep. Erlenborn: ...If we abandoned the language in the House amendment, we are going against the clearly expressed will of the House and, I might even point out...an amendment that was voted for and supported by six of the House conferees as well as the vast majority of the House.
>
> ....
>
> Senator Javits: Mr. Chairman, I point out the fact the Senate is just as determined as the House. The vote in the Senate was 69 to 32...I agree with both chairmen. I don't want to foul up the works. I don't want to load it either way, but I don't want to accept an amendment which on its face will invalidate a Supreme Court decision...[10]

[10]House-Senate Conference on S210, September 13, 1979.

An impasse seems to have been reached. But Chairman
Brooks provided an opening for agreement when he supported
a compromise proposal in the language, and noted that
the House conferees were given some leeway concerning
the type of language they would accept:

> Rep. Brooks: ...Let me say, Senator, the
> House was very adamant in its adoption of
> this language, but when it instructed the
> conferees it was not quite so adamant, and
> that vote was 214 to 202. So it indicated
> a more reasonable attitude on the part of
> the House to fixing in concrete what this
> language ought to be as you examine the conse-
> quences of it. That is the difficulty of
> writing legislation on the Floor --as you
> and I know.
> ...I hope we can adopt this [compromise]. I
> think it is probably a good compromise. Certainly
> it cannot be used to discriminate against
> anybody....[11]

The compromise preserved the House's intent to warn
against the use of specific quotas, but did not specifically
mention them as such. When the House conferees agreed
(on a six to three vote) to this compromise, Representative
Erlenborn attacked his own Chairman for acquiescing
to a Senate position which undermined the version the
Chairman himself had supported on the House floor.

Such examples reveal both the flexibility of language,
and the ingenuity employed in using this flexibility
to find acceptable middle grounds on apparently dichotomous
questions. Indeed, several senators reported that
they are most willing to compromise on questions of
language, rather than on matters of substance. They speak
about not being "wedded" or "married" to specific language. But, once again, such a distinction can be misleading. As in the case of the connection between appropria-

---

[11]Ibid.

tions figures and human need, specifics of language
usually reflect different substantive understandings
of government programs. Certainly there are exceptions,
such as the altering of the title of a bill. In most
cases, however, willingness to alter language means
willingness to alter substance.

In addition, such a distinction merely reinforces
the already rather morbid attention in Congress to
a legalistic wrangling over language. Perhaps the best
example of this mentality occurred in the recent discussion
in the Senate Ethics Committee of the appropriate action
to take against Senator Talmadge. Unwilling to censure
him, and uncomfortable with the more lenient option
of reprimanding him, the Committee finally recommended
that the Senator be denounced. The Senate accepted
this solution, with some senators objecting that it
was too harsh, others that it was too lenient. We might
marvel at such an imaginative compromise, one which
clearly falls within our third category of middle ground
solutions on ordinal questions. But we might also sympathize
with the objection raised by a staff member: "What
are you going to do in such cases, solve them by sending
people off to the thesaurus?" Such compromises of language
do increase the likelihood of finding a middle ground
in such difficult cases. If the language is used to
fashion a creative position, we might rest easier than
if it is used as a cloak to hide remaining distinctions
and disagreements.

As a final example, consider briefly a discussion
in the Senate Banking Committee during the markup of
the Chrysler aid package. The question concerned what
criteria would be used by the new board regarding the
repayment probability to be demanded before new loans
would be issued. The bill as drafted said "reasonable

assurance," Senator Heinz suggested "substantial probability," and Senator Tsongas countered with "substantial
assurance." This discussion appears ludicrous, until
we recognize that each of these phrases is tied to
a particular percentage figure in the minds of the
senators. Again, what appears to be a purely "semantic"
debate is in fact a crucial substantive disagreement.[12]
The observer may be forgiven for viewing such compromises
as both important and muddled. But the muddled character
is largely intended, to hide from the members (and
often from the public) the continuing existence of
such conflicts. To say, and to believe, that one has
"merely compromised on language" can provide a comforting
way to yield valued ground.

4. Blending Values

Our first three types of compromise share a crucial
common element: their ordinality, allowing conflicts
to be resolved by moving to a middle ground between
ranked options. Our fourth type occurs when the conflict
is not between different locations on a common scale,
but between two apparently opposed values. In most
such cases, both sides accept the importance of both
values, but disagree concerning the relative weights
to be assigned. In the search for a middle ground,
what is compromised is not the desire for more of a
particular social resource, but the selection of one
criterion over another. Let us examine one of the most
common disputes of this type: the battle over the role
of the federal government.

---

[12]Senate Committee on Banking, Housing, and Urban Affairs,
markup of The Chrysler Corporation Loan Guarantee Act
of 1979, November 29, 1979.

Consider first a case from the windfall profits tax debate over the income assistance plan. Examining the Committee transcripts, one is struck by the range of arguments put forth for each proposed compromise. As we noticed, much of the dispute concerned regional demands for more assistance. But, interwoven with such concerns, we find appeals to certain deeper arguments concerning the definition of governmental action.

Part of the debate concerned not only how much assistance to give, but how to give it. Should the funds be given directly to recipients, or to the states, or to a federal agency? Several arguments were used to support each position. What is most interesting for our purposes is that one can perceive two different emphases here. As a general rule (although one with many exceptions), Democrats and liberals tended to be primarily concerned about making sure that no poor people "slipped between the cracks" of the program; thus, they preferred to err on the side of giving too much money to a region or an income group, even though some "unneedy" persons might then receive funds. On the other hand, most Republicans and conservatives seemed primarily concerned about guaranteeing greater state control over the disbursement of funds, and avoiding duplication and unnecessary expenses; they were more likely to prefer grants which gave the states more discretion, and which limited the number (and income) of the recipients.

There was no dispute concerning the validity of either of these two goals. Rather, the question concerned which would be incorporated more fully into the final program. One could state the choice as one between compassion and efficiency, but this would be too harsh. (The conservative argument that the poor are the ultimate

beneficiaries of efficiency is largely, but perhaps
not entirely, a cover for class interests.) These are
essentially differences of emphasis, a fact which has
two results.

First, there is relatively little difference between
the two sides, particularly if one compares these disputes
to those in many European countries. Second, the stage
is set for compromises which, rather than forcing the
politician to choose one value over another, can blend
two favored values. Thus, the Committee could decide
to give block grants to states (thus preserving state
discretion in some respects) while also establishing
minimum levels of aid to be given to each state (thus
assuring than a certain level of aid would be given
to persons in all states).

A closely related example reveals that concern
over governmental power and size is not necessarily
the ultimate value for more conservative senators. The
Senate Governmental Affairs Committee considered a
bill to "sunset" all existing governmental programs;
the legislation required a review of such programs
periodically to avoid entrenchment and expense from
unnecessary and duplicated programs. At one point,
Senator Danforth (a moderate Republican) objected to
the bill on the grounds that it would add more uncertainty, while Senator Glenn (a moderate Democrat) insisted
that it was important to cut down the size of government. In
the following exchange, note particularly the extent
to which both men accept the same premises, disagreeing
only on the relative weighings:

> Senator Danforth: ...I certainly agree with
> the concept that government is too big and
> out of control...[But] the best argument
> against the sunsetting...[is] the uncertainty
> that is created throughout the country by

having programs which are in existence for
a finite but uncertain period of time....That
is, the marketplace really needs a degree
of certainty....It seems to me that if you
have a system where a program is going to
lapse simply by the passage of time, then
that creates a degree of uncertainty which
really becomes intolerable...
Senator Glenn: ...I share the concerns about
the uncertainty introduced...What we are
saying is certainty is more important than
controlling government growth, that certainty
is more important than controlling a government
bureaucracy that is out of control and that
certainty is more important than seeing cost
continually escalate for government expen-
ditures. I think a little uncertainty in
these areas would be the best thing we could
introduce....
Senator Danforth: ...Obviously I think the
size of the Government is a serious problem.
Anything that I can do to reduce its costs
and to reduce its burdens on the American
people, I would certainly consider with great
enthusiasm. But I think that at least of
equal importance is the fact that for many
people dealing with the Federal government
is very much like the plot of a Kafka novel,
people just don't know what is going to happen
next. The rules are changing with breath-
taking speed...
    Therefore, size, and reducing the size
of government, is obviously something that
is very, very important, but to build within
a system which keeps people guessing without
any kind of concern for how much they guess
or whether or not they are able to predict
what the future is going to bring, I think,
is to exacerbate perhaps the most serious
problems we have created.[13]

This example provides an interesting twist on the relative

weights of two traditionally conservative concerns: the

size of government, and the stability of the market-

place. Glenn was more concerned with the former, while

---

[13]Senate Governmental Affairs Committee, markup of S2,
June 12, 1980.

Danforth was more worried about the latter. Neither disagreed with the importance of either concern. The search for a compromise was made easier by this fundamental agreement. Indeed, several senators more conservative than Danforth joined with Glenn to support the bill. But several compromise solutions were made to try to deal with Danforth's concerns. The Committee considered (and rejected) a proposal to review only selected programs, and it passed an amendment to extend the period between reviews, in order to minimize uncertainty.

Most complex compromises in the Senate reveal some such dispute over the relative weighings of shared social values and goals. The acceptance of similar values makes compromise possible, while the differential weighing makes compromise necessary.[14] The result is an effort to blend these opposing emphases, to satisfy both sides. Unlike our first three types of compromise, we cannot be sure that a solution is in fact a middle ground; no ordinal ranking is possible, other than a more intuitive sense that one's concerns have been attended to. What is interesting here is that each side tends to insist that its own concerns have been honored no more than those of the opponent; neither side wishes to be seen as winning a clear-cut victory, precisely because both values are appealed to.

Another example is seen in the Chrysler aid bill, a complex piece of legislation developed in its final form as a compromise between two ideologically opposed Senators: Tsongas (liberal Democrat from Massachusetts) and Lugar (conservative Republican from Indiana). Listen to the following arguments given by the two members

---

[14]This sentence is adopted from a similar point about democracy made by Reinhold Niebuhr.

as the bill finally came to the Senate floor, and attend
once again to the agreement on the basic values, as
well as to the insistence upon the importance of the
opponent's views:

> Senator Lugar: I suggest that anyone looking
> at this legislation in a compassionate sense
> must be impressed with the possibilities
> of alleviation of unnecessary human suffering
> in our country if we are to act with prudence
> and with wisdom. I think Americans find this
> idea appealing.
>
> The question asked by Americans as taxpayers
> as opposed to Americans as compassionate
> human beings is simply what is the degree
> of the Federal involvement, what is the risk,
> what are the possibilities that tax dollars
> will be lost?
>
> ...we have a very solemn obligation
> in fashioning a compassionate remedy to make
> certain, it seems to me, of these vital principles.
> ....
> Senator Tsongas: When I meet my liberal labor
> constituency, I get [the following reaction]: why
> am I in concert with those who want to impose
> a wage freeze [on Chrysler employees]?
>
> ...Nobody should walk through this door
> again as an alternative to self-discipline,
> as an alternative to good management. That
> applies to Chrysler and the unions, in particular.
>
> The goal is not to seek to satisfy anybody,
> and if anybody gets up in a union hall or
> in a Chrysler plant or in a boardroom and
> gives the final details and gets a standing
> ovation, something is wrong.
>
> What is the middle ground between Scrooge
> and St. Nick? That is what the bill is all
> about.[15]

The conservative Republican emphasizes the need for
compasssion for the workers, as he reiterates his (primary)
concern for self-discipline and protection of government
funds; the liberal Democrat emphasizes the need to
discipline the unions and force the workers to sacrifice,

---

[15]Congressional Record, December 18, 1979, S18983-88.

as he reiterates his (primary) concern for protecting
their jobs and their future role in the economy. The
existence of automobile plants in Lugar's home state
merely intensifies the complexity here. The compromise
is thus a blending of the two values, seeking to assure
each side that its needs have been met without thereby
adopting the visage of either Scrooge or St. Nick.

Such choices can be found in most legislative
decisions. Their resolution in a particular type of
compromise suggests the importance of such mechanisms
for the passage of any legislation at all. Senators
do not simply "throw up their hands" over such disagreements
and conflicts between shared values. Indeed, they cannot
do so, for many of the organizational factors we have
discussed earlier. But such compromises do remind us
as well that compromise can be achieved between shared
values, without thereby sacrificing the values. Indeed,
this may be the model for the more complex and difficult
social problems confronting American society, few of
which involve the distribution of a single social resource. This type of compromise will become even more
important in American politics, as we seek new ways
to blend the often conflicting emphases placed upon
our shared goals.

5. The Lesser Evil: Accepting the World As It Is

All the compromises we have considered thus far
have one comforting attribute: they are made with a
view that, even though I cannot get all of what I want,
I am achieving something of positive value in the compromise. But our next type does not provide such a
feeling, for it involves the cases where the only thing
to be said for the decision is that things would be

worse without it.[16] The distinction is an important
one: do we see compromises as positive accomplishments
moving us toward what we want, or are they simply decisions
to stave off a greater evil?

In a sense, all compromises could be seen as falling
into this category. Because of the nature of compromise,
we are seldom willing to sacrifice something of value
unless we believe we will be worse off if we fail to
do so. This is in part a trivial assertion, however. To
say that we only compromise when we choose to avoid
a less desirable alternative places our reasoning in
an infinite regress of saying that we do what we want
to do because we want to do it rather than something
else. We certainly will compromise only when we feel
this is better than alternative decisions; but this
is part of _all_ decision making by definition.   To
decide is to prefer one option over another, which
means that one rejects the less preferable choice. But
surely this is not what we mean when we speak of choosing
the lesser of two evils.

There is a less trivial meaning here. Compromises
are made in situations, and we cannot define the boundaries
or details of many of these situations. We might prefer
to have another option, but it is unavailable; we want
to fly but our arms are too weak. Although this is
also inevitable, there is an important difference between
compromising a _perfectionist_ (or ideal) model of what
we want, and compromising a _satisfactory_ (or acceptable)
model. In our first four types, we dealt with situations
where perfection was impossible, but where the remaining

---

[16]One is reminded of Churchill's comment that democracy
is the worst form of government, except for all the
others.

options were still acceptable or desirable. In our fifth type, we deal with those cases where the only attraction of the preferred option is that it is less horrible than all the others.

Thus, when we speak of the lesser evil, we are not simply referring to the fact that all human action is the choice of the best option. We are dealing with situations which present us with a series of alternatives, all of which are unacceptable but between which some choice must be made. The resulting compromise is accepted rather than made. The emphasis thus shifts from the actor's decision between valued options, to the unmanageable and unchangeable aspects of the situation which provide us with such bleak alternatives.

The windfall profits tax bill can be seen as one large example of this type. The bill was introduced to Congress after President Carter decontrolled the price of gasoline. The White House made it very clear that its decontrol decision (to go into effect several months later) was contingent upon the passage of a strong bill, and that, if such a bill was not passed rapidly, the controls would be reintroduced. Thus, the southern senators from oil-producing states were caught in a dilemma: accept the tax on oil, and thereby allow the oil companies to reap profits from decontrol, with many of these profits then being returned to the federal government; or refuse to accept the hated tax, thus depriving the companies of the very profits the bill was designed to control. With such a choice, it is not surprising that much of the debate has the aura of children walking gingerly around a spinach-covered chocolate pie.

Senators from oil-producing states adopted different approaches. But the predominant view was represented

in the following statement by Senator Long of Louisiana,
the Chairman of the Finance Committee (and therefore
the eventual floor manager of the bill), at the beginning
of the discussion of the bill in Committee:

> Senator Long: ...I am going to vote for such
> a tax. The precise amount of the tax is a
> different matter. I am going to vote for
> it for a very simple reason: there is no
> doubt in my mind if we do not pass the tax,
> the President is going to withdraw his decontrol
> plan, just withdraw the whole thing, and
> leave us right back in the same mess that
> we were before.
>   Anyone who is upset about the tax better
> take a look about what the situation is going
> to be when the President withdraws his order. If
> they look at the alternatives, it is sort
> of like this person who is complaining about
> getting old. When you think about the alter-
> natives, you do not feel so bad about it.[17]

Long thus viewed himself as backed into a corner, and
wanted to make it clear that he was supporting the
bill under duress. His willingness to accept it was
not a compromise between two attractive options, but
between two despised scenarios.

One reason for Long's willingness to work for
the bill stemmed from his role in the Senate. As Chairman
of the relevant committee, and as a senior Senator
who is relatively safe in his state, he could afford
to adopt such a stance on the grounds of pragmatism. But
some other senators remained unalterably opposed, perhaps
none so firmly as Senator Gravel of Alaska. Gravel
responded to Long's opening statement by making two
points. First, Gravel claimed that the President was
already committed to decontrol, having made promises
to foreign governments. Second, he insisted that, since

------

[17]Senate Finance Committee, markup of HR3919, September 11,
1979.

there were no windfall profits in the first place, it was ridiculous to speak about taxing them. This objection met with cautious agreement from Senator Dole, the ranking minority member who also represented an oil-producing state. However, Dole ended up adopting Long's argument:

> Senator Dole: ...There will be a tax. I know Senator Gravel does not share that view, but...there is no doubt in my mind that there will be a tax. I guess our obligation is to structure the tax so that it is productive and not punitive, and hopefully we can do that...
> Senator Gravel: ...There is no question that death and taxes are certain, so I would never quarrel with that statement on the surface.
> There may be a tax. It may be in the judgment of this Congress that we are going to pass a tax, but I hope that [Senator Dole] would not emphasize --and certainly I would not join him--in saying that a tax is never punitive. A tax is always punitive, and for him to gloss over the fact that we are going to pass a tax here, that is a given.
> Senator Dole: Less punitive?[18]

To try to circumvent the force of Gravel's argument, Long asked for a show of hands among Committee members concerning whether some tax should be passed. Gravel immediately objected, saying: "What kind of vote is that? Some kind of tax that this committee does not want to go on record as passing?"

But the difficulties of adopting Gravel's "all-or-nothing" strategy here are enormous. For, at some point, one may have to deal with the claim that the alternatives are worse than the passage of the admittedly bad bill. Gravel insisted upon exempting Alaskan oil entirely from the legislation; when the Committee moved

_____

[18] Senate Finance Committee, markup of HR3919, September 11, 1979.

toward his position, he objected to the claims of the majority that they were giving his region equal treatment:

> Senator Gravel: Do not salve your consciences by saying that you are giving me equal treatment when, in point of fact, it is not equal treatment. I would rather you vote that we are not going to give Gravel and Alaska equal treatment, and that is a vote. I will take that vote.[19]

But Gravel eventually votes "aye under protest" to the compromise, which passes the Committee unanimously. When Dole says, "We did it for you," Gravel icily replies: "Do not tell me it was good."[20]

We see a similar division between opponents of any windfall profits tax during the House-Senate conference committee. When a compromise between the two chambers was agreed upon in private, two southern House members responded in opposite ways to a bill which both considered to be ill-conceived and poorly drafted:

> Rep. Archer: ...perhaps it can be argued that this final compromise is the best that can be done....[But] I have spoken already about my opposition to the size of the tax as a deterrent to [oil] production. I must reiterate these figures do not include any provision for supply response in anything other than new oil. I think this is a fatal flaw....I personally cannot approve this so-called compromise or vote for it...for fear that it will be and should be construed as approval for the entire amount of the tax, and it is a deterrent on production which we so desperately need if we are going to really and truly fight OPEC....
> Rep. Moore: ...I don't think a windfall profits tax is going to produce one barrel of energy....I have to agree with the comments of the gentleman from Texas along those lines. However, that question is not before the Conference. We

---

[19]Senate Finance Committee, markup of HR3919, October 9, 1979.
[20]Ibid.

> go to conference with a bill from the House
> and a bill from the Senate, both of which
> pose a substantial tax, and the question
> is what can we do as conferees to come forward
> with the best possible compromise, given
> those two bills to work with. And I think
> that this compromise we have before us is
> the best possible. I...would have much rather
> seen a simple flat tax rate...but it appears
> that the possibility of putting together
> a simple flat tax rate is not possible for
> a number of reasons, so... [I] will be supporting
> this compromise as being the best possible,
> given the fact there is going to be a tax
> and the two bills we had to work with.[21]

The proposal passed overwhelmingly.

Such compromises are very important in an organization where the members represent different and often conflicting interest groups. If one can argue convincingly that a bill is indeed the only alternative to a far worse situation, and that there is simply no better bill which can be passed, then one has added leverage. This is one of the most common battles fought in the Senate between the committees and the full body: is the bill, considered at length in hearings and markup in the committee, to be amended and tinkered with on the floor? Particularly in the case of a complex piece of legislation, committee members will try to insist on a "take it or leave it" strategy. Those objecting to specific provisions run the risk of being left without a passable bill.

We saw earlier the dispute in the Senate Finance Committee over the question of the degree days formula to be used in apportioning funds to different regions of the nation. The compromise which was adopted moved the bill substantially toward the position of the southern

---

[21]House-Senate Conference on HR3919, January 22, 1980.

senators. As we might expect, when the bill came to
the floor, the task was then to convince northerners
who were not on the Committee that the bill did represent
the lesser evil. The bill was defended in precisely
these terms by the Committee members:

> Senator Dole: ...I do not know anybody who
> will hold out just because somebody may have
> a better formula. But frankly after weeks
> and weeks in the Senate Finance Committee,
> we compromised, as is so often the case,
> and I think it is a good compromise. It is
> probably one that did not satisfy everybody
> completely.
> ....
> Senator Nelson: I think we came out with
> a compromise, where those who represent parts
> of the country that do not have the same
> problem respecting degree days as the North
> does made compromises. Those who represented
> States that had the higher degree days made
> compromises. It seems to me we struck a
> fairly happy medium respecting the formulas
> we adopted...[22]

But several northern senators (particularly Muskie
of Maine and Boschwitz of Minnesota) attempted to amend
the bill on the floor. The following comments indicate
both the difficulty of maintaining such a fragile compromise, and the attempt by the supporters of the committee
bill to define the compromise as the best possible
alternative to a number of admittedly bad options.

> Senator Muskie: I am perfectly willing to
> compromise in the direction of whatever urgent
> needs exist in any State. But I think that
> the problems of the poor and the cold States,
> States where I campaigned in January in tempera-
> tures of 45 degrees below zero, day after
> day--I am talking about the middle of the
> afternoon, not midnight--the problems of
> those States and those poor have not been
> adequately addressed by the bill before us. And
> I do not question the good faith or the motivation

---

[22]Congressional Record, November 14, 1979, S16607-08.

of any member of either committee. The Senator
from Wisconsin is a man whose compassion
is well written in the record. I do not criticize
him on his motive or his attempt to compromise. But I just do not believe that this
formula in the committee bill, however well
motivated, addressed the problems of the
cold in this country.

....

Senator Boschwitz: We ask for equity. We
are not greedy, as has been suggested. We
ask for equity and we ask that the original
intent of this legislation be adhered to...

....

Senator Nelson: Now, we struck a compromise
which, I think, is reasonable. There is no
perfect formula. As I said, I would rather
have the formula the Senator from Maine and
the Senator from Minnesota are advocating,
but that was not what we could get passed.

....

Senator Dole: I tried in committee to do
what I think the Senator from Maine is trying
to do. I did not succeed. We went around
and around for about a week in the Finance
Committee.

As the Senator suggests, certainly everybody
has a right to question the wisdom of our
committees. All wisdom is not lodged in
the Finance Committee or in the Human Resources
Committee; but, we finally came up with something
that there was nearly unanimous support for
in the committee. I would suggest that the
Senator from Kansas was travelling down the
same road the Senator from Maine is now on,
and I was derailed.[23]

Muskie threatened to filibuster the bill, and
a series of private meetings ensued to find a new compromise. The strongest argument in the arsenal of the
defenders of the Committee's bill remained their insistence
that, however flawed the bill was, it remained the
best that anyone would get.

---

[23]Congressional Record, November 14, 1979, S16611-13.

Such arguments can always be disputed in at least two ways. The senator can argue that the bill is not the lesser evil, and that another alternative exists. This was the line taken by Senator Gravel, when he insisted that the President would not rescind the order to decontrol gas, and that therefore the entire bill was unnecessary. Similarly, Senator Muskie tried to make this argument, saying that there were still other plans which would be preferable.

The other approach is to attack the compromise solution as itself a sell-out of the goals of the legislation. One could argue that, if the bill is passed as drafted, it is no less evil than the absence of any bill. Such a case can itself be made in two ways: from a purist position, or a more pragmatic one. The first approach insists that it would be better, on principle, to have nothing than to have a partial victory, while the pragmatist sees the actual effects of such a partial victory as not worth the costs.

Let us clarify this distinction by looking at an example where the pragmatic claim is being made in opposition to a proposed compromise. The sunset legislation was attacked in Committee by those who insisted that it was both unrealistic and expensive. The supporters of the bill insisted that neither charge was accurate, and that any effort to water down the bill would destroy it completely. The two senior Senators on the Committee supported an amendment which would have limited the number of programs to be targetted in each session of Congress. This amendment (introduced by Senator Javits with the support of the Chairman, Senator Ribicoff) was attacked by the two strongest proponents of the bill, Senators Glenn and Roth:

<u>Senator Roth</u>: It would be a mistake, a serious
mistake, in my judgment, to pass legislation
which has the name of sunset which, in fact,
means maintenance, which is watered down
to basic provisions which would make it more
difficult to make a cohesive, efficient system
of Federal assistance, and I, for one, shall
oppose any efforts to water it down...
...There is no purpose in passing something
that appears to be doing something that it
isn't. There is no purpose in enacting watered
down legislation that will give the public
at home a perception of reform when, in fact,
it means nothing....
              ...I believe this committee ought to
either   report out this legislation in substantially its   present form, or if it does not
want to do that, then we ought to send it
back to our subcommittee and look for whatever
changes are essential. I just want to go
on record that I cannot support this kind
of legislation, sunset legislation, if it
is gutted   in such a matter that it really
means sunsetting of sunset.
....
<u>Senator Glenn</u>: ...The limited approach that
Senator Javits suggests would be a step. I
question whether it would be a step that
we would then move on to the bigger steps
that I think are really necessary. I am questioning in my own mind whether I want to
fight for the full sunset and resist this
completely, or whether I am willing to take
a tiny, tiny step as I see it, in the right
direction, one that could be expanded maybe
ten years from now into something   really
meaningful.
        This is part of compromise in the Con-
gress. In my own mind at least at this point
I think we have compromised too far on that
one....[24]

When the supporters of the Javits amendment claimed
that the unamended bill would be unable to pass the
full Senate, they were met with the response that the

---

[24]Senate Governmental Affairs Committee, markup of S2,
June 11-12, 1980.

passage of a weakened bill would be worse than the passage of no bill at all. The amendment was finally defeated, nine to eight, with the five senior Senators voting in favor of the weakening amendment.

In such cases, it is important to distinguish between the pragmatic and the purist versions of the arguments. One staff member, referring to senators who refuse to compromise, scornfully commented: "Some people are happy being ideologically pure and politically impotent." But, in the quotes cited above, Senators Roth and Glenn are not adopting purist positions. They are not saying, "I want the whole pie or none at all," but "I won't accept a piece of the pie under the guise of the whole pie." This second argument insists that failure to pass a bill is better than passing something which simply creates the illusion of progress. The judgment called for is complex, of course; how much of what is central to a bill can be sacrificed, without thereby destroying the very essence of the legislation?

A Senator gave another interesting example of this quandary. He favored federal funding for abortion, and he was willing to compromise. But he was confronted with a choice between two proposals, both of which severely restricted the funding. One proposal would allow funding in about six hundred cases, the other in about twelve hundred. He viewed both bills as so restrictive that the differences between them were, in his words, "purely symbolic"; passage of the less restrictive bill was seen as only pretending to adopt a more lenient stance. As a result, he voted for the more stringent proposal, arguing that he could thereby make his point that, if they were going to be restrictive, "they might as well go all the way."

Such arguments are still pragmatic ones, waged on the same terrain as the proponents of the lesser evil compromise. For this Senator, it was not a lesser evil to have six hundred more abortions funded, if in doing so the appearance is given of adopting a less restrictive stance. Similarly, for Senators Roth and Glenn, it is not a lesser evil to have a watered down sunset bill, if in doing so public pressure to pass a stronger bill will be diminished.

Let us look briefly at several more examples. A conservative southern Senator insisted that the major determinant of his own voting record is his understanding of the limits the Constitution places upon the federal government. He made it clear that he is opposed to government "interference" in areas such as health care, education, and civil rights. However, he voted for the establishment of the Department of Education, in spite of these objections. A staff aide explained that "you can't swim against the tide all the time," and that, since the government obviously was already deeply involved in education, the Senator wanted it to function as effectively as possible. Thus, to vote against the creation of a new department would have continued an even worse system of inefficient and overlapping bureau-cracies.

Consider next a liberal Senator struggling to maintain the scope and range of the food stamp program. A House-Senate conference committee is considering a bill which includes a plan to place a ceiling on the income of eligible food stamp recipients. The Senate has consistently refused to accept such a ceiling, and our Senator remains strongly opposed to the idea. But the House has passed such an amendment, and the debate in the conference centers around the House's threat to scuttle the entire program if a limit is not imposed. Does the Senator, who is one of the leaders in the fight for this program, accept a ceiling in order to save the bill?

In this case, the Senator accepted the compromise, convinced that only by doing so would he save the entire program. This was a pragmatic decision, made between two unappealing choices. He did ask himself whether the heart of the bill was being destroyed; he decided that it was not, and thus he could vote for the amendment. He may have answered his own question differently and voted against the bill, on the grounds that the very point of the food stamp program was to keep it open to everyone. This refusal would still have been a pragmatic one. But what he did <u>not</u> do, and what the purist would begin and end with, was consider the question primarily in terms of the ideal view of "feeding the hungry," and refuse to consider any bill which threatened to leave any person without food.

We find similar examples when liberals deal with military appropriations bills. The range of responses is represented by three Senators interviewed in my study. Senator A adopts a pragmatic position. Admitting that he is opposed to the size and nature of most defense appropriations, he attempts to cut selected portions of the budget when he can, but he refrains from making the case on the basis of moral views. When questioned further on this point, he replied: "It is easy to go out in the name of intellectual purity and call for massive cuts in defense spending--but the result would be to hurt people in other ways." He noted, for example, that such cuts, even if they were effective, would result in retaliation by conservatives against poverty program funding. For this Senator, an admittedly bad

defense budget must be accepted on lesser evil grounds;
in his own words, "I get the best deal I can to get
as close to my position as possible."

Senator B adopts a purist approach. Although he
introduces amendments to alter certain portions of
the defense budget, he consistently votes against all
such bills, arguing that they are unduly militaristic. He
believes that to vote for such bills would be to identify
himself with the style and extent of American military
power, and he refuses to do so. But he knows that his
position places him in a small minority; indeed, he
even admitted that he is able to act in this way precisely
because his is only one vote out of one hundred. When
confronted with the choice between an unacceptable
military budget or no budget, he takes the latter choice,
because he refuses to view himself as someone who could
vote for such a bill at all.

Senator C adopts a middle position. He is willing
to vote against a defense budget, but only if convinced
that everything has been done to change it, and that
the only way to indicate his dissatisfaction is to
cast a negative vote. He is more willing to accept
a lesser evil compromise, on the grounds that the alternative would be worse; but he pays more attention to
the symbolic nature of the vote than does our first
Senator.

Such examples indicate that compromises of this
sort must meet challenges from several directions at
once. But they also suggest that the very willingness
to ask the question about what is the lesser evil commits
the actor to a pragmatic orientation. I may oppose
a compromise because I am convinced that no bill is
better than this bill, but I thereby accept the logic
of the bill's supporters. Only Senator B steps outside

of this arena, refusing to even consider the choice as one between evils. Rather than weighing the effects of the two bills, or of the bad bill against no bill, he views the vote itself as the crucial question. He cannot bring himself to vote for a bad proposal, because to do so undermines a value he holds dear. His refusal to compare the given options challenges the proponents of the lesser evil compromise, because what is at stake is not limited to the available options.

There is, therefore, something highly coercive about the effort to define decisions as lesser evil choices. The coercion is cognitive; the actor is told not merely to act but to see the world in a certain way. It is this attempt to define the world of available activity as consisting of two and only two choices, which constitutes its coercive force, and it is against this coercion that the purist tries to rebel. The pragmatist who rejects a compromise remains part of the game, accepting the two alternatives as the only options but weighing them differently.

The lesser evil compromise is often the compromise of last resort. If I cannot arrive at a compromise on other grounds, I can always try to appeal to the lesser evil argument as my justification. But it is precisely for this reason that we are wary of such compromises. When presented with a choice between two evils, we may have to compromise by choosing one or the other. But the call to accept these two alternatives as the only available lines of action must be viewed with suspicion.

6. Trading for Future Benefits

We turn now to compromises which involve action which seems wrong from the viewpoint of the actor. Persons may go against their own best sense of how to act, for the sake of some future benefit in another situation. What is compromised here is the decision that one feels is correct, and the justification is simply that something else--another bill, or the bill as a whole, or another issue--is simply more important. What is crucial in such compromises is not our assessment as observers, but the assessment made by the compromisor.

A common type of compromise in the Senate involves what is often called logrolling. The most usual situation involves trading between different parts of the same bill; I will vote for your pet provision if you will vote for mine.[25] We are interested in those cases where the senator knows that she is supporting a bad provision in a bill, and compromises her judgment or conscience or values on this issue for the sake of an eventual

---

[25]Having adopted a broad definition of compromise, I will treat logrolling as one of its subtypes. Such a position is also taken by Joseph Carens in "Compromises in Politics," op. cit., p. 127. For two articles which distinguish between compromise and logrolling in most cases, see: Golding, "The Nature of Compromise," op. cit., pp. 13-14; Lewis A. Froman, Jr., and Michael D. Cohen, "Compromise and Logrolling: Comparing the Efficiency of Two Bargaining Processes," Behavioral Science 15 (1970), pp. 180-183.

gain in another area.[26]

Let us look first at an example from the conference on the windfall profits tax bill. The two sets of conferees went back and forth on each aspect, with each side insisting on receiving something for each item it gave away. When the House Chairman (Representative Ullman of Oregon) insisted that he would accept a Senate provision only if the Senate receded (that is, gave in) on something else, Senator Long responded:

> Senator Long: ...we fellows on that Senate Finance Committee have not just stricken out of this tax bill provisions that the House enacted that had merit. Where the House provisions had merit we have kept them...Now, I do not think the Chairman of the House committee or anybody else on the House side wants to set a precedent here of rejecting a perfectly good Senate provision that they had not considered before merely to trade that for something else. We have not done business that way with anything else in this bill, and if we are not going to be appreciated in that respect, we will have to change our way of doing business....
> Rep. Ullman: ...Let's leave this one out and move to another one. If I have a night's sleep maybe I will see it a little better.
> Senator Long: I know the Chairman is getting a little tired. We will move on to the next thing, one that is easier for you to grasp.

---

[26]There is a complex philosophical problem here which we cannot go into in much detail. Some philosophers argue that it makes no sense to speak about acting incorrectly if one can give reasons or overriding considerations for that action; the balance swings one way or the other, and what one should do depends upon that balance. Such consequentialist arguments are powerful, but seem to ignore the fact that we often feel that we have done something wrong when we lie or give in or refuse to compromise, even if we can also justify that action in terms of other consequences. The question of whether such actions really are wrong need not concern us here.

And Long gets his revenge on the very next item, a provision on which the House asks the Senate to recede:

> Rep. Gibbons: I was hoping the Senate would recede on that item.
> Senator Long: If we can come to terms on the other part--
> Rep. Gibbons: Oh, we are trading?
> Senator Long: That might be what Mr. Ullman is looking for, a trade. I think we ought to go on.

The House quickly recedes on the next item, and Representative Ullman makes it clear that he did so with expectations of a trade:

> Rep. Ullman: I am more concerned about the next item than I am about this one...I hope that my friend [Senator Long] will look with some consideration of this next item.

And when the next item comes up, Ullman expects delivery:

> Rep. Ullman: ...I am adamantly opposed to this kind of provision....the House would take a very firm position against this provision....In the spirit of good will and cooperation, the gentleman was so persuasive we gave on this last number and without making a big fuss. Now I would think that in the same spirit...[27]

What is crucial here is that the compromise was not reached on the merits of each amendment, nor was there any attempt to find a middle ground within each section of the bill. Rather, the compromise was reached between amendments, with each side's view accepted totally in one case, with the understanding (explicit or implicit) that the other side would win on the next one. We have here a very different type of compromise, external to the merits of or arguments for each particular proposal.

Such compromises need not occur in such a short

---

[27]House-Senate Conference on HR3919, January 22, 1980.

time span. Often they are more implicit; a vote reflects
a willingness to go out of one's way, with the unstated
assumption that the tables will soon be turned. There
may be a verbalized hint of such expectations, however.
The phrase "reserve the right" is often used to indicate
that a senator will go along with something for the
moment, but that "the chickens will come home to roost"
later on. When Senator Moynihan accepts a tax credit
plan for homeowners, for instance, he notes that his
own state has a large number of apartment dwellers:

> Senator Moynihan: ...We are giving $5000
> to people here. That is a big credit. I just
> say I would like to reserve the fact that
> there are people who live in apartment houses,
> people who rent. We will have to find some
> equity for them as well.[28]

Often the willingness to recognize someone else's
interests is tied explicitly to the expectations of
receiving comparable recognition for one's own. Unlike
our earlier examples of regional arguments over income
assistance to cold states, however, such acceptance
can be approached as a trade-off of different parts
of a bill, rather than as an attempt to reach a middle
ground on one provision. In the Committee on Energy
and Natural Resources, the discussion of a conservation
bill turned into a sectional dispute over natural gas. The
Chairman (Senator Johnston of Louisiana) tried to push
through an amendment over the objections of Senator
Ford of Kentucky. In the following exchange, note both
the implicit threat given by Ford, and the more explicit
threat (and offer of a compromise trade-off) by Senator
Tsongas of Massachusetts:

----

[28]Senate Finance Committee, markup of HR3919, September 18,
1979.

Senator Johnston: This is what you call coalition
building?
Senator Ford: Mr. Chairman...I am willing
to give where it will help the country, but
I will be darned if I am willing to give
where it is just going to help a State.
....
Senator Tsongas: ...I am inclined to support
the Chairman...for reasons that are somewhat
different... My concern is that, from a
purely Machiavellian point of view, if the
Chairman succeeds in getting this through
now, how willing is he going to be to look
at other issues that the other members of
the committee might be interested in?
Senator Johnston: Very willing.
Senator Ford: May I just make one comment,
Paul? If this amendment is passed, half this
room will walk out and will not support a
damned word of [this bill]...
....
Senator Tsongas: That is what I am talking
about. I think there are competing interests
here and I would like to see a package put
together in which all of the interests are
somehow accommodated, including the environmental
concerns, and that I would like to state
for the record now so that as we wend our
way down the rest of the legislation, there
will be a sensitivity on the part of those
who are strongly supportive of the amendment. It
shouldn't be 'I will get mine now, and the
rest can be down the road.'[29]

Such compromises are common. The committee members
work with each other over a long period of time, and
they learn the interests and needs of each constituency.
They view each piece of legislation as a carefully
crafted and balanced piece of work, and each senator
wishes to contribute to its formation without thereby
losing the respect of the other people around the table. Trading compromises allow senators to accept other interests,
without demanding a specific defense for the particular

---

[29]Senate Committee on Energy and Natural Resources, markup
of S2470, May 29, 1980.

amendment under consideration. In this type of compromise, the merits of each case can be largely ignored, being seen instead in terms of the broader process of give and take on each bill. The balance is thus struck between, not within, particular aspects of each bill. Indeed, one result of such compromises is that many bills resemble ad hoc combinations of grab-bag-like proportions, in which each senator's pet project has been included.

But such trading is also limited by certain features of the Senate. There are so many pieces of legislation under consideration at one time, and so many parts of each bill, that members cannot remember precisely how many favors are owed. In addition, because each senator is intimately involved with only a small fraction of the pending legislation, the favors given and received can be expected to even out over a number of years. Indeed, it is viewed by some senators as dysfunctional to tie one's vote on a bill to a trade-off on another one, since the favor may be called in at an unpropitious moment. To ask someone for a favor is seen as acceptable, provided one does not do so often; but to call on someone to return an earlier favor is usually considered inappropriate. Due largely to the difficulties in such explicit trading, many senators report that they try to avoid asking favors whenever possible. Trade-offs thus occur primarily between provisions within a particular bill, especially when broad coalitions are sought to pass out a complex and controversial bill.

7. Compromising Judgment for the Constituency

We turn to compromises where, once again, the senator acts in a manner contrary to the merits of the case on the particular vote. This type involves those cases where the conflict is between the judgment

of the merits of a bill, and the desire to maintain
one's job. The conflict reflects our earlier discussion
about role conflict, particularly the tension between
representing the constituency and voting for what one
may believe to be correct.

This sort of compromise is both very common and
very troubling to the senators themselves. Most members
I interviewed made it very clear that they would not
compromise in this way on certain matters: issues of
principle, or foreign policy questions, or situations
where they had much more information.[30] Regardless
of how accurate their claims may be, the point is that
such compromises are not merely defended but are actually
used to justify other compromises. In other words,
most senators, while believing that they draw limits
concerning their own action, seem to assume that most
of their colleagues will act out of an inordinate fear
of constituency wrath, and they will then use this
perception to justify their own compromises.

Consider the debate in the Finance Committee concerning
Senator Danforth's proposed amendment to the windfall
profits tax. Danforth wants to tax the profits of oil
on state-owned land, a proposal benefitting his state
and harming Louisiana. Listen to the following exchange,
and pay particular attention to the assumption that
one must represent the interests of one's state:

> Senator Danforth: ...some of the biggest
> winners [of decontrol] are some of the States. I
> do not happen to represent one of those States.
> Somehow, I am going to have to go back to

---

[30]See chapter 6 for a detailed discussion of this response.

> my people in Missouri and say, 'Folks...let
> me tell you what else I have done for you: I
> have just bought new limousines for the Governor
> of Louisiana and the Governor of Texas.'
> I do not know how to explain that....
> Senator Long: Why not go back and explain
> to them that you have tried to tax Louisiana,
> you have tried to tax the State government
> itself. You have tried to remove the State's
> taxing power. You tried all that, and it
> did not work. Now, if you got the votes,
> it did work. Of course, we will see you in
> court if it does. [Laughter] In any event,
> you had your chance.[31]

The very next day, we find Long using Danforth's argument
in opposing Senator Gravel's effort to exempt Alaskan
oil from the tax:

> Senator Long: ...It is kind of hard for me
> to go back and tell my people that I am sorry
> I could not get those folks out from under
> all these darn taxes, but thank God we did
> save Alaska. They will probably say that
> it is too bad that they don't have that guy
> from Alaska representing them in the Senate
> as Senator from Louisiana.[32]

The logical extension of this argument is to view
the entire policy-making process as nothing more than
a clash between interest groups represented by different
senators, with each compromise based solely on the
desire of each member to get as much as possible for
the relevant groups. In the following quotation from
Senator Moynihan, to which we referred earlier, we
see the force of this argument, as well as the way
in which it leads into a plea for one's own interest
groups:

---

[31]Senate Finance Committee, markup of HR3919, October 3,
1979.
[32]Senate Finance Committee, markup of HR3919, October 4,
1979.

<u>Senator Moynihan</u>: ...I've got to tell you why I'm not going to vote for Senator Danforth's bill, although everything he said is right, in my view. Everything he said is right. I'm not going to vote for it because it would cause severe difficulties for Senators around this table who represent communities which would be affected. They would be thought not to have protected the interests of their States, and a Senator is sent here to do that. And I wouldn't want any Senator in a situation of heightened emotion to be thought that he could not protect the interests of his own people.

On the other hand, I think it behooves us to observe our behavior. We [on the Finance Committee] are not a random selection of the Senate....we are disproportionately on this committee because of the mineral resources that our states have. And this committee has been disproportionately concerned about those mineral resources.

I don't object to concern. I am a Madisonian. I think that we are here to represent interests; but there are more interests than just the oil and gas companies of this country. And I was struck the other day when we were talking about relief for low income people as part of this package, and we had had a most attentive full committee, full attendance all through the week as we discussed [natural resources], and suddenly we were talking about low income people, and there were five of us around the table, and only one of them, the Chairman, came from the state that had any oil or gas...[33]

Note that there is no defense in such situations of the substance of the interests, nor of the claimed (and assumed) connection between these interests and the particular bill. The argument rests on the view that each senator must be willing to compromise with better judgment in order to attend more fully to constituent needs. Or, to put it somewhat differently, one's better

---

[33]Senate Finance Committee, markup of HR3919, October 10, 1979.

judgment is defined in terms of representing the interests of the constituency. Such compromises share with trading compromises a relative disdain for the merits of the proposals; but they are justified not by referring to a more important section of the bill, but by pointing to the need of each senator to defend the interests of each state.

Few senators seem to believe that they should always compromise in this way, and some argue that such decisions are not compromises at all. I am considering only those cases where the senator does perceive a conflict between judgment and constituency interests, and hence might be more willing to enter into a compromise. Although attention to constituency interests is a background factor in all compromises, there are examples where the very essence of the decision involves using the interests of the constituency as the basis. In the above example, Senator Moynihan's willingness to recognize the interests of the Senator from Louisiana is based on an interest-oriented view of politics; what is compromised here is the actor's capacity to decide on the basis of the merits of an issue. This is not to suggest that such decisions are wrong, but simply that, in so acting, the actor compromises with another understanding of the role of being a senator.

Perhaps one way to understand this type of compromise is to use the terminology of "bad faith."[34] I act in bad faith when I claim that my actions are totally

---

[34]The major reference is to Jean-Paul Sartre, Being and Nothingness (translated by Hazel Barnes) (N.Y.: Simon and Schuster, 1966 [1943]), pp. 86-116. See also Peter Berger, The Precarious Vision (N.Y.: Doubleday and Co., 1961), esp. chapters 5 and 10; and Berger, Invitation to Sociology (N.Y.: Doubleday and Co., 1963), pp. 142-163.

defined by my roles. Thus, a senator may insist that it is her job to represent the interests of the constituency. This argument can turn into an example of bad faith when the senator forgets that she has chosen to follow this definition, and to act out of that particular role at that moment. When a senator defends an action purely in terms of service to constituents, without weighing this responsibility over against others, the action has moved from the category of role-influenced to that of role-controlled.

We might wonder whether a senator would ever be justified in acting against her better judgment on a particular issue. If we define "responsible action" as action guided solely by constituent interests or desires, then there is no difficulty. But if we see multiple constituencies and responsibilities, such compromises can be justified in terms that sound like bad faith. To enter into an agreement with an opponent purely on the grounds that he is representing his interests while I am representing mine, is to draw a misleading picture of our action. We are both free to choose which interests we represent, and to decide under what circumstances we will choose to represent them. The need to weigh conflicting constituencies provides a context for compromise here.

We should recognize that the failure to attend to constituent interests is equally a compromise, of course. We seldom speak about cases where senators resist constituent pressure as being compromises; this can probably be explained by remembering the somewhat derogatory force of the term. But we should be careful here--as one Senator angrily pointed out to me, it is elitist to assume that one's judgment is always superior to that of one's constituents. It would be better to recognize that the senator can compromise either of the two senatorial role obligations: to serve the constituency and to do what one believes is correct. These two obligations may conflict, but they need not do so. When they do conflict, it is by no means clear which choice is to be preferred in all cases. Our own individual assessments depend largely upon our view of the proper mix of the two obligations, as well as upon our attitudes toward the particular compromise being made.

8. Compromising Judgment for Senate Pressure

Another type of compromise where one may act against one's judgment pits that judgment against the interests, not of the constituency, but of the Senate itself. The senator may wish to act in a particular way, but will compromise for the sake of getting along with colleagues or maintaining her position in the organization. We are concerned here again with substantive issues, not with questions of courtesy or honesty.

An interesting example occurred in the Budget procedure adopted recently in the Senate. The new Budget Committee must struggle with the other committees to establish and enforce spending limits. Although the Senate established the Committee, senators often refuse to go along with its recommendations, and the Committee has little direct power. When members of the Finance Committee objected to some proposed changes in the process, particularly to the establishment of limits to which the individual committees would have to comply, Senator Packwood (who served on both the Budget and Finance Committees) responded:

> Senator Packwood: ...you know, I love this
> Committee and the Budget Committee is tough. But
> at some stage we are going to come against
> this rock and a hard place.
>   What are going to be the ultimate powers
> of the Budget Committee?
>   I am not quite sure how you harmonize
> a committee that sets an overall budget that
> has no power to enforce it, with committees
> that are not unlike many of the interest
> groups in this country, all of whom want
> to balance the budget, except for them.[35]

The battle over turf is acute. Senator Long, admitting
that "I guess if I served on the Budget Committee and
I did not serve on the Finance Committee or Appropriations
Committee, I would think it is a great idea," fights
for control over budgetary matters in his area. He
refers to an old saying by ex-Senator Bob Kerr that
"I am against any combine that I'm not in on." The
central concern is power: who can tell the senator
that he must compromise with the Budget Committee's
figures?

> Senator Long: Tell us, Mr. Expert, do we
> have to comply with this budget or not? I
> would just as soon not comply if we had the
> option.
> Senator Packwood: I suppose, Mr. Chairman,
> the bottom line comes down to the fact that
> the majority of the Senate can do anything
> it wants...whether that is on a point of
> order that somebody objects to and you overrule
> the Chair. That is your bottom line.[36]

The senator must decide whether to abandon her
own position, pet projects, and established arguments,
all for the sake of the whims or conclusions of another
committee, or the arguments or projects of a colleague. Once

---

[35]Senate Finance Committee, executive session, April 15,
1980.
[36]Senate Finance Committee, executive session, June 17,
1980.

again, such a willingness to move toward another senator
should be seen as a compromise of the position with
which we begin; whether for reasons of convenience
or of pressure, we choose to give up our better judgment
on a particular issue.

Senators adopt various stances here. Chairpersons
of powerful committees are loathe to compromise in
this way with other committees, but they compromise
continually with their own committee members. Indeed,
much of the Chair's power resides in the good will
provided by the other members, because many of the
recent rule changes stripped the chairperson of many
prerogatives. The same can be said of the majority
leader, as we noted earlier. Senator Byrd was selected
as majority leader not because of his legislative skills
or parliamentary maneuvering, but primarily because
of his assiduous courting of other members and his
willingness to recognize their needs and concerns.

In what sense is this a compromise? What is Senator
Byrd sacrificing by acting in this way? He gives up
a degree of freedom of action and decision making,
a freedom which "comes with the territory" of being
a senator. After all, time and resources are scarce,
and one can quickly use them up in such continuous
attention to the needs of one's colleagues. But the
value of maintaining autonomy and judgment conflicts
with the desire for increased influence and opportunities. Every senator is in this situation, and each
must choose an appropriate balance; the majority leader
is simply an example of someone who has opted for the
"responsiveness" end of the continuum. Such a choice
may be a highly instrumental one, of course; to have
more autonomy in the future, I may have to be more

responsive now. But such a choice remains a crucial compromise.

Of course, even the most independent senator cannot avoid making such compromises. One Senator admitted that he is somewhat uncomfortable making "the little compromises that you rationalize as not being compromises, such as when I am leaning fifty-two to forty-eight [percent] on the merits of a bill and I vote the other way under pressure of a senator who did me a favor recently." Note that, unlike the trading compromises we discussed earlier, the merits of the bill are relevant here, although they are overridden by the perceived need to attend to senatorial relationships.

In another example of such a compromise, a Senator explained his opposition to stronger disciplinary measures by the Senate Ethics Committee. Admitting that such discipline was justified in many instances, he argued that the reputation of the Senate as a public institution would be undermined by focussing attention on the personal moral behavior of its members. Thus, he favored such discipline only when the reputation of the Senate itself had been brought into disrepute. He did say, however, that he believed other "malfeasances" should be disciplined, and that there was something appropriate about the organization's efforts to enforce discipline. His willing-ness to compromise on this point reflected his view that the reputation of the Senate was the most significant concern.

Once again, our evaluation of such compromises depends largely upon what we expect these politicians to be doing as senators. I would merely suggest that such compromises are so common that they are seldom viewed as compromises at all. To focus attention upon them is to call into question not merely the quality of life in the Senate, but the ease with which such decisions become seen as necessary for the continued functioning of the organization. What is compromised is a style of autonomous action and initiative on the part of the actor; the compromise may pay off, but it remains an action requiring careful oversight and continual explanation.

9. Compromising Judgment for Reference Group

Another type of compromise involves situations where one's judgment is sacrificed for the sake of a perception of one's broader reference group. This term refers to any set of persons (or ideal persons, such as God) whose opinions and evaluations matter greatly to the actor. For the senator, in addition to the obvious attention paid to constituency and colleagues, there are other persons and groups whose opinions may influence decision making. Exactly who these groups are, is dictated largely by past experience as well as present needs and beliefs. Thus, the senator may be torn between a vote for a bill which is seen as correct, and the belief of a particular reference group that the bill contradicts its image of what "their senator" will do.

It is the perception by the senator of the beliefs of the reference group, not the actual beliefs, that is crucial here. As we shall discover in chapter 5, political rhetoric consists largely of appeals to such reference groups as justifications for action. When such appeals are evidently self-serving, one may wonder whether these other groups really do feel this way at all. But we are concerned here merely with the compromises made or refused in terms of such perceptions.

For example, a conservative Senator's refusal
to compromise on the abortion issue was explained (by
a staff aide) by a desire not to displease the broader
group of ideological conservatives who looked to the
Senator for leadership. In this case, the refusal to
compromise is related to the views of the reference
group. Even if the Senator believed that the particular
compromise was desirable, he would hesitate because
this reference group "would have to take you down from
your pedestal if you compromised." Similarly, a moderate
Senator votes consistently for education programs and
legal services bills, even when he questions their
quality and relevance for his constituency. He explains
this unerring support by referring to his long term
association with both teachers' organizations and lawyers. Perhaps partly because his parents were both
teachers, he is loathe "to go against their impressions
of me."

Such background loyalties can lead toward or away
from compromise in various ways. Note that, in the
above examples, the senator might be less willing to
compromise. In doing so, however, he is compromising
his judgment on the bill at hand. There are situations
where attention to the reference group may lead to
a more substantive compromise than the senator may
be comfortable with on other grounds.

Such compromises are somewhat less direct than
our previous two types. In American politics, it is
more appropriate to be swayed from one's better judgment
by constituency or Senate pressures than by the more
hidden and pervasive influences of background or organizational loyalties. We came across this problem earlier
when we considered the question of representation;
we stumble across it again as we see that compromises

between judgment and the desire to please are often unavoidable ones.

One interesting issue concerns the precise role of party affiliation as a reference group in the Senate. The decline of party loyalty and power in the Senate has contributed to a greater degree of independence for most senators. But one still sees examples of senators "bowing" to pressure from party leaders, although this pressure is exerted rather gingerly. One particularly independent Republican admitted that he had switched a vote on the floor in one instance: after casting what he believed (and continued to believe) was the correct vote, he was called up to the desk by the party leaders and shown that he was the only Republican voting against the bill. In explaining his vote switch, he claimed that such pressure was rare. What was compromised here was his judgment on the merits of the bill, for the sake of the desire to honor his party loyalty.

10. Compromises of Honesty

We discussed earlier the norms of courtesy and reciprocity, and some of their effects upon Senate conduct. We want to ask here whether such a situation creates a distinctive type of compromise: namely, a compromise of manners. We are dealing with compromises of honesty or expression. One tones down a sentence, refers to someone in an inaccurate way, pretends to respect an admittedly abhorrent argument, or goes along with an outmoded custom. What is compromised is a standard of honesty and directness.

Several senators reported that they saw manners as totally unrelated to ethics or compromise. As one Senator pointed out, "manners are the oil--and it does get pretty oily around here. But I see no relationship

between manners and honesty." Yet, there are some ethical
issues here. The somewhat hypocritical nature of such
over-familiarity is evident; when everyone is everyone
else's "close personal friend," we begin to wonder
about the relationships these persons are capable of. Alben
Barkley's advice to a freshman Senator is relevant
here: "If you think a colleague stupid, refer to him
as 'the able, learned and distinguished senator,'
but if you know he is stupid, refer to him as 'the
very able, learned and distinguished senator.'"[37] In
a similar vein, a junior Senator told me that, on his
very first day in the Senate, he was introduced to
Senator Muskie, and the two men simply said hello. Several
weeks later, during floor debate, Senator Muskie referred
to him as "my good personal friend," prompting a staff
aide to say: "He should have said 'my good personal
friend who I am looking forward to meeting.'" Such
overkill undercuts both the clarity of language and
the credibility of public statements in general, particularly when one discovers that there are in fact few
close friendships between senators.[38]

   A part of the function of senatorial courtesy
is to separate political and personal disputes. Senate
insiders point proudly to the shared dinner engagements
and back-slapping which follow acrimonious floor debate. But
this separation is troubling as well. One staff member
reported that he feels uncomfortable with his boss'
ability to stay on such close personal terms with a
colleague who is ideologically opposed to him on almost
every issue. The staff member believed that, if the

[37]Quoted in Matthews, U. S. Senators and Their World,
p. 99.
[38]See, for example, Ross Baker, Friend and Foe in the
U. S. Senate (N. Y.: The Free Press, 1980).

Senator really felt strongly about these matters, it would be difficult to carry on such a relationship. We might recognize the value of courtesy here, without dismissing the complaint too easily. Perhaps there are some issues which we would want our representatives to feel so strongly about that they are not able to maintain easy personal contacts with opposing members.

Furthermore, there is something questionable about a process of decision making which occurs in an aura of such superficial and generalized familiarity. The public sees only the close side, as the more hostile moments are usually hidden from view (or quickly expunged from the Congressional Record before it is printed). Perhaps this is unfortunate, for a process which seems to drip with sincerity and unabiding respect calls into question both the honesty of the participants and their commitment to underlying values.

I am not suggesting that such norms should be abandoned, even if that were possible. Rather, senators and the public should be aware of the hypocrisy involved in compromising with a more honest or direct use of language. To live in a context of superficiality and deference can undermine one's ability to distinguish between genuine friendship and distanced respect, and we should expect our legislators to be able to do so. Once again, such compromises are important and are often desirable, but they are always in need of explanation.

Perhaps several other examples will clarify this point. Language is almost infinitely malleable, as Alice learned much to her chagrin; but the "almost" is crucial. Because our politicians speak for a living, we know them almost exclusively through their words. Hence, a senator who uses speech dishonestly presents not just a false front but a false self. One Senator made a rather strong distinction between "capitulation on substance" and "finessing of language." He uses terms such as "the man" when speaking to black audiences, arguing that "the whole point of language is to communicate." Such a mild example might not be troubling, although even here the adoption of such language is used to disguise his obvious differences with this wing of his constituency. But, when we consider our examples of referring to someone we have just met as "my close personal friend," we may feel that something other than "just language" is being compromised.

Similarly, what one says may be less important than what one does not say. We are inevitably selective in our speech and our descriptions of our actions. But there are limits here. Senators are very concerned about how their activities are viewed by the public; what is crucial is not what is done but what is reported, emphasized, and stressed. Thus, a Senator from a fairly conservative state has compiled a liberal voting record, and he carefully selects certain aspects of his record to speak about. He favors a balanced budget, and he talks about this position whenever he has the chance. But one consequence of his support for a balanced budget is his opposition to deductions for the use of gasoline, a position which (due to its unpopularity) he skirts whenever possible. Do we want to fault him for this choice? We are not surprised when a politician tries to "put his best foot forward," of course. But we should be concerned, nevertheless, to look below the surface here. Such choices may make it impossible for the constituents to understand (and therefore to evaluate) what is involved in the Senator's support for the popular balanced budget. If the result is to mislead and misrepresent one's voting record, then selectivity takes on a serious ethical dimension.

One of the most revealing moments in my interviews occurred during a discussion with a Senate staff assistant. Reflecting on her years in the Senate organization, she found herself marvelling at how her own actions had changed. In particular, she admitted that she is now much more likely to "lie" in numerous situations. She will tell someone that she has just spoken to the Senator about an issue, when she has not done so; she writes speeches which the Senator then delivers verbatim; she overlooks private uses of the free telephone line. Whether we consider such actions to be morally problematic, she saw them as such. While such activities seem relatively harmless, the pattern they establish is disturbing. They are compromises which reflect an unwillingness to live by certain "everyday" standards of honesty. The conflicting values of courtesy and honesty are often difficult to mesh, and this is true of the non-political world as well. The problem is merely compounded in the world of politics, where language is so important and where such major decisions are made. This staff member seemed somewhat surprised, and a little horrified, to recognize the distance she had come.

11. Compromises of Maneuvering

Our final type concerns the minor maneuvers engaged in by members of the Senate. Such actions, taken by themselves, seem harmless enough. Many of them concern matters of timing. For instance, when does one report out a bill, or introduce an idea? Is one willing to wait? A Senate Chairman said that "you always make some compromises to get legislation through, and we're always rationalizing here." He will put off a vote

on a bill for a year, even though he knows it should
be passed now, because different people may be on the
Committee later on. He is careful to refer to such
actions as "tactical, not moral, compromises." Another
Chairman, trying to guide a difficult amendment through
his Committee, admitted during a markup session that
"I don't want to have a premature vote on this, premature
being defined as before you have a majority."[39]

Sometimes such compromises of timing are used
by one committee against another. When the Finance
Committee was confronted with a budgeting limit which
it was in danger of exceeding, a staff member suggested
a way to avoid cutting back on desired programs:

> Staff aide: ...The question is whether you
> do nothing, you pull it back for, in effect,
> one month, to satisfy the Budget Act requirements
> by increasing our cash flow...and then restore
> it on October 1 for fiscal year 1982 and
> subsequent years, or you just withdraw it
> permanently.
> Senator Dole: Is that kind of a trick to
> satisfy the Budget Committee?
> Staff aide: We wouldn't call it a trick. It
> is a device. [Laughter][40]

The concluding hours of each session are notorious
opportunities for such compromises. Both sides can
maneuver throughout the session to leave selected controversial bills for the last moment. Once again, there
is nothing intrinsically wrong with such activities,
but they are compromises of the normal flow of business,
or at least of the expectations that the timing and
ordering of the legislative process will be dictated

---

[39]Senator Johnston, in Senate Committee on Energy and
Natural Resources, markup of S2470, May 29, 1980.
[40]Senate Finance Committee, executive session, June 18,
1980.

by considerations other than one's desire to get the
bill passed in any way possible.

Conclusion

We have examined a number of types of compromise. In
spite of the differences between them, all have in
common the crucial elements we identified in chapter 1.
The actor, torn between two desirable goals, or between
a desired goal and the real world, seeks a solution
which will avoid the hard choice. The argument for
extending coverage of the term "compromise" to many
of these activities is based on the view that they
remain choices which must be justified. In seeing them
as compromises, we gain a richer sense of the alternatives
available to the actor, and of the values between which
the choice must be made.

The reader may wonder whether anything of value
is being compromised, particularly in the last several
types. One might suggest that a rigorous ideal of honesty
is simply out of place in politics, and that therefore
there are no compromises of honesty. But the examples
I have provided share an important feature: such ideals
were held and cherished by the actors in the situation. All
of these types were drawn from, and suggested by, the
participants themselves. I think we are warranted in
seeing them as compromises, and in asking about the
sorts of justifications we should demand for their
occurrence.

In chapter 7, we will return to the ethical question
of assessing the appropriateness of these types. I
have already suggested some arguments here. I would
simply add that one's assessment can involve two different
aspects. First, we can feel uncomfortable about a compromise
because we disagree with the result; compromises on

certain issues will be justifiable, when they lead
to solutions we approve of. In this sense, each compromise
demands to be examined and evaluated on its own terms. But
we can also question certain compromises on more <u>categorical</u>
grounds; if I insist on a high standard of honesty,
then I will question compromises of honesty, regardless
of the particular bill or the particular result of
the compromise. We should be clear which of these arguments
we are using when we ask our elected officials to justify
their actions. By suggesting such an extensive typology
of compromises, I hope to make it easier to do so.

CHAPTER 5. THE RHETORIC OF SENATORIAL COMPROMISE

In chapter 3, we looked at compromise from the standpoint of the organizational features of Senate life. In chapter 4, we focused on the types of compromises resulting from these organizational features. Now, we turn the lens once again, and ask about the <u>language</u> used to justify and explain compromise.

The use of language in the Senate poses some major problems for us. First, we have already discovered that such language is quite malleable, and that senators are quite adept at adopting it for their purposes. Indeed, senators (and all politicians) speak for a living; the words they use are more than tools of the trade, they are the very substance of the trade as well. As outsiders, we should therefore be wary of accepting any statement at face value.[1]

Second, such wariness does not solve the central problem of political discourse. Because of the public nature of politics, the practitioners see the world as a stage with a continuous series of performances. The metaphor of role fits human action quite well, but it fits political action all too well. Are these people "acting," in the sense here of "posturing," when they say anything? This question is not posed simply as a criticism voiced from outside. One Senator complained to me about this problem, suggesting that the entire world of the Senate is "unreal" and "fantastic" (in the literal sense of resembling a fantasy). Whether delivering a flowery statement on the Senate floor, wrangling over a bill in committee, or speaking to

---

[1]In the use of interviews and transcripts in this book, I have tried to find systematic patterns of responses. But we are still dependent finally upon the language used, in public or in private, when conducting this type of research. Indeed, such problems constitute both the curse and the excitement of engaging in such study.

a constituent or an interviewer in the privacy of an office, the senator can adopt a variety of styles of language, leaving the observer uncertain about where, if anywhere, the "real" senator is to be found.

The importance of such acting is clear. Any slip, any word spoken out of context, can be used in future years to undermine a political career. In no other area is the value of each sentence spoken quite so critical; as a result, in no other area is the staged nature of each sentence quite so apparent. If we have to think twice before saying anything, it is tempting not to think at all, substituting hedged generalities or safe platitudes for potentially hazardous positions. But, at the same time, language is a potential weapon, to be used to further one's purposes and to present an image of self to the voting public. In both of these ways, the public relations aspect of political discourse undercuts the observer's ability to trust what is heard.

Once again, we should not overstate the difference between political language and all other language. We never know whether someone means what is said. The political figure is simply an extreme case; we do not know this person intimately, the job calls for a constant stream of words on all subjects, and the public nature of the role demands caution before saying anything. Unless we become close friends with the individual, we must listen and weigh what we are told.

Third, the language we hear is not always the language which determines action. Much policy making occurs behind closed doors, in private conferences and phone calls. There are some sound arguments for conducting much of the decision making in private; if the degree of posturing is indeed as acute as we have suggested, then the amount of rigidity and demagoguery will be decreased by private discussion and decision.

In spite of these difficulties, we do possess a wealth of information. What is revealed in public is not simply window dressing. If we are careful in sorting out the different types of language used, and in forcing ourselves to ask probing questions, we find that the words chosen do reflect some important features of the decisions themselves. We can view all public statements as rationalizations for action; the politician decides what to do, and then searches for a reason which can be given in public for that action. Such a view is often expressed in condemnatory or cynical tones, leading us to distrust what we hear. But such a reaction misses the point of political language. One crucial aspect of political language--indeed, perhaps the most important single aspect--concerns the need to justify and explain the action in a public arena. Politicians are acutely aware of this need, and decisions often reflect, and depend upon, the language chosen to explain them.

I cannot emphasize this point strongly enough. The very categories we have to think about policy questions are generated by language, and the outcomes of policy decisions are themselves largely controlled by the choice of such language. In this sense, the place of appearance in politics is central. There is little reality behind the arguments we give to support our decisions, because the decisions themselves are largely determined by our ability to give reasons for them. If we ask "But what really happened?" we are denying the reality and centrality of the language.

I am indebted here to two writers who have developed this point in some detail. C. Wright Mills, writing in 1940, speaks of <u>motives</u> of human action in a distinctive way. Instead of seeing motives as underlying causes of action, he suggests that our motives are "the terms with which interpretation of conduct <u>by social actors</u> proceeds."[2] Our motives are the words we use to justify our action. But we do not simply arrive at these words after a decision is made; often, before we decide, we ask ourselves: "If I did this, what could I say? What would they say?"[3] Mills goes on to ask about the vocabularies of motives, suggesting that we learn a great deal about human action by understanding the ways in which motives are put forth. If I provide a particular set of motives for my action, you are given information concerning not only my choice of words but about my choice of meaning and action as well.

This approach is relevant for our discussion of political language. The political actor must justify a decision to a large audience of constituents, media watchdogs, political supporters and potential opponents. Much time and energy is spent in the Senate finding appropriate motives for decisions, and some decisions are not made because such motives are not available. The senator who will vote against better judgment for fear of disappointing a long-term constituent group, or a senator who reluctantly goes along with a colleague's compromise to pay off a previous favor, may be unable to find an appropriate motive for acting otherwise. Or, more accurately, the senator is able to find the appropriate motive, but cannot use it as

---

[2]Mills, "Situated Action and Vocabularies of Motives," op. cit., p. 904.
[3]Ibid., p. 907.

a motive, without thereby being seen as either disappointing
or dishonest.

Thus, the language used in politics is often a
rationalization, but it is not a "mere" rationalization. The
need to find and use an explanation as a motive for
action itself affects the action in major ways.

A similar point has been made by Murray Edelman,
who emphasized that our beliefs and categories are
controlled by the language in which our political discourse
proceeds:

> Political and ideological debate consists
> very largely of efforts to win acceptance
> of a particular categorization of an issue
> in the face of competing efforts in behalf
> of a different one; but because participants
> are likely to see it as a dispute either
> about facts or about individual values, the
> linguistic (that is, social) basis of perceptions
> is usually unrecognized....[4]

Edelman provides an example where political language
not merely explains but actually creates a context
for action and evaluation:

> Some linguistic forms generate important
> beliefs that are uncritically and unconsciously
> taken for granted....Vivid metaphors, sometimes
> including statistics respecting actual or
> hypothetical events, can create benchmarks
> that shape popular judgments of the success
> or failure of specific programs. An announcement
> that the government plans to reduce unemployment
> to the 6.8 percent level within a year or
> to hold an expected increase below the 7.5
> percent level creates a benchmark of success
> against which future trends are then evaluated.
> Attention focusses on meeting the publicized
> goal, rather than upon the seven or eight
> million people who are still without jobs. Such
> a cognition even more completely takes for
> granted the institutional arrangements that

---

[4]Edelman, Political Language (N.Y.: Academic Press,
1977), p. 25.

make it probable that there will always be
four to six million people unable to find
work and others who have given up hope....[5]

Mills and Edelman direct us to take seriously
the language we find in politics, but not to take it
"literally." Language is important, both as a provider
of justifications and as a creator of contexts. In
politics, perhaps the central aspect of action lies
in the search for, and the use of, appropriate language
in which to express (and upon which to base) action. To
focus upon language is not to be hoodwinked by what
we hear, provided we can look behind the sentences
for the motives and beliefs expressed and created by
them.[6]

Senators themselves are often quite aware of the
use of language as tool and creator. During a committee
debate on a bill to reform the requirements for lobbying
disclosure, the term "lobbying" is used in strikingly
different ways by the proponents and opponents of the
bill. Senator Chiles is finally prompted to say:

> Senator Chiles: ...[The discussion] kind
> of reminds me a little bit when we were talking
> about the lobbying bill here, somebody says,
> like the old story, when you say 'whiskey,'
> do you mean that lubricant of the soul, that
> elixir that allows men to get together in

---

[5]Ibid., pp. 35-37.

[6]For an older, but still depressingly relevant, discussion,
see Jeremy Bentham, The Handbook of Political Fallacies
(1788) (N. Y.: Harper, 1952). See also Kim Ezra Shienbaum,
"Ideology vs. Rhetoric in American Politics," The Midwest
Quarterly 21 (Autumn 1979), pp. 21-32.
     Richard J. Burke approaches the subject of political
rhetoric from a slightly different perspective, but
one which also underscores the centrality of persuasion
in politics. (Burke, "Politics as Rhetoric," Ethics 93
(October 1982), pp. 45-55.

fellowship, warmth of friendship and companion-
ship, or when you say 'whiskey,' do you mean
that devil's brew that breaks up families
and renders the breadwinner incapable? That
sounds in a way like we are talking about
lobbying....[7]

Before turning to particular tactics of rhetoric
used in the Senate, we need to ask precisely what sort
of language we are dealing with here. It may be helpful
to use a distinction developed by Edelman between four
styles of language in government. (1) Hortatory language
is used to appeal for support, and is directed at "the
mass public"; much of the language used in floor speeches
and press conferences is representative of this type. (2)
Legal language is more ambiguous, and is used in statutes
and court decisions. (3) Administrative language resembles
the legal type, but is directed to public employees
who are "directed" to act in particular ways. (4) Bargaining
language is usually restricted to private settings,
and is aimed at finding a solution without having to
appeal to the public.[8]

For our purposes, the two crucial types are hortatory
and bargaining language. Let me quote an extended passage
in which Edelman compares these two types of political
language:

> Like hortatory language, [bargaining
> language] involves an effort to gain support
> for a political position; but the two styles
> are fundamentally different in respect to
> the occasions of their use, the parties involved,
> and the meanings conveyed by the respective
> media. A lobbyist arguing his case in the
> office of a congressman or administrator
> normally uses hortatory language; he suggests

---

[7] Senate Governmental Affairs Committee, markup of S2160,
June 12, 1980.
[8] Edelman, The Symbolic Uses of Politics (University
of Illinois Press, 1964), chapter 7.

a rationalization that would justify the public official in granting him what he wants. But the rationalization, if it is persuasive, is so precisely because it would satisfy an interested public. The whole interaction can be understood as an effort to feed some premises about a potential public reaction into a legislative, administrative, or judicial decision-making process.

The bargainer, on the other hand, offers a deal, not an appeal. A public reaction is to be avoided, not sought. A decision is to be made through an exchange of quid pro quos, not through a rational structuring of premises so as to maximize, or satisfy, values. It is a prerequisite to bargaining that values be incompatible, not shared.[9]

Most of our evidence from floor speeches is clearly hortatory. But how are we to understand the language used in interviews or committee sessions? The latter present interesting challenges to Edelman's point that bargaining occurs in private. Although much of the discussion in committees is certainly directed toward the public, and although a certain amount of self-censorship and posturing is inevitable whenever a transcript is recorded, there is also much bargaining which does occur there. We might want to distinguish between two types of committee meetings. All of my evidence is drawn from _markup_ sessions, in which the draft of a bill is discussed, amended, and either rejected or passed along to the Senate floor. It is clear that much bargaining takes place in these meetings, with trades suggested and agreed to, amendments discussed and passed, and promises asked and given. These sessions are often sparsely attended; when the bill is controversial, the room may be packed, but the sessions are seldom (if ever) televised. By contrast, committee _hearings_

---

[9]Edelman, _The Symbolic Uses of Politics_, pp. 145-146.

precede the markup sessions; witnesses parade before the committee, giving arguments to a handful of members. When the bill is controversial, however, television cameras are usually present.

Hearings are examples of the pure use of hortatory language. Markup sessions usually combine hortatory and bargaining aspects. But, when an individual sits down in the comfort of a senator's office and asks about the nature of political compromise, what sort of language is involved? I believe that certain features of the interview setting create a context in which another sort of language--self-reflective language-begins to occur. [10] I am not suggesting that I established much "rapport" with these senators, or that they "bared their souls" to me. But, along with a healthy dose of hortatory language, these conversations provided an opportunity for the politicians to sit back and think about how they acted. Although such conversations must be interpreted with caution and skepticism, they do provide a window into another sort of political language.

Let us turn now to several types of rhetoric used in the Senate.

1. "What we have here is a failure to communicate"

Because compromise is an ambivalent term, senators are not sure precisely how to respond when they are asked to discuss examples of its occurrence. The two tactics they adopted in the interviews reflect the ambivalence of the word. The first response was to make <u>distinctions between different sorts of compromises,</u>

[10]See the Appendix for a further discussion of the interview context.

some of which were good and some of which were bad. Examples
of such distinctions include the following:

> compromise on judgment, not on
>   substance
> compromise on language, not on
>   principle
> compromise on policy, not on political
>   philosophy
> compromise on pragmatism, not on
>   substantive issues

Twenty-three of the thirty-four senators made some
such distinction.

Such responses do not deny that compromise is
necessary or frequent. But they do give the actor the
right to make the distinction, particularly when we
see how vague these distinctions are in practice. It
would be hard for an observer to challenge a senator
on a particular compromise, for how could we ever prove
that a decision was really a matter of substance rather
than of judgment? Thus, by drawing such distinctions,
the actor retains the freedom to make whatever compromises
are desired, while still sounding as if there are some
compromises which are off limits.

The alternative response was to draw <u>distinctions
about the meaning of compromise itself</u>. Here, rather
than finding certain situations in which compromise
is allowed and others in which it is forbidden, the
speaker suggests that compromise is to be compared
with another category of action entirely. The argument
may contrast compromise with a negative category, in
which case compromises are defended. Or compromise
can be juxtaposed to a positive category, in which
case compromises are attacked. Senators made the following
distinctions between compromise and something negative:

compromise/rationalization
compromise/arm-twisting
compromise/spinelessness
compromise/capitulation

They made the following distinctions between compromise and something positive:

compromise/balancing
compromise/synthesizing

Nine senators made at least one of these distinctions.

Once again, the actor demands the right to decide when a compromise is justified. But this time one does so by deciding when a compromise has actually occurred. Thus, the potential critic is disarmed before the arrow can be put in the bow: "Oh, you thought I was compromising; that wasn't a compromise at all, that was simply balancing." Or: "I was compromising there, not capitulating; you have overlooked the difference between the two." By controlling the language in which the action is described, the politician maintains an enviable ability to undercut objections.

Both of these responses attempt to distract our attention from the substance of the action to its definition. One important task of such definitional work is to convince the listener of the necessity and value of the adopted course of action. For example, when an interviewer asks a question about compromise, one way to defuse the potentially negative overtones of the compromises one has made is to suggest that the activity under consideration is in fact the most common and ordinary occurrence imaginable. The following comments from the interviews reflect this strategy:

Compromise is a daily exercise, and the art is to get what you can out of it....It is all too second nature to us here that this whole discussion seems artificial.

> You have to compromise to get any legislation
> through; you can't always get everything
> you want.

> Life is a matter of compromise; it helps
> you get through life....Modification of objectives
> is part of all of life, and the Senate isn't
> much different.

> Compromise involves finding a middle ground;
> this is necessary for government.

> The ability to make a worthwhile compromise
> is what legislation is all about.

These senators may indeed view compromise in this
way. But we must then ask what purpose is served by
such a taken-for-granted meaning of the term. The distinctions drawn are highly general; the word compromise
is used in widely disparate senses, both to cajole
and to criticize. The advantage of being able to compromise
repeatedly and easily without drawing sharper distinctions
is clear: an activity repeated so frequently cannot
be thought about without thereby calling its validity
into question in at least some of its manifestations. An
honest reaction of "What do you mean by compromise? We
do it all the time here" is itself a reflection of
the use of compromise as a motive for action in the
Senate. Someone may criticize you for a particular
compromise, but not for the willingness to compromise
itself.

By thus controlling distinctions beween good and
bad compromises, or between compromises and something
else, senators have accomplished two important tasks. They
have developed a highly malleable vocabulary enabling
them to escape from the charges of "bad compromises"
or "capitulation" by redefining the very nature of
the action. And they have turned the question of compromise
into an outsider's problem reflecting the questioner's

ignorance about the way the Senate (and politics in general) "really" works.

2. "Passing the buck", or "The Devil made me do it"

Senators often want to compromise, and decide that they cannot; they may not want to compromise, and decide that they must. In cases of such strongly conflicting desires, one common device is to do what one wants to do, but pretend that the situation is out of control. The actor thus tries to avoid responsibility for the decision by shifting the blame onto someone (or something) else.

There are various ways in which this can occur. Perhaps the most obvious way (and therefore the least satisfactory) is to avoid consideration of the issue completely. Because every senator must take a stand on each bill which comes up for a vote (or be recorded as not voting), this option is difficult to adopt. Committee chairpersons may keep a bill from coming to the floor at all, and there is constant battling concerning which bills will be subjected to a direct "up and down" vote. Indeed, most votes are in the form of a motion to table, allowing a senator to vote for a motion killing the bill, without being called upon to vote directly against the bill itself. But this procedure is so well established that it no longer hides what is going on.

But there are other ways of deciding not to decide. Let us consider an apparent impasse between the House and Senate, and examine how the responsibility for compromising is transferred to the respective chambers and to the legislative process itself. As the conference on the windfall profits tax begins, the House Chairman (Representative Ullman) notes that the House resolution gave binding instructions to the conferees. Thus, even though the members of the conference might wish to compromise, they were apparently prohibited from doing so.[11] When the difficult issue of tax credits arises, the following comments are made. Note particularly the attempt to insist that whatever compromise occurs is due to (and constrained by) the views of other members of the two chambers:

> Senator Long: ...I think our House friends ought to understand that the Senate is very serious about this matter, and so much so that I doubt very much that the majority of the Senators would sign a conference report unless we had a reasonable compromise for our suggestions in the way of credits...
>
> ....
>
> Rep. Ullman: Mr. Chairman, this is an important item but I think what we perhaps should address ourselves to it, there are many members of the House conference that are strongly opposed to credits, period, who think that it is possible to get a bill now and perhaps take the credits up somewhere else; and I think perhaps we should address ourselves to that issue, because if that is one way to go, then certainly we ought to consider it.
>
> ....
>
> Senator Long: ...if anybody could sign a conference report that leaves out these alternative sources, I suppose I could. But I am fully convinced that I could not get a majority of the Senate conferees to go along with any such thing...Even if you could get a majority to sign the conference report, you still have got to get 61 Senators or 60 Senators to vote cloture on the Senate floor because [Senator Packwood] wouldn't let you vote on it as long as he could stand and talk, and he is a pretty vigorous young man.[12]

Thus, both Chairmen insist that other members of Congress are unwilling to compromise. These others insist on

---

[11]House-Senate Conference on HR3919, December 19, 1979.
[12]Ibid., February 7, 1980.

a more rigid position than the Chairs might otherwise accept (or, at least, than they might want to be seen as accepting).

It is common for chairpersons to make such an argument. Indeed, they usually are more willing to compromise, due to their desires to pass a bill and their relative safety in their home districts or states. In this case, Ullman is quite unrepresentative of his House colleagues on the issue of tax credits, a fact revealed in the following comment by one of his junior colleagues:

> Rep. Gibbons: ...really, to ask Mr. Ullman to speak first on this is unfair to Mr. Ullman ...[in the House committee] he only could rally three more members to vote with him...so a total of four of the House conferees voted with the chairman...and it is a shame to put him in the position of trying to explain the House conferees' position...I want to say, frankly, I am not for any of [the credits]. I am not for any of them. I think they are all a bunch of biomass. But I want to get a conference. I am willing to give. But I want to look at the whole cost of these...[13]

When the House later pushes the idea of refundable tax credits as an alternative solution, Long uses the distance between his own position and that of the rest of the Senate in a similar way:

> Senator Long: ...I think it is a great idea but I have some doubts about taking something back to the Senate that they said they would not let us pass.
> Rep. Ullman: Why don't you do the big bold thing and accept it now?
> Senator Long: ...I do not mind, Mr. Chairman, being bold. I do not like to get beat...[14]

---

[13]Ibid.
[14]Ibid.

Such comments are largely rhetorical devices. Binding instructions are binding so long as the Senate wishes to consider them as binding. Nothing prevents the Senate from accepting a conference report which ignores its earlier instructions; the decision remains in the hands of the conference committee, which will then try to persuade the full chamber of the wisdom of its compromise.

But such protestations serve a more important purpose. By convincing the other side that my hands are tied, I gain an important bargaining advantage. Thomas Schelling has spoken of the importance of commitment, particularly of the ability to tie oneself to a course of action. The actor actually gains power by being seen as tied irrevocably to a course of action, because the opponent must then yield if any solution is to be reached. Schelling discusses the bargaining power of an extortionist. If I wire myself with explosives, you will be more likely to give in to my demands. But if I am unable to disarm the explosive myself until you meet my demands, I have even more credibility, since you cannot then argue or plead with me to change my mind. In a somewhat more relevant example for our purposes, Schelling writes:

> Something similar occurs when the United States Government negotiates with other governments on, say, the uses to which foreign assistance will be put, or tariff reduction. If the executive branch is free to negotiate the best arrangement it can, it may be unable to make any position stick and may end by conceding controversial points because its partners know, or believe obstinately, that the United States would rather concede than terminate the negotiations. But, if the executive branch negotiates under legislative authority,

> with its position constrained by law, and
> it is evident that Congress will not be reconvened
> to change the law within the necessary time
> period, then the executive branch has a firm
> position that is visible to its negotiating
> partners.[15]

By being less free (or, more precisely, by being perceived as less free), the bargainer gains power, if the opponent wants a solution. Representative Ullman is therefore the best possible spokesperson for the House position, by virtue of his own _un_representativeness. If his opposition to tax credits stemmed from his own feelings, the senators could argue, cajole, or threaten. But such tactics are useless against someone constrained by the views of others.

The burden of responsibility can be shifted in other directions as well. If there is difficulty in arriving at a compromise, one can defer the decision, promising both sides that satisfactory provisions will be written into the legislative report or into the guidelines for future implementation. In this way, the burden of decision is foisted upon either staff members or an executive agency. In the conference committee on the new Department of Education, several compromises were arrived at in this way. In one case, the House accepted eliminating a section on abortion, insisting that the report language state that the new Department follow the general policy of the rest of the government.[16]

In another example, as the debate over income

---

[15]Schelling, _The Strategy of Conflict_, op. cit., pp. 27-28. For an equally fascinating study of blackmail, and some blackly humorous illustrations, see Daniel Ellsberg, "The Theory and Practice of Blackmail," Rand Corporation Paper P-3883 (July, 1968) (first delivered as a lecture in 1959).
[16]House-Senate Conference on S210, September 13, 1979.

assistance dragged on in the Finance Committee, the Senate as a whole passed (by voice vote) an amendment by Senator Javits to provide more than one billion dollars in such aid for the present fiscal year. A somewhat tired and exasperated Senator Chafee then asked:

> Senator Chafee: What did Senator Javits do that permitted him to cut through this Gordian knot so swiftly and achieve by one voice vote something that we have been mulling over here for a week?
> Staff Aide: He avoided making a decision. In other words, he simply gives the money to the Director of the Community Services Administration; so he has not made a decision about who will get the money on the other end.[17]

Javits' move is an end run around the dispute; whether we describe this move as an imaginative solution or as a cop-out depends upon our view of the appropriate locus of decision-making responsibility.

Such avoidance occurs between committees and the floor as well. I overheard a conversation between a committee Chairman and a senior staff member, where the former was complaining about a controversial amendment being considered in the committee. The staff member suggested that they simply wait and introduce the amendment on the floor, to "allow the blame to be placed on the whole Senate." As the staffer later commented to me: "That's politics." The burden can be shifted to the floor, to another committee, to the executive branch, to an administrative agency, or to the process itself. In all cases, the senator tries to avoid being seen as the determiner of policy. This tactic explains much of the importance of the conference committees; they

---

[17]Senate Finance Committee, markup of HR3919, October 16, 1979.

possess little inherent power to make difficult compromises, but the other members often prefer to allow them to make such decisions. The non-conference senators can then "reluctantly" vote for the finished compromise as the best possible solution.

When the buck is passed, the evasion of responsibility is often delayed. The senator is confronted later on with the decision, made by an executive agency or by the Senate as a whole. At that point, the compromise seems to be out of that actor's hands. Whether this rhetorical device occurs before or after the compromise, however, it provides a useful tool for passing along a responsibility which is both cherished and feared.

3. "Motherhood and apple pie"

In the search for justifications for compromise (or for the refusal to compromise), senators seize upon certain phrases which represent the "higher interests" to be served by American politics. In so doing, they appeal to certain reference points, identifying them in terms such as "the public interest," "public opinion," "the public," "the American people," "the working people," or "the poor." They establish such entities as the reference groups to which decisions can be addressed and in whose names decisions can be defended.

Edelman points to the importance of such reference points, using the example of "public opinion" here:

> Perhaps the archetypical device for influencing political opinion is the evocation of beliefs about the problems, the intentions, or the moral condition of people whose very existence is problematic, but who become the benchmarks by which real people shape their political beliefs and perceptions....
>   'Public opinion,' then, is an evocative concept through which authorities and pressure groups categorize beliefs in a way that marshals

support or opposition to their interests,
usually unselfconsciously. Public opinion
is not an independent entity, though the
assumption that opinions spring autonomously
into people's minds legitimizes the actions
of all who can spread their own definitions
of problematic events to a wider public.[18]

We have already seen many examples of such appeals. The debate on income assistance in the windfall profits tax bill involved various efforts to claim the turf of "representing the best interests of the American people," "the poor," and similar entities. The extent to which such rhetoric can be taken is revealed in the following interchange in the Finance Committee, after Senator Moynihan criticized those who seemed more concerned about the oil companies than about the poor. Senators Dole and Bentsen objected that they also were concerned about the poor, and the Chairman responded:

> Senator Long: Could we agree, by unanimous
> consent, that everybody here--in fact, all
> members of the   Committee--are very concerned
> about the needs of the poor, and if we could
> agree to that--
> Senator Moynihan: I so move.
> Senator Long: Without objection, agreed.
> Senator Roth: Mr. Chairman, I just would
> like to say, while we are concerned about
> the poor, we must also be concerned about
> the working people. That is another group.
> Senator Moynihan: I so amend.
> Senator Long: We love the working people
> just as much as we love the poor. We will
> include that.[19]

Such groups as "the poor" do exist, in the sense that there are persons who are poor, and they do sometimes organize to demand that their needs are met. But such

---

[18]Edelman, Political Language, p. 51.
[19]Senate Finance Committee, markup of HR3919, October 11, 1979.

categories are appealed to here more for their rhetorical
power than for their descriptive accuracy. How could
one's position be called into question, when one merely
has "the interests of the poor" at heart?[20]

    We saw another example of such appeals in our
earlier discussion of the Chrysler aid package. Senators
Lugar and Tsongas appealed to various groups throughout
their defense of the compromise: the poor, the working
people, the taxpayers. When Senator Sarbanes suggested
omitting specific figures for salary limitations, Lugar
responded by saying that the large wage increase (negotiated
earlier by the union) is simply not acceptable to the
press and the public:

> Senator Lugar: ...I think we are talking
> here about something that is acceptable to
> the American public, quite apart from those
> of us in this Committee, and they are looking
> to that wage contract, to raises by Chrysler
> management...I think it is a very practical
> consideration and an important one in the
> political stability of this whole idea.[21]

To whom is Lugar appealing here? Who is "the American
public"? What Lugar needs is an image of a concerned
taxpayer who would not want his tax money used to support
a company which had given large salary increases to
its workers. Perhaps the reader shares his vision of
the taxpayer, depicted in old political cartoons as
"John Q. Public" with the wife and kids, the car in
the garage of the nice suburban house, reading his
evening newspaper and complaining about rising prices

---

[20]I am not suggesting that concern for groups such as
the poor is illegitimate. Indeed, in chapter 7 I shall
insist on such concern. The point here is merely that
such appeals are often (usually?) empty.
[21]Senate Committee on Banking, Housing, and Urban Affairs,
markup of The Chrysler Corporation Loan Guarantee Act
of 1979, November 29, 1979.

and governmental inefficiency. Such figures are of course constructions, and we can draw the picture in any way we choose. The politician decides upon the needed reference figure, constructs it (or, better yet, simply appeals to it, since we share a common culture of such figures), and uses it.

4. "For Brutus is an honorable man"

As Marc Antony recognized, no tactic of language is as effective as the caricaturing of an opponent. In his speech following Caesar's assassination, he details the conspiracy against the Emperor, closing each charge with the clever disclaimer that, surely, Brutus would not have engaged in such nefarious activities, for Brutus is an honorable man. By the end of the speech, the refrain drips with sarcasm, and the opponent has been painted into a corner.

We find such tactics in the Senate. They are generally aimed less at individuals than at positions, however. Let us discuss two sets of examples: the attempt to describe the opponent's motives as "purely political," and the desire to see one's own action as "independent."

One of the more common expressions in the Senate is used when someone's bill is opposed on the basis of a regional or state interest. The affected party will refer to the problem as "a case of whose ox is being gored." In this way, the charge is made that the opponent is being narrowly political, putting the interests of a region above that of the nation, and allowing such questions to obscure the "true" nature of the problem. The windfall profits tax bill again provides numerous examples here. When Senator Muskie threatens to filibuster the bill on the floor unless the interests of the colder states are recognized,

Senator Long makes the following comment:

> Senator Long: ...whatever we come up with
> here should be a compromise because a number
> of states, feeling that they are being victimized,
> have every right, and when they feel strongly
> their Senators will stand on this floor and
> do just what the Senator from Maine is doing...
> ....
> ...the Senator has a good point when he says
> he proposes to stand here and fight as he
> has the capability to fight for what he believes
> is right, and I hope he understands that
> he is not the only Senator who has the talent,
> the ability, and the inclination to do that
> when he really feels that his State is not
> being treated fairly. That is why this Senator
> believes that what we need is something that
> takes into consideration the arguments of
> all and the views of all parts of the Nation,
> not just something that one section of a
> nation imposed on another, but something
> where we all try to consider the viewpoint
> of the others and bring something that shows
> respect for the point of view of all Senators...[22]

At least three different points are involved in
this fascinating statement. First, Long is trying to
maintain a certain amiability in the disagreement;
as the floor manager of the bill, he wants to avoid
drawing clear-cut "us against them" lines. Second,
Long is laying the groundwork for his own impending
filibuster against an amendment introduced by Senator
Danforth. Third, he is taking a sizeable piece of revenge
on the north for the earlier civil rights struggle
in the Senate in the 1950s and 1960s; read the quotation
again with an eye toward the southern filibuster of
that legislation, and note Long's obvious glee in seeing
the roles reversed.

---

[22]Congressional Record, November 14, 1979, S16615-16.

Muskie is quite aware of this third point, as he indicates during the beginning of his filibuster attempt:

> Senator Muskie: I am not practiced in lengthy debate, certainly not as practiced as the distinguished Senator from Louisiana, and I could use some of his experience at this point to stretch this discussion out. Also, I suspect before I get through I might be able to use some of the physical resources which have sustained him on the many occasions on which he has held the attention of the Senate at great length.
>
> I envy my southern colleagues who now serve by silence, whereas I have to serve by the unaccustomed tool of talk. In any case, I would hope that I might be as effective as my Senate colleagues have been in the past in dealing with problems about which they felt very intensely and very strongly as they affected and impacted upon their regions.[23]

The effect of such language is to turn the disagreement into one of conflicting interests represented by each senator. In this manner, Muskie can appeal to the spirit of compromise; since each senator can identify with the need to represent one's home base, the implication is that the opponent is simply being stubborn or rigid. At the same time, by claiming that all such disputes are simply cases of ox-goring, the senator undercuts the claim by the opponent to be representing any broader values or shared interests.

The battle over language is often fought out on precisely this terrain. One group denies that its opposition to a program is really connected with local interests; the other side turns the guns of ox-goring rhetoric upon them; and they reply by either denying the charge, or by accusing the opponent of the same thing. The

---

[23]Congressional Record, November 14, 1979, S16619.

result is often a frustrated sense of having arrived at a dead end where nothing can be discussed in any other terms. For example, when southern senators from oil-producing states opposed a minimum tax provision, they denied that they were simply representing the large oil companies. Senator Stewart of Alabama replied: "I say one thing to Senators who are opposing this minimum tax. If they are not defending the large-sized oil interests in this country, then please pray tell us who they are defending."[24] And Senator Muskie, objecting to a proposed amendment sponsored by seventy-eight of his colleagues, noted: "For most of my Senate career, I have marveled at the ability of Senators to rationalize the popular course they have determined to take. I no longer marvel at it. I accept it as a matter of course."[25]

The reaction to such a charge can thus take two different tacks. One can deny that there is anything wrong or unusual about it, or one can deny that it is true at all. The responses we have given so far represent the first approach. In another such example, taken from the conference committee on the windfall profits tax bill, Senator Long and Representative Ullman locked horns over the value of depletion allowances for oil companies. Taking advantage of what is clearly an uncomfortable situation, in which he was defending the oil-producing states, Long turned the tables on Ullman by suggesting that both of them were equally representing narrow regional and political interests:

---

[24]Congressional Record, December 12, 1979, S18312.
[25]Congressional Record, December 17, 1979, S18818.

> Senator Long: ...Mr. Ullman doesn't see much
> merit to the depletion allowance. If I didn't
> have any people producing oil in my state,
> I don't guess I would see much merit in depletion
> allowance either, but I have got good news
> for the whole United States, the whole free
> world. Oil has just been discovered in Oregon,
> and it is just a matter of time...before
> every farmer and landowner out there in Oregon
> are going to get very quiet about this depletion
> allowance.
> Representative Ullman: It hasn't been discovered
> in my district.[26]

Long thus paints Ullman into the same corner in which
he finds himself, depriving the opponent of the use
of the higher ground.

In another example, during the floor debate on
the Chrysler aid package, Senator Riegle argued for
the bill by drawing an analogy between Chrysler and
American Motors, a company which received federal aid
earlier, and which is located in the home state of
the major opponent of the loan guarantee, Senator Proxmire.
Proxmire responded:

> Senator Proxmire: It is not the same at all.
> Mr. President, that is outrageous....The
> Senator is making a big point of the fact
> that American Motors happens to be in my
> state.
> Senator Riegle: I am not at all.
> Senator Proxmire: Of course he is; that is
> all the Senator is arguing about. I will
> always fight for people in my State.
> Senator Riegle: I will, too.
> Senator Proxmire: There is nothing wrong
> with that.... That does not mean that any
> time somebody else comes around and wants
> something that the Senator says will be the
> same, I have to support it.[27]

The other response is to deny that these narrow
political interests are operating in the decision at

---

[26]House-Senate Conference on HR3919, January 17, 1980.
[27]Congressional Record, December 18, 1979, S19006.

all. Introducing an amendment to the windfall profits
tax bill, Senator Durenberger of Minnesota takes pains
to indicate that the subject (cogeneration plants)
is not merely one of personal political gain:

> Senator Durenberger: Mr. President, so that
> my colleagues will know that this is not
> another one of those parochial amendments
> to the windfall profit tax to benefit one
> or a few States at great expense to the Federal
> Treasury, I would like to point out that
> the most successful examples of cogeneration
> applications do not occur in Minnesota.[28]

In arguing for his compromise on the Chrysler plan,
Senator Tsongas says:

> Senator Tsongas: If we look at these arguments
> on balance, it is my opinion, as someone
> who has no Chrysler plant in his State and
> has received no support of any significance
> that I am aware of from any Chrysler dealer,
> that...it is in the national interest to
> have a Chrysler bill....
>   We came out to the four billion dollars
> through some negotiations and we set in motion
> a fire storm. Well, that fire storm was endorsed
> by the New York Times and condemned by the
> Washington Post, so we knew we were somewhere
> close to where we should be.
>   I might also say it was condemned over-
> whelmingly by the Lowell, Massachusetts Sun
> [his home district newspaper when he served
> in the House].[29]

And Senator Levin of Michigan, who obviously cannot
deny the interests of his state in the Chrysler decision,
tries to deny a direct connection: "I am not here carrying
Chrysler's water. I am carrying the water of commonsense."[30]

Indeed, the Senate norm of courtesy, and particularly
the Senate Rule prohibiting the imputation of unworthy
motives, can be applied to the charge of narrow political

---

[28]Congressional Record, December 15, 1979, S18723.
[29]Congressional Record, December 18, 1979, S18986-88.
[30]Congressional Record, December 17, 1979, S18943.

leanings. One amendment to the windfall profits tax bill involved mandatory conservation efforts, a highly unpopular measure for most senators. Senator Weicker berated his colleagues for their opposition, asking: "I understand it is a drastic step to ask for mandatory conservation, but is anyone willing to risk a few votes in exchange for a few lives [of the hostages in Iran]?" Senator Javits, a supporter of Weicker's amendment, rises and defends his other colleagues from this attack:

> Senator Javits: ...I do not think that Members are going to be deterred here from voting for this mandatory law because they are afraid of losing some votes....
>   This is something real, tangible, and effective in terms of the kind of efforts we need to make, and I admire the Senator for having authored it.
>   That is what really takes the kind of courage that he speaks of.
>   But I would not say what he says about my colleagues. They have their reasons. We have had different experiences with price control and with rationing, and there have been injustices and leakages and national difficulties.
>   But we are right, and therefore, being right, without being overly critical of anyone else, let us keep pressing the issue.[31]

Javits is in ideological agreement but tactical disagreement with his Republican colleague here. He suggests that the use of such rhetoric must be tempered, not that the underlying point is incorrect.

Whether reacted to with denial of fact or denial of importance, such tactics reveal the balancing act engaged in by members of the Senate. They need to appeal to broad constituencies and reference groups, while defending (and being seen as defending) the narrower interests of their electing groups.

---

[31]Congressional Record, December 6, 1979, S17942-43.

Our other examples of this type of rhetoric concern the very effort to escape from the tension by denying that the wishes of the constituency should be determinative at all. In the interviews with senators, I found a similar caricaturing of opposing arguments here, intended to create the following impression: "of course I follow my own judgment; what else could I be expected to do?" The following quotes from the interviews are representative here:

> Some of my colleagues take a poll in the morning to see what the statesmanlike thing to do is, and then take another in the afternoon.

> You're sent here to use your brain.

> We're not a poll-taking operation here...you have to be a leader and use your judgment.

> I'm not here to be a computer to poll my state.

We find similar comments made by senators wishing to caricature anyone who denies the importance of compromise in the Senate:

> You don't just walk away from the job if you can't get a bill passed as is on the floor...This is good judgment and good ethics... more people today are set in cement on one issue.

> The easiest thing to do is to be an ideologue and not retreat from your pristine principles....This frees you from the burden of making hard decisions... or, horror of horrors, changing your mind.

The justification provided here allows the senator to turn the tables on anyone who might ask whether the constituents should be represented. Since the best defense is a good offense, the language does not so much defend the adopted stance, as it caricatures any

alternative solution. Voting for the constituents'
views is not identified as a value which must be blended
in with other needs; rather, it is made to sound ridiculous
by being defined as "a poll-taking operation." Once
again, the language which shapes the categories we
use to understand or assess political action is employed
most effectively.

5."But we've already compromised"

Let us look briefly at several other rhetorical
devices used to justify or reject Senatorial compromises. First, the claim can be made that one has already
compromised, and that the position to which one has
moved is the final offer. Of course, one's bargaining
power determines whether the opponent is likely to
believe this claim. During the debate on degree day
formulae, for example, each side claimed repeatedly
that it had already given up significant ground. Although
each side had in fact done so, a compromise still depended
upon more yielding. The rhetorical purpose of such
arguments is to insist that future yielding should
be done only by the opponent.

Such language will be effective only if a threat
is implied.[32] In the Senate Judiciary Committee's markup
of the Criminal Code, Senators Hatch and Thurmond both
supported a proposal to allow the government to prosecute
labor union extortion and violence. This proposal was
opposed by Senator Leahy. Hatch warned Leahy by referring
to the fact that the House version of the bill was
even less acceptable to Leahy than the present Senate
version:

---

[32]See our earlier discussion of Schelling's comments
on commitment in bargaining situations.

> Senator Hatch: ...What our Chairman has done, and I think in a very reasonable way, has been to compromise this so both sides can feel good about it. Neither side feels terribly good about it, but at least it is an effective compromise. The House would have gone all the way.
>
> ....
>
> Senator Thurmond: Mr. Chairman, this is already a compromise. This amendment seeks to establish the middle ground between labor and unions seeking the right to demonstrate freely during a labor dispute, and the ability of law enforcement to punish violent acts that reach the level of extortion....This amendment is fair to both sides of this issue, and should be adopted. If this amendment is not adopted, I am not too sure, Mr. Chairman, whether I can support this code.
>
> Senator Leahy: Mr. Chairman, obviously I don't want to scuttle the code. I worked with the Brown Commission, years before I was in the Senate, to try to put together the first criminal code. I have a great deal of concern here...[33]

The two threats are based on an argument that the compromise process has reached its end. If the proposed solution is not accepted, then either the House version will become law, or the entire bill will be undermined. Leahy's response indicates the power of this tactic, as it puts the burden of "being reasonable" back on his shoulders.

To prove reasonableness, a senator may take great pains to detail the compromise which has already been made. In consideration of the sunset legislation, Senator Sasser (the major sponsor of the bill) says that "I have made a good faith effort to compromise," and insists that this effort has not been reciprocated by other committee members:

---

[33]Senate Judiciary Committee, markup of S1722, November 20 and 27, 1979.

> Senator Sasser: ...the bill was originally
> scheduled to be first on the mark-up agenda
> a week ago. To accommodate other Senators
> because it was important legislation, I agreed
> to allow the anti-terrorism bill with its
> controversial amendment to come up first. Then
> I agreed to postpone consideration until
> other Senators with an interest in the sunset
> bill could be present...Then I agreed to
> a week's further delay in order to make a
> good-faith attempt to comply with the Chairman's
> suggestion...that a middle ground be found.
>   Mr. Chairman, we worked throughout the
> week and weekend and fashioned what I and
> my staff thought was a true and meaningful
> good-faith compromise which, as a matter
> of fact, gives up so much ground...that I
> frankly lost some of the original supporters
> of S2. But during that entire week, not a
> single Senator opposed to S2 made any movement
> to accommodate the positions of the supporters
> of S2...If last week I said the compromise
> meant that the supporters of S2 should accept
> carte blanche, we could have saved the committee
> and the staff a lot of time...[34]

Once again, the point of this language is to put the
burden for the next move on the opposition. The tactic
may not work, but it is at least an effective stalling
device while planning one's own next move.

6. "This hurts me more than it hurts you"

In discussing the compromises on the abortion
funding amendments, we saw Senator Exon's claim that
he was merely putting forward an admittedly unsavory
proposal in the interests of compromise. This tactic
is also a common one. The actor attempts to have it
both ways: one sides with the supporters of the compromise
through actions, while appealing to the opponents by
referring to one's "true feelings" on the subject. The

---

[34]Senate Governmental Affairs Committee, markup of S2,
June 11, 1980.

senator also appeals to the underlying valuation of compromise in the Senate, calling into question the person who is not willing to agree to an apparently reasonable solution. After all, the senator seems to be saying, if I can accept this proposal (and remember that I really agree with you on the issue), then surely you can do so as well.

During consideration of a bill ordering a study of the effects of Agent Orange on Vietnam veterans, Senator Percy objects to the compromise worked out by the conference committee. He is reassured by Senator Cranston, who stresses his agreement with Percy on this point:

> Senator Percy: Although I believe I understand the reasons for the compromise, I frankly find the compromise language a bitter pill to swallow. The Senate has been forced to yield to jurisdictional concerns of House Members that, in this instance, are not in the best interests of our Vietnam veterans.
> Senator Cranston: As I have said, the compromise was not what I have wanted or thought best, but I believe that we had to do what was necessary to get a study underway as soon as possible.
> ....
> ...I agree with the Senator that, ideally, HEW should conduct the study. I believe that the compromise language we hammered out is the best that could have been achieved and that the V. A. will be able to do the job under the provision....[35]

Whether Cranston actually shares Percy's concern is irrelevant. By saying that he does, and that even he could accept the compromise as the lesser of two evils, he adopts an effective ploy for assuaging a colleague.

---

[35]Congressional Record, December 7, 1979, S18072-73.

Another version of this type of language occurs in attempting to stall a bill while denying that one is really doing so. Senators seldom use the term "filibuster" to refer to their own efforts. When they introduce a stack of amendments, or call for roll call votes on minor procedural matters, there is an element of farce, as if they are deeply unhappy about their own actions. In one odd example, during the floor debate on the Chrysler aid bill, Senator Proxmire, as the Chairman of the Banking Committee, was the floor manager for a bill he opposed. Senator Riegle, one of the strongest supporters of the bill, was holding up the debate to try to gain more concessions, while insisting that the bill be enacted quickly. The following exchange reveals the sensitivity of senators to any charge of delaying Senate business:

> Senator Riegle: ...Should I have a chance to finish my opening statement?
> Senator Proxmire: Senators do not have to make their opening statements before we act on amendments when we have the opportunity...I would be willing to postpone my opening statement, even though I am managing the bill.
> Senator Riegle: That is easy for the Senator from Wisconsin to do after he has made his opening statement. The chairman made a very eloquent, very passionate, and a very long and detailed statement.
> Senator Proxmire: My statement was 30 minutes less than that of the Senator from Michigan. I have just checked the record, and it was 30 minutes less.
> The Senator from Michigan is filibustering his own bill.
> Senator Riegle: I have no desire to get into a quarrel with the chairman. He is my friend, and we have worked together on a lot of things. We do not always agree on things.
> As to the point he has just made, in terms of the amount of time and my statement earlier, before I yielded to the Senator

> from Connecticut, at his request, versus
> the amount of time others have spoken, it
> is not different by 30 minutes. That is not
> true, and I do not want it to stand in the
> RECORD as being true.[36]

Attention to such apparently insignificant details reveals a deep concern about appearing to be an obstructionist. When one is slowing down the process, the preferred interpretation is: "I don't like to do this, but...." The Senator can thus deny that she intends to act in the way she is acting; the listener may be forgiven, of course, for not being very impressed by the argument. But other senators may be soothed by such language, for they often will find themselves in similar predicaments. At least, by using such language, the senator demonstrates a sensitivity to the problematic nature of such stalling, and to the frustration this creates for the supporters of the compromise.

7. "But how will it look?"

We have discussed the importance of impressions and appearances in political life. One common rhetorical move in the Senate is to call into question a compromise proposal on the basis of how it will look. What happens here is that a senator will admit that, since there is no easy or comfortable justification for the proposal which can be given to the public, the compromise will not work. In doing so, the opponent calls the other senators to consider, not so much the substance of the legislation, but the appearance it will create.

Let us look at two examples from the windfall profits tax bill. Senator Chafee of Rhode Island is uncomfortable with the income assistance formula arrived

---

[36]Congressional Record, December 18, 1979, S18999.

at in the Senate Finance Committee. Because the compromise takes account of low income populations and transfer payments as well as degree days, the state-by-state results look somewhat suspicious to the northern Senator. But he expresses his objections not in terms of his own views but in terms of the expected opposition of other members of Congress: "Well, Mr. Chairman, I can just see us running into a buzz saw on this thing, coming to the Floor with a proposal that gives Florida as much as the District of Columbia, for example."[37] Later, when Senator Long suggests a minimum payment for each state as a compromise for the income assistance program, Chafee again objects, but now Long responds with the same argument about how it will look on the Senate floor:

> Senator Long: Senator, you have a good point. On the other hand...let me remind you that we may need sixty votes to pass this bill because we have reason to believe that we may be confronted with a filibuster out there on that floor. If that develops and we are looking for sixty votes to pass the bill, people start voting against it if they can find anything in there that they are opposed to....Look at Arkansas. Arkansas has about 1.75 percent, almost 2 percent of the population. Look at what they get [in income assistance]: 0.00.
>   You can understand when a fellow from Arkansas looks at that, people get cold up there in Arkansas and they get very hot, too. And he looks at that thing. If I were a guy from Arkansas, I think I would be in the filibuster, you know?
>   It is one thing to say we get very little. By the time you get down to where you cannot even find the second decimal point, you begin to get upset.[38]

---

[37]Senate Finance Committee, markup of HR3919, October 18, 1979.
[38]Senate Finance Committee, markup of HR3919, October 24, 1979.

Long uses the example of Arkansas here, but he later objects that Louisiana also has two percent of the population and receives only .03 percent in the plan. The attempt to focus attention upon how the bill looks to others is an important diversion from how the bill looks to him.

But we do not want to minimize the substantive importance of appearances in political decision making. If "things are seldom what they seem," they are at least largely determined by how they seem. If one cannot feel comfortable with a justification for a proposed compromise, then the compromise probably will not be agreed to anyway. The discomfort may be due to a feeling that it will not pass, or that "it will not sell in Peoria." Indeed, the appearance probably should be an important criterion for legislation, since one of the most important tasks of the legislature is to form legislation which not only is fair but which also looks fair. Although one hopes that the latter will lead to the former, part of the former inheres in the latter. The consent of the governed must involve a feeling that, even if the content of particular laws is questionable, the process and general nature of policy determination is fair.

Conclusion: The Ritualization of Political Language

The use of language in the Senate is highly ritualized. Senators do not often sit down and decide which tactic to use, or which style of language fits the occasion. Such choices of words and style are usually second nature. Listen to the following statements made during the interviews: "In the end, it's your own conscience that people will respect." "Politics is the art of compromise." "Don't compromise on matters of principle."

Such comments are somehow deadening; repeated endlessly
in numerous settings, they provide the semblance of
meaning in the form of an easy but empty phrase.

Consider these statements from committee and floor
sessions as well:

> Senator Moynihan: ...I thought we were going
> to share this burden a bit...
>   ...it is going to be hard, and a question
> of equity. Do we share a tight situation
> together, or do we not?[39]

> Senator Riegle: ...I would hope that, while
> we expect and ask for a maximum sacrifice
> from the [Chrysler] workers and all of the
> other parties at interest, that we will find
> a way to balance that in such a fashion that
> no single party at interest is asked to go
> beyond, substantially beyond that degree
> of sacrifice that anybody else is facing...[40]

> Senator Muskie: We are going to talk about
> this nonsense and this injustice until somehow
> we get the message across to my colleagues
> in the Senate.
>   This body is made up of a lot of people
> who have different opinions about a lot of
> subjects. But I find we are not all totally
> parochial in our view. We are not totally
> insensitive to concepts of fairness and justice.[41]

> Senator Johnston: The Constitution of the
> United States is to a lot of people an ana-
> chronism. It is a worrisome document that
> gets in the way of trying to accomplish some
> ends they want to accomplish.
>   But, Mr. President, that Constitution
> lives, whether it is inconvenient, whether
> it is 200 years old, it lives today. We have
> all taken an oath...to uphold it.[42]

---

[39]Senate Finance Committee, markup of HR3919, September 28,
1979.
[40]Senate Committee on Banking, markup of The Chrysler
Corporation Loan Guarantee Act of 1979, November 29,
1979.
[41]Congressional Record, November 14, 1979, S16614.
[42]Congressional Record, December 15, 1979, S18658.

Appeals to such principles are important in politics, as we shall discuss in our last two chapters. All I want to emphasize here is the rather innocuous and meaningless way such appeals are used in most political discourse. The speaker often seems to be mouthing the words to a pre-recorded message; the ability to deliver impromptu speeches may be a mixed blessing indeed. George Orwell referred to this feature of political language in the following terms:

> When one watches some tired hack on the platform mechanically repeating the familiar phrases...one often has a curious feeling that one is not watching a live human being but some kind of dummy: a feeling which suddenly becomes stronger at moments when the light catches the speaker's spectacles and turns them into blank discs which seem to have no eyes behind them. And this is not altogether fanciful. A speaker who uses that kind of phraseology has gone some distance towards turning himself into a machine. The appropriate noises are coming out of his larynx, but his brain is not involved as it would be if he were choosing his words for himself. If the speech he is making is one that he is accustomed to make over and over again, he may be almost unconscious of what he is saying, as one is when one utters the responses in church. And this reduced state of consciousness, if not indispensable, is at any rate favorable to political conformity.[43]

Senators catch each other occasionally. Listen to Senator Biden's objection to the use of high-sounding language in discussions of the Chrysler aid bill. Admitting that the impact of the bill on his own state of Delaware

---

[43]Orwell, "Politics and the English Language," in A Collection of Essays by George Orwell (N.Y.: Harcourt, Brace, Jovanovich, 1946), p. 166.
  Murray Edelman makes the same point, referring particularly to bureaucratic settings of American politics. (Edelman, Political Language, esp. p. 98.)

is acute, he argues against those senators who question the legislation on the principle that large companies should not be given special consideration:

> Senator Biden: I do not like bailing out Chrysler, loan guarantees or otherwise, even if it costs the Federal Government no money. That is one of the things we all have to grapple with. Why? The Senator from Pennsylvania made a very strong argument. I thought it was interesting: Is the message we are sending that we have welfare for the rich and not for the poor?
>
> That sounds good, it even feels good when I say it, Mr. President. It fits right in with my democratic principle, my skepticism about major corporations and their interest in the American economy, and it sounds great. I feel like a true American, a true Democrat, with a capital D. But, quite frankly, it does not mean a whole lot, because the fact of the matter is that we are going to have a whole bunch of folks affected directly, about half a million jobs....
>
> I hope we come along and see to it that if we do not help Chrysler in the manner we are suggesting, we also all stand firm here on the floor next year while we are buffed by the winds of unemployment and higher inflation and we all go back to our constituencies and make those speeches about free enterprise and let it work. I am all for that.
>
> If everybody would sign on right now, all of us right now, or if we made our votes conditioned on our commitment to sign on right now, and not be here on the floor asking help for our States, I think maybe we might set a new policy and trend in this country. I think we would go to heaven in a handbasket in the meantime, but it might happen.[44]

Political language is an amalgam of interested and disinterested reasons, pragmatic considerations and high-sounding appeals, regional concerns and national interest. As observers to the use of such language,

---

[44]Congressional Record, December 18, 1979, S19015-16.

we should be attuned to the way in which such language
is generated for justificatory purposes. We might consider
how important such language is in determining policy;
I have suggested that it is vitally important, particularly
because a policy which cannot be defended in words
will probably not be adopted.

But the tension between language and policy is
a significant one. The actors want us to believe that
the language means what it says; when politicians refer
to the public interest, they want us to praise them
for making a decision using this criterion. We might
wonder, however, whether the term is often anything
more than a nice phrase to cover actions taken, compromises
made, and trades arrived at on other grounds entirely. Such
a view is reflected in the following brief exchange
during a committee meeting, when a tired Chairman directs
the staff to develop a new compromise:

> Senator Johnston: We are giving the staff
> broad latitude to do justice, equity, and
> give us a bill we can pass.
> Staff Aide: Could we also have a room in
> the basement of the Capitol where there are
> no phones and no lobbyists?[45]

---

[45]Senate Committee on Energy and Natural Resources, markup
of S2470, May 29, 1980.

CHAPTER 6. COMPROMISING PRINCIPLES IN POLITICS

> In politics, man must learn to
> rise above principles.
> > --H. L. Mencken

> Business and political leaders
> don't mean badly; the trouble with
> them is that most of the time they
> don't mean anything.
> > --Walter Lippmann

Introduction

In chapters 6-7, we turn to more explicitly normative questions, and broaden our scope from the Senate to politics in general. Having seen the prevalence of compromise, we ask whether there should be any limits to compromise. In this chapter, we examine one particular answer often given to that question: namely, that persons should not compromise on matters of principle. In the final chapter, some specific criteria for limiting political compromise will be suggested.

Can we speak about ethical norms in the political arena at all? It is important to understand why this question is asked not only by political philosophers but also by the proverbial "person in the street."[1] We often think of ethics as a world of right and wrong, where certain actions or intentions can be examined, evaluated, and recommended. We deal there with obligations, with what we ought to do, with the central rights, responsibilities, and duties of human beings toward one another. We can recognize the ethics of limited social roles (such as professional ethics for lawyers

---

[1] My efforts to explain to people that I am writing a book on political ethics in Congress have met almost invariably with comments such as the following: "It must be a very short book," "Did you find any ethics there?" "They certainly will need to read it."

or physicians), but we are likely to look for broader
values or obligations underlying our lives as human
beings. As part of this realm of ethical action, the
notion of principles plays a prominent role. Such principles
need not be construed as binding in all situations
or as overruling all other considerations, but they
are important building blocks with which we attempt
to structure our ethical decisions. Whatever the significance of such principles, we look toward them when
we are thinking ethically.

By contrast, even the most optimistic and uncritical
observers of American political life would recognize
a very different tone in politics. Our politicians
are less concerned with determining rightness than
with balancing interests, less with right and wrong
than with better and worse, less with principles of
morality than with practicalities of politics. The
key words of commendation in politics are not "good"
or "moral", but "prudent" or "realistic." This is not
to suggest that principles of morality are irrelevant,
but only that they are viewed more as incidental than
as fundamental.

We want to explore the question of the connection
between these two worlds. The problem arises in speaking
to politicians about their own actions. In the interviews,
the senators were asked whether there were any political
decisions concerning which they would not be willing
to compromise. In more than two-thirds of the interviews,
the senators used some sort of "principle/non-principle"

distinction to indicate where they tried to draw the
line.[2] The following responses were typical:

> It depends on how deeply the issue is one
> of conscience; you have to live with yourself.

> You have to just bite the bullet, decide
> what's right, and stick with your principles
> through thick and thin.

> You draw the line on principle; don't compromise
> principles.

> It's hard to compromise on fundamental questions
> of ethical, as distinct from economic, problems.

I was struck by the consistency of this sort of
response, from persons of different party, ideological,
regional, and intellectual persuasions. The responses
simply reveal how like the rest of us these individuals
are, however; it is a piece of common wisdom, of accepted
truth, that one can compromise on the less important
things, on issues that "don't really matter." But one
should "hold firm," "stand one's ground," "bite the
bullet" on matters of principle. In this chapter, we
examine this notion as it applies to American politics. Is

---

[2]Other reasons for drawing the line included such diverse
factors as whether this vote would affect the outcome
of the bill, consistency with one's prior voting record,
degree of knowledge of the issue, and the closeness
(both in time and in degree of difficulty) of the next
campaign.

it a coherent idea? Does it work? Would we even want
it to work?[3]

Principles and Politics

Note first the effect of making such a move within
the Senate. There are some very good reasons for politicians
to desire their decisions to be seen as matters of
principle. Many people--staff, colleagues, lobbyists,
constituents--are less likely to ask for reasons or
arguments, or to continue to badger the representative,
once the decision has been labelled a matter of principle. Further, senators are less likely to ask each
other for favors in such situations. In addition to
peace of mind, the individual gains respect and a sense
of self-worth in being perceived as a person of principle. In the words of one Senator, "most people prefer

---

[3]Among the most interesting discussions of the place
of principles in politics are the following: Hannah
Arendt, "Truth and Politics," op. cit; Peter Berger,
Pyramids of Sacrifice: Political Ethics and Social
Change (N.Y.: Doubleday, 1974); R. N. Berki, "The Dis-
tinction between Moderation and Extremism," in Bhikhu
Parekh and R. N. Berki (eds.), The Morality of Politics
(London: George Allen and Unwin, 1972), pp. 66-80;
Wayne Leys, Ethics for Policy Decisions: The Art of
Asking Deliberative Questions (N.Y.: Greenwood Press,
1968 [1952]); T. V. Smith, The Ethics of Compromise
and the Art of Containment and The Promise of American
Politics, op. cit.; Kenneth Thompson, Christian Ethics
and the Dilemmas of Foreign Policy (Duke University
Press, 1959) and The Moral Issue in Statecraft (Louisiana
State University Press, 1966); and the articles by
Benditt, Carens, and Kuflik in Pennock and Chapman
(eds.), Compromise in Ethics, Law, and Politics, op. cit. In
addition, the classic works of Burke, Weber, Reinhold
Niebuhr, and others raise all of the most important
issues.

it if he's not just another politician"--the last three
words implying someone who deals and compromises on
any issue without exception.[4]

Senators are surrounded by people vying for attention
and votes; in their effort to be convincing, these
other people quickly learn to phrase their arguments
in terms of principled language. After all, who could
consider mere mundane interests with all these principles
floating around? The senator is likely to join this
procession, saying, in effect: "I know you feel strongly
about this, but so do I--it is a matter of principle
for me, and so I can't act otherwise." The decision
seems to be taken out of our hands somehow when it
becomes a matter of principle, for who would ask us
to be untrue to a principle? The senator thus gains
both the stature of being seen as a person of moral
character, and a shield from the continual reconsideration
and reassessment of every difficult issue that comes
down the legislative chute.

The fact that appealing to principle has these
positive functions does not make it illegitimate. But
it does make it suspect, particularly when the only
evidence we have that certain issues _are_ matters of
principle is the testimony of the prime beneficiaries
of the claim. Because the appeal is so self-serving,
the represented should be very cautious about accepting
it too readily.

What do we mean when we speak of principles? Under
a very broad definition, no decision could ever be
made without appealing to principle. If our principles
are simply the grounds, the fundamentals, the bases,

---

[4]See Garry Wills, <u>Confessions of a Conservative</u>, op.cit.,
pp. 171-174, for a fine discussion of this question.

upon which we act and decide, then all decisions rest
upon them (however ill-formed, sub-conscious, or incon-
sistently held they may be). But such a definition
is not very helpful, and does not correspond to what
we usually mean. A somewhat narrower definition covers
the arena of ethical principles more adequately. Sometimes
we are referring to central values (such as the sanctity
of human life, or the requirement to keep promises);
sometimes we mean ideals or visions of how the world
ought to be (such as utopian visions, or calls for
equality of distribution). What is involved is a statement
of value which (a) involves concrete action, (b) revolves
around the dimension of "right and wrong" or "good
and evil" (rather than around other possible dimensions,
such as the "beautiful and ugly" of aesthetic principles),
and   (c) has a broad range of application. I will use
the term principles to refer to such moral principles.[5]

What, then, is the role of such principles in
politics? What does it mean--what could it mean--to
believe that such beliefs or values or visions should
serve as the grounding for our political decisions,
or at least as the key limiting factors? How would
we know such principles when we saw them?

Let me suggest three different ways in which the
role of such principles might be understood. I shall

---

[5]There is another sense in which moral philosophers
often speak of principles: namely, as the criteria
by which we judge our other values or beliefs. Universalizability and generalizability are two such principles. For
our purposes in this chapter, I will not consider such
broader criteria. See chapter 7 for a suggestion of
some closely related guidelines, however.

refer to these as <u>substantive</u>, <u>motivational</u>, and <u>functional</u> meanings.[6]

Substantively, principles are recognized by the substance of the issue addressed or covered by the principle. For example, some argue that matters of human life or suffering are matters of principle, and therefore have a stronger (or, at least, a different) claim upon our attention. Similarly, matters of national security or constitutional questions might be identified as principled considerations.

Alternatively, a motivational view holds that what distinguishes our principles is the strength by which certain beliefs are held. Principles are those views about which we feel very strongly, or to which we have committed ourselves, or which define us as the persons we are. I may therefore refuse to compromise on a matter of principle simply because I feel so strongly about this particular view. The nature of the issue is less important here than the intensity with which I hold to my position on it.

Finally, a functional view defines principles, not in terms of the nature of the issue nor in terms of the strong feelings toward it but rather by the very refusal to yield. The principle, as a principle, is something which is irrevocable, inalienable, over-riding. When it ceases to fulfill this function, it ceases to be a principle.

These three views of principle may overlap, and it is often difficult to see which meaning is operative in a given case. But the distinction is helpful, capturing

---

[6]These categories were developed from content analysis of the responses given in my interviews. They do overlap considerably with much of the prior literature on this subject, however.

some significant differences in the way persons understand and speak of appealing to their principles. Let us examine each of these meanings, asking whether they provide a coherent way to speak about the place of principles in political compromising.[7]

Substantive understandings

Are there certain issues, or sorts of issues, which call forth decisions of principle? I have already suggested the most commonly mentioned possibilities: life and death, human suffering, national or public interest, constitutional obligations. If such a distinction is useful in politics, we must be able to discriminate between those decisions which concern such matters and those which do not. I want to suggest here that the substantive understanding of politics usually represents a confused view of the nature of political decision making.

Let me distinguish here between an issue which is a matter of principles, and an issue which is a matter of a principle. The former means that a political decision raises questions of principle. Substantively, we would want to identify such issues, and see them as different from issues which could be decided without such appeals. The most common approach is to use human life or suffering as the substantive key; one compromises on matters of economics or money but not on issues such as abortion or capital punishment.

---

[7]For a somewhat different understanding of the roles of moral principles, see Joseph Gilbert, "Features of Morality," The Personalist 51 (Autumn 1970), pp. 470-476. He suggests that three features of morality (universalizability, over-ridingness, and socially important ends) often work together to give force to moral principles.

But connections can easily be made between questions of human need and almost any spending measure. All social legislation can be seen in terms of the lives affected by seemingly minor changes in wording or applicability of funding. In spite of one Senator's claim that "there is no moral principle between choosing five billion dollars and three billion dollars in an appropriations bill," there is no such bill or government program which does not have ramifications in terms of most substantively stated ethical values. The connection may be easier to see in some cases, of course, but that is a different question.

On the other hand, when we speak substantively, we could mean that certain issues are matters of <u>a</u> principle: to vote yes is to sacrifice the principle, to vote no is to uphold it. The problem here is not whether all political decisions fall under such a description, but whether <u>any</u> do so. Consider the abortion example, appealed to and defended often as a clear matter of principle. This question indeed raises principled considerations, but not in a clear choice between principle and expediency. Rather, we are confronted with the all-too-frequent situation of conflicting principles. It is hard to conceive of a policy stance on abortion which posed only one principle directly to the actor. Indeed, this is the norm, rather than the exception. We always find many principles embedded in policy decisions.[8]

We must remember that substantive views of principles have beneficial results for the politicians themselves. Certain policy decisions do not somehow intrinsically possess a principled aura by virtue of their subject matter; politicians consciously choose to <u>invest</u> certain kinds of issues with the evaluative term "principled." Why, then, do certain issues of public policy tend to be seen in this way?

First, it is simply easier to see the connection in certain cases. If human need is a criterion of a principled area, then a child labor law is more easily subsumed under this rubric than a complex package of appropriations for governmental agencies. In a world of minimal time and maximal pressure, such distinctions gain more credence than they may deserve.

Second, there are historical and cultural reasons why certain issues become seen as matters of principle. Special interest groups, religious traditions, powerful social movements--all make us more likely to view questions of personal morality rather than broader social issues of economic justice, as raising questions of principle. All the major so-called "social issues" of our time (capital punishment, abortion, prayer in schools) are particularly nonsocial when

---

[8]The failure to distinguish between matters of principle and matters of a principle accounts for much confusion in the literature on this subject. For example, William S. White writes of the Senate: "...this is no place for the man who has <u>only</u> principle; for every genuine political fanatic is simply awash with principle as he understands the term." But a fanatic is awash with a <u>single</u> principle, not with principle itself. (White, <u>Citadel: The Story of the U. S. Senate</u> [N. Y.: Harper and Brothers, 1956], p. 115.)

compared to economic and organizational arenas of public
policy. There are always strong ideological elements
operating in the choice of which issues become seen
as principled. For example, the revolution of the 1950s
and 1960s in civil rights occurred, not simply in changing
attitudes toward race, but in focusing the country
(and, by 1964, the Congress) to deal with this problem
as a matter of principle. Willingness to override
filibuster attempts may depend upon such a redefinition
of a problem area; those in control of essential power
resources may well prefer to define such questions
as political rather than as principled.[9]

To see the problem in this way undercuts much
of the force of a substantive interpretation of principles
in politics. There are rare occasions where a substantive
principle is indeed threatened by a political proposal
(as we shall discuss in the final chapter). But once
we recognize that our politicians generally decide
which issues count as principled ones, and that these
choices are likely to be made more on political than
on logical grounds, we will be less likely to accept
the label as an explanation for action. If virtually
all issues are matters of principle, and virtually
no issues are matters of a single principle, then we
must look elsewhere to find a relevant meaning for
such values in the political world.

There is one final point here. Even if certain
policy issues could be distinguished on substantive
grounds, why would this therefore provide a reason
for not compromising on such issues? It might be argued

---

[9]We might consider in whose interests it would be to
turn energy conservation policy, or the distribution
of wealth, into such a principled arena for legislative
policy making.

that such issues are so important that we ought to be willing to do more, rather than less, to protect the values carried in such principles. If abortion is wrong as a matter of principle, then perhaps more compromising is demanded in order to save more human lives; if the Constitution is to be protected, then perhaps compromise becomes more important in establishing legislation to interpret and implement it. In any event, the mere labelling of an issue as a principled one need not undercut the necessity of compromise.

Motivational understandings

Motivational understandings of principles rest upon the strength with which the particular view is held. We stand fast on matters of principle because they are so important, because we feel so deeply about them. Almost one-third of the senators interviewed expressed such an interpretation of the term, and seemed to take it as axiomatic that one would never act against such strong feelings. But if an elected official feels strongly about something, does this serve, by itself, as an argument for viewing the action as a principled one? I think not, for three reasons.

First, one does not have to be a Kantian philosopher to recognize that inclination is not necessarily the best guide to moral obligation. It is one guide, and a highly informed one in many cases. But to call our strong feelings "principles" is to miss the mark somehow. We indeed ought to feel strongly about doing our duty, but the strong feelings are an impetus toward, not the defining element of, that end. Persons can be mistaken about what they ought to do, strong feelings notwithstanding.[10]

Second, there are many reasons why someone may feel strongly about a particular question. In politics, an upcoming election campaign creates exceedingly strong feelings toward particular votes, and the desire to remain in office may become the basis for most action. In the words of one Senator, "Your intense anguish on a particular issue is proportional to the number of intense people." But we should be wary of terming such motivations principled ones, or of allowing such a person to use the language of principle to explain what is happening. Some such reasons, and some such feelings, may indeed be matters of principle, but it is not the strength of the feelings that makes them so.

Third, we might note the difficulty of using strong feelings as determinative in our political organizations. We do want our representatives to have strong feelings, and we want them to be able to act on them. But this may not be the most appropriate model for policy making in such settings. We usually want them to represent us, and this demands the ability to gain some distance from strong feelings of their own. The very ability to compromise at all depends upon some perspective here. The alternative need not be a wholly dispassionate computer-like mind, but our elected officials should at least be able to make decisions apart from the strength of their feelings on the given issue.

---

[10]A powerful philosophical defense of this point can be found in Richard Brandt's Ethical Theory (N.J.: Prentice-Hall, 1959), pp. 244-252.

Once again, the appeal of such an understanding
of principle is largely self-serving. Who would criticize
someone for acting according to such strong feelings? But
the very existence of strong feelings is not sufficient
to explain why certain questions, as principled ones,
are immune from compromise.

Functional understandings

We turn now to the understanding of principles
which emphasizes the place these views play in politics.
What defines a position as a principled one here is
that it is overriding, definitive, and clearly determinative. Principles serve to make difficult decisions
for us; if we hold them--or, perhaps more accurately,
if we are held by them--then we cannot do otherwise.

On first glance, there is something circular here. If
I use principles as the explanation for why I stand
fast, and my principles are defined as those views
on which I stand fast, then I have explained nothing. Indeed, the course of many discussions with political
figures reveals such a circular route. But let us try
to dig more deeply to see what is at stake in this
common understanding of the place of our principles.

The attraction of this meaning stems not only
from the sort of self-serving motives mentioned earlier. If
we are trying to understand how politicians make complex
and difficult decisions, and if we see that some sort
of rationality must be present, then we recognize the
value of believing that, under many of these decisions,
a principle lurks as the key. Similarly, from the actor's
standpoint, how better to understand one's own decisions
than as the logical working out of an overriding value?

But, if appeals to principle are to work in this
way, then we must be able to agree that there are such

overriding values, and that they can, or should, be
followed in such settings. It is this issue which poses
the problem in the political world.

First, the very nature of principles calls into
question the model adopted by this functional approach. Are
there principles which could function in this way? It
has often been noted (usually in the context of attacks
on the whipping boy of "absolutist" ethics) that principles
must be specified and detailed before they are useful. It
is hard to think of a principle which could be applied
directly without some such specification. General guidelines
such as "strive always to prevent suffering" or "preserve
life" could be relevant in all cases, but they help
us very little without adaptation and interpretation.[11]

But it is precisely in the adaptation and interpretation that the hard ethical decisions arise. In
Burke's words: "Reason is never inconvenient, but when
it comes to be applied."[12] Principles, in the form
of rules or action guides, seldom function as overriding
in the abstract. Moral decision making (not only in
politics) consists of weighing various conflicting
principles, or of conflicting interpretations of a
single principle. Indeed, as Joseph Gilbert has pointed
out, this functional understanding of principles excludes
the possibility of conflicts between principles; if
overridingness is the key, then the overridden principle

---

[11]For an interesting effort to develop three principles
of a very general sort, see Charles Anderson, "The
Place of Principles in Policy Analysis," American Political
Science Review 73 (Sept. 1979), pp. 711-723.
[12]Burke, "Tract on the Popery Laws," VI (in Bredvold
and Ross [eds.], The Philosophy of Edmund Burke [University
of Michigan Press, 1977], p. 26).

is no longer a principle at all. There is clearly something wrong with such an account.[13]

One may have reasons for choosing one principle over another, or for interpreting the principle in a particular way. Indeed, we should have such arguments, and be prepared to defend them. But such arguments are just that--arguments, which return the actor to a context of mutual searching, not to a stance of intransigence defending a clearly overriding principle. If the principle is to be followed in this situation, then we must know why this is the case. It will not do to say that the principle is overriding simply because it is a principle.[14]

This calls forth another objection to this understanding of how principles work. Can particular political decisions be derived from principles at all? Peter Berger speaks of this difficulty:

> I'm very suspicious of abstract ethical principles in general, and doubly so when these principles are to be applied to policy options. Such principles tend either to be so general that they are of no practical use, or to produce blindness to any alternatives to the one course prescribed on principle.[15]

The blindness mentioned here is particularly significant in a highly pluralistic society. If what happens in decision making is not simply a process of finding

---

[13]Gilbert, "Features of Morality," pp. 471-472.
[14]For discussions of the overriding nature of moral and political principles, see especially: Ronald Dworkin, "Liberalism," in Stuart Hampshire (ed.), Public and Private Morality, op. cit., esp. pp. 116-117, fn. 1; David Gauthier, Practical Reasoning (Oxford University Press, 1963), ch. 7; Stuart Hampshire, "Public and Private Morality," in his Public and Private Morality; William David Solomon, "Moral Reasons," American Philosophical Quarterly 12 (October 1975), pp. 331-339.
[15]Berger, Pyramids of Sacrifice, p. 245.

an overriding principle, but rather a process of weighing various principles and interpretations, then some criteria must be found to do this weighing. In politics, it is a question of great significance whether these weighing criteria will themselves be viewed as matters of principle. All of the biases of American politics mentioned earlier in chapter 2 (decisional, pressure, pluralistic, and representative) lead toward an accommodating and compromising approach to policy making. We may well want politicians to have their own views about which principles are overriding, and which interpretations are preferable. But we may not want them to adopt this position before the fact, thereby refusing to consider alternative weighings or interpretations.

Furthermore, once such a derivation is attempted, how persuasive can it be in a pluralistic society? It is interesting to consider the frustration and anger generated by the effort of the "New Right" to define a set of "Christian" voting positions, ranging from support of Taiwan to opposition to the establishment of a Department of Education. (Perhaps the strangest example was reported to me by a Senator who was told to support the Chrysler aid package by a constituent who had been called by God to run a Chrysler dealership.) What strikes us as odd about such positions? The derivation is simply not very believable; what is it about the Christian faith, for example, that leads to opposition to a Department of Education, or to support for the Taiwanese government? We may seem more comfortable with such a derivation when we are dealing with abortion, or capital punishment, or segregation.

But we should be aware that, in all situations, the derivation is highly problematic, depending both upon our interpretation of the principle and of our support for the policy position being derived. Support for civil rights may strike us as a more valid Christian or principled position because we have built into our understanding of Christian ethics a notion of social justice and political relevance, and because we are operating within a political stance of opposition to segregation.

Because of these difficulties of understanding and justifying such derivations, one only obscures the reasoning process in moving the argument from the level of policy dispute to the level of underlying principle. If we believe that the derivation is both direct and believable, then there is nothing wrong with making such a move. But such occasions are rare indeed, and the politician is more effective (and probably more honest) providing reasons for support of a policy decision without trying to derive it directly from a principle.

There are two other problems here with the idea of deriving a policy stance from an overriding princi- ple. One is a question of intolerance or arrogance involved in the derivation. Such arrogance can be intel- lectual (claiming to know the facts and consequences well enough to identify the preferred policy as a principled one) or moral (claiming to know the status of the principle as clearly applicable and overriding in this situation). The unanticipated consequences of social action, combined with the finitude of human knowledge and perception, undercut any confidence in such derivations. In theological terms, notions of human sinfulness call into question our capacity to make such connections. Senator Tsongas once suggested that "in this world, the fewer people we have who deal in absolutes, the better off we are going to be."[16] A member of the House of Representatives similarly reported that "Hell hath no fury like a vested interest masquerading as a moral principle."[17]

Such observations need not paralyze us, however. We act as best we can, making decisions with available facts and preferred interpretations. But we are less likely to adopt a mode of reasoning directly from principle to policy on the claim of an overriding view of the principle. Principles can be discussed, evaluated, and used, but seldom as absolute warrants for our highly uncertain actions.[18]

The other problem stems from the detrimental effects of drawing such connections. This is most apparent when we consider direct appeals to religious beliefs, but it is true of moral beliefs of any sort. Kenneth Thompson once pointed out that "policies cloaked in religious and moral terms tend to become frozen, intractable, and absolute."[19] Conflict may indeed be preferable in many situations, but there are strong reasons to oppose conflict at the level of unyielding principles as the model for legislative decision making in our society. This is the observation that has led many writers to link up American pluralism with democracy, pragmatism, and compromise.

One consequence of such functional appeals to principle is particularly troubling, not from the standpoint

---

[16]Congressional Record, December 18, 1979, S18987.
[17]Representative Clarence Brown, quoted in Helen Dewar, "Liberals Lose Four Skirmishes in Budget War," The Washington Post, May 1, 1980, A6.
[18]For a related discussion, raising these same issues but drawing somewhat different conclusions, see Benditt, "Compromising Interests and Principles," op. cit. See also chapter 7, below.
[19]Thompson, Christian Ethics and the Dilemmas of Foreign Policy, pp. 125-126.

of legislative efficiency but in the interests of public oversight. To see policy decisions as principled in this functional sense is again to remove the discussion from the realm of further reconsideration and evaluation. If there really is an overriding principle involved, a short circuiting seems to occur: to ask about other reasons or to demand justification is undercut by the claim that a decision was simply a matter of principle. Once we ask whether the principle was applicable, or whether the derivation works, we are asking for other sorts of reasons, and the defense of principle seems to be a diversion. Why is this principle overriding in this situation? If the legislator can give us a reason, then it is this reason which is central. If there is no such reason, then the appeal to principle is simply a subterfuge for an arbitrary decision.

There are other arguments to be made against such appeals to principle in politics. There may be certain issues which we feel do raise matters of principle directly, and where the derivations are sound.[20] But if there are such cases, they are only obscured by the all-too-frequent sounding of the alarm in cases where the appeal to principle is clearly inapplicable. Unless we want to consider any difficult and dangerous political decision as a principled one, we might try to restrict the claim to those rare cases where it does apply.

This observation becomes more important when we recognize that work on a particular issue can create a type of commitment which is easily defined as one of principle. For example, a staff member who worked on the development of the National Health Service Corps

---

[20]See chapter 7.

wrote about how the issue quickly developed major ethical
proportions in his mind:

> I felt by this time personally committed
> to the NHSC...as an important program in
> its own right....I had read a great deal
> of literature on the medical plight of the
> poor....In melodramatic fashion I began to
> think: there are people alive today who
> will die because they can't find a doctor;
> creating the Corps means saving at least
> a few lives.[21]

Such a bill may indeed involve principled questions,
and study of a policy problem may create heightened
moral awareness. But from the standpoint of the elected
official, every person with a position is similarly
heartfelt or committed. The result is that one's appeal
may not be heeded unless some moral principle is called
upon, with a consequent blurring of all such distinctions.
When everything becomes an issue of principle, nothing
has legitimate priority. We may be better off if we
can purge our political discussion of such language,
and then begin to discover those rare situations where
the derivation from principle to policy makes sense.

There are two final philosophical issues which
I will mention briefly. First, if someone does hold
a principle in this functional sense, then should we
want that person to act against it, if we are convinced
that it is wrong? Another way to ask this question
is: Should a person ever act against the claims of
conscience? It is obviously difficult to make such

---

[21]Eric Redman, The Dance of Legislation (N.Y.: Simon
and Schuster, 1973), p. 76. For an effective argument
that we choose the ways in which we use principles,
see Edward W. James, "Working in and Working to Principles,"
Ethics 83 (October 1972), pp. 51-57; and his "A Reasoned
Ethical Incoherence?" Ethics 89 (April 1979), pp. 240-
253.

a case, for to what could we appeal? If we can convince
the other person of the incorrectness of the principle,
fine; but then the principle no longer functions as
such. What if we cannot convince the opponent? Are
we to say, "Yes, I know you are convinced, utterly
convinced, of the rightness of your position, but you
must act against it, on moral grounds"?

I can see no argument for expecting persons to
act against such principles, without being able to
convince them that the principles themselves are unsound. We
may be forced, therefore, to question the nature of
the application of principles to policy decisions. It
may be impossible to undercut someone's principles,
but it may be possible to point out that the specific
policy decision does not follow so closely from the
principle as the person believes. In this way, we can
avoid asking people to act against their principles.

Second, merely calling a belief a principle gives
it no claim either to our attention or our consideration. If
we respect someone, we will expect to respect the principles
on which she acts; but we may find that those principles
are not only "not ours," but are not even plausible
as principles for us. People do indeed believe all
sorts of strange things, and calling them principles
does not make them less strange. Jonathon Harrison
made this point well:

> I am inclined to think that any principle
> can be a moral principle, provided that certain
> formal requirements are fulfilled....Though
> I may be (linguistically) eccentric, I personally
> would say that a man who exhibited signs
> of remorse when he stepped on the black lines
> of the pavement, tried to persuade others
> not to tread on them, tried to make unlined
> pavements by law compulsory and so on, did
> hold this as a moral principle. It is true
> that I should also say that he was very probably

mad, but why should not insanity manifest itself in moral as well as in factual delusions? And though we may think his moral views erroneous, is he otherwise so very different, logically or psychologically, from ourselves? I have little doubt that his moral promptings are just like ours-- which suggests that morality may be no more than the manifestation of a socially useful compulsive neurosis--and no doubt at all that he can give as good reasons for his moral view as we can for ours, i.e., none at all.[22]

Whether we agree fully with Harrison's analysis of moral principles (and I do not), it is correct in recognizing that people claim as moral principles beliefs which may strike us as absurd. Even if we refuse to admit such beliefs to the status of moral principles, we must live with such persons, and it is important to undercut the claim that, simply because a belief functions in a particular way, it has a right to be followed, heeded, or implemented.

Conclusion

I have identified several reasons for being cautious about appealing to principle in the political world. Such appeals err in overlooking conflicts of principles; they cut against the element of pragmatism and tolerance in the American political system; they are often incoherent in their claim of derivation from principle to policy; they obscure those rare situations where such a principle

---

[22]Harrison, "When is a Principle a Moral Principle?" A Symposium. The Aristotelian Society, Supplementary Volume 28, 1954, pp. 111-134 (quotation appears on pp. 112-113). For an opposing view on this question, see Phillipa Foot's article in the same symposium, pp. 95-110.

may truly be at stake; and they are poor guides to action when used by persons of limited knowledge and imperfect character (a category into which we all fit). The aspect of the self-serving nature of such appeals simply reinforces our skepticism.

But where does that leave us? Are principles ever effective appeals? If not, then are there any limits to the process of political compromise? Are there any ways to try to distinguish appropriate from inappropriate compromises in American politics? We turn to this question in our final chapter.

CHAPTER 7. LIMITS TO COMPROMISE

> There does exist for man, therefore,
> a way of acting and of thinking which is
> possible on the level of moderation to which
> he belongs. Every undertaking that is more
> ambitious than this proves to be contradic-
> tory. The absolute is not attained nor, above
> all, created through history. Politics is
> not religion, or if it is, then it is nothing
> but the Inquisition.
>   --Albert Camus

Introduction

Our examination has basically supported the traditional claim that compromise is the heart and soul of American politics. The nature of political action requires it; the institutions of American politics cannot function without it; the complexity of the legislative process mandates it; and the nature of political language is built upon it.

Are there, then, no limits to the appropriateness of compromise? In chapter 6, we saw that there are major problems with the most common answer given to this question. Must we then conclude that our politicians are free to compromise at any time and in any manner they please? John Kennedy recognized the problem here when he wrote: "[T]he question is how we will compromise and with whom. For it is easy to seize upon unnecessary concessions, not as means of legitimately resolving conflicts but as methods of 'going along'."[1]

In this final chapter, drawing upon the earlier sections, we ask whether there are any criteria for

---

[1]Kennedy, <u>Profiles in Courage</u> (N.Y.: Harper and Row, 1964 [1955]), p. 5.

judging compromises as legitimate or illegitimate.[2]
The task here is not an easy one, for many of the reasons
we have already discussed. American society is highly
pluralistic, and it is difficult to find agreed-upon
values or standards for such judgment. In addition,
the complexity of political compromise undercuts the
search for a stable and clear judgment, or even for
a clear understanding of all the factors involved in
any given decision.

But we must make some such effort, for the alternative
is to throw up our hands in despair. I shall suggest
some criteria, drawn both from the requirements of
political activity and from the reflections of many
other people. The criteria are broad, but they do provide
a set of questions which must be asked of any political
compromise. By using examples from the study, we can
try to ground these criteria sufficiently to see how
they might be applied.[3]

I shall suggest four criteria here: concern for
broader interests, concern for consequences to others,
progressivity, and nonviolation of principles. The
discussion of the fourth criterion will be more detailed,

---

[2] The term "legitimate" is used to suggest that the standards
are bound up with their context of application. A legitimate
action is one which is seen as appropriate or correct
or right not only by an outside observer, but also
by someone familiar with, and sympathetic to, the action
required by the context. Legitimacy is not essentially
a legal concept, but a moral and social one.

[3] Of course, the reader may not select the same set of
criteria, or may find the brief arguments given in
their behalf to be unsatisfactory. The major concern
here is to demonstrate how some such criteria are both
plausible and necessary. If the reader has alternative
standards for assessing political compromises, let
her/him ponder how they would be applied and defended.

building upon our discussion in chapter 6. Several
types of compromise are then examined, providing an
opportunity to see how the criteria can be applied. The
chapter concludes with some more general comments about
the place of compromise in American politics.

I. Criteria for compromise.

I would suggest the following criteria for evaluating
political compromise in institutions such as the United
States Senate.

> I. The representative must represent a range
> of interests. Such interests should be paramount
> in justifying compromises, and the <u>broader</u>
> interests have a prima facie claim to recognition
> over the narrower ones.

This criterion follows from the discussion of
the complexity of the representative role. We cannot
establish any general rules concerning whose interests
should be represented in every case. But we can suggest
that compromises are illegitimate if made without serious
consideration for the full range of constituencies
and interests. The senator may argue that a refusal
to protect the interests of the voters of the state
is justified in terms of some wider interests, but
some such argument must be made.

What are these wider interests? Perhaps the one
most commonly cited is "the public interest." I do
not want to enter the ongoing battle concerning whether
this term is merely an ideological tool, or precisely

how we would know the public interest if it did exist.[4]
But there are cases where some such concept may be
required in political debate, such as when we are confronted
with the existence of collective or public goods. Such
goods are those benefits or resources which, if available
to any of us, must be available to all. Resources such
as clean air and water, national security, and democratic
political institutions are either shared or they do
not exist.[5] Because one of the central tasks of government
is to provide for (or at least protect) such goods,
any compromise which overlooks or acts against them
is likely to be illegitimate.

---

[4]For discussions on both sides of this issue, see, for
example: Carl J. Friedrich (ed.), The Public Interest
(N.Y.: Atherton Press, 1962); Brand Blanshard, "Morality
and Politics," in Richard T. DeGeorge (ed.), Ethics
and Society (N. Y.: Anchor, 1966), pp. 1-23; Brian
Barry, "The Public Interest," op. cit.; Richard Flathman,
The Public Interest: An Essay Concerning the Normative
Discourse of Politics (N. Y.: John Wiley and Sons,
1966); Hanna Fenichel Pitkin, Wittgenstein and Justice
(University of California Press, 1972), esp. pp. 216-
217; Glendon Schubert, The Public Interest: A Critique
of the Theory of a Political Concept (Illinois: Free
Press of Glencoe, 1960).

[5]This is somewhat overstated, of course. The more affluent
can move to those parts of the nation with cleaner
air or water, or can enjoy democratic rights while
depriving the poor or the outsiders of the right to
vote. Often, the attempt fails, either because it is
difficult to pretend that the "others" are not one's
fellow citizens, or because the dirty air ends up contam-
inating the clean. But efforts to deny the collective
nature of such resources are recurrent and sometimes
successful.
    For an excellent and influential discussion of
this issue, see the consideration of social goods in
Richard A. Musgrave and Peggy B. Musgrave, Public Finance
in Theory and Practice, 3rd edition (N.Y.: McGraw-Hill,
1980), esp. pp. 56-86.

Much of the anger generated in the windfall profits tax bill debate stemmed from the existence of this criterion. As we have seen, Senator Gravel of Alaska repeatedly refused to accept any compromise proposal which would harm the oil interests of his state. Such a refusal (especially in the adamant form in which it was expressed) was perceived by many of his colleagues as an effort to ignore the broader energy and security interests of the nation as a whole. By raising the spectre of the collective good of energy as a national resource, the other senators demanded a compromise which would guarantee that resource to all.

The potential self-interestedness of such an appeal is evident, and we need not believe that every such appeal to broader interests is valid. Illegitimate compromises might be made by appealing to the public interest or collective goods, but any compromise is illegitimate if it cannot make such an appeal.[6]

II. Concern for consequences to others must be the primary factor in political compromises.

Such a claim is an attempt to find some tentative resolution to the pragmatic/purist debate we discussed earlier. The politician should not view the call to compromise primarily as an opportunity for personal purity or as a challenge to personal integrity. Such

------

[6]By limiting appeals to the public interest to these cases of collective goods, I am adopting what William Connolly calls the "thin theory" of the public interest. Although I tend to agree with his call for a more robust model which can incorporate more substantive notions of the collective good, I can see no coherent way to argue for such a model within the context of present-day American legislative politics. (See Connolly, Appearance and Reality in Politics [Cambridge University Press, 1981], esp. pp. 90-119.)

challenges may arise, of course, but the represented have a right to demand that compromises made or refused on their behalf are justified first in terms of their interests. If the interests of the constituents are to be overridden, it must be to further a higher interest, not to maintain the purity of the political actor. Concern for personal integrity must be measured largely in terms of the requirements of prudential decision making.

A famous statement of this position is found in the following comment by George Bernard Shaw, writing about a fellow politician who had refused to give up his own moral code for the sake of political expediency:

> When I think of my own unfortunate character, smirched with compromise, rotted with opportunism, mildewed by expediency--dragged through the mud of borough council and Battersea elections, stretched out of shape with wire-pulling, putrefied by permeation, worn out by 25 years pushing to gain an inch here, or straining to stem a backrush, I do think Joe might have put up with just a speck or two on those white robes of his for the sake of the millions of poor devils who cannot afford any character at all because they have no friend in parliament. Oh, these moral dandies, these spiritual toffs, these superior persons. Who is Joe, anyway, that he should not risk his soul occasionally like the rest of us?[7]

Politics does not require us to be devils, but our representatives do have a prima facie obligation to

---

[7]Quoted in Stephen K. Bailey, Ethics and the Politician (California: Center for the Study of Democratic Institutions, 1960), p. 6. For similar discussions, see: Cranston, Politics and Ethics, op. cit., esp. pp. 19-22; Robert E. Goodin, Political Theory and Public Policy (University of Chicago Press, 1982), esp. ch. 1. For an interesting consideration of prudence in political action, see R. L. Nichols and D. M. White, "Politics Proper: On Action and Prudence," Ethics 89 (July 1979), pp. 372-384.

place public need above concern for personal purity.

There are two closely related dimensions to this problem. The first concerns the choice between purity of intentions and consequences, while the second involves attention to the interests of others rather than oneself. In the case of political action, concern for consequences to others should be paramount. But we might recognize that these two issues are separable; to act for others need not commit us to a purely consequentialist style of reasoning. In the political arena, however, the two dimensions overlap considerably, largely due to the representative nature of the legislative role.

We should not overstate the problem here, however. Thomas Nagel has pointed out that we are seldom forced to choose between maintaining personal moral integrity and doing the correct thing:

> ...there are two confusions behind the view that moral self-interest underlies moral absolutism. First, it is a confusion to suggest that the need to preserve one's moral purity might be the <u>source</u> of an obligation. For if by committing murder one sacrifices one's moral purity or integrity, that can only be because there is <u>already</u> something wrong with murder. The general reason against committing murder cannot therefore be merely that it makes one an immoral person. Secondly, the notion that one might sacrifice one's moral integrity justifiably, in the service of a sufficiently worthy end, is an incoherent

notion. For if one were justified in making such a sacrifice (or even morally required to make it), then one would not be sacrificing one's moral integrity by adopting that course: one would be preserving it.[8]

Although we may confront tragic choices in politics, we are better served to begin by using the criteria of prudence and effectiveness as tests of the rightness of political compromise. Whether we would want to say the same thing about compromise in the rest of our lives is another matter.

> III. Compromises should be progressive, opening up the possibility for future compromises and agreement, and for the resolution of underlying problems.

Such a criterion stems from the very nature and purpose of compromise. As an aspect of, and a tool in, negotiation, compromise is appropriate only as a method of reaching agreement in situations of social conflict. It is not the only such method, and often it is the wrong one. But if it is going to be selected, then its justification must include a claim that certain results will follow.

There are two types of results we might desire here. The first involves peace, stability, predictability, or a lessening of tension--goals expressed well by Stuart Hampshire in referring to Spinoza's view of moral progress as "the increasing dominance of gentleness

---

[8]Nagel, "War and Massacre," in Marshall Cohen, T. Nagel, and T. Scanlon (eds.), War and Moral Responsibility (Princeton University Press, 1974 [1972]), pp. 12-13. Nagel does admit, however, that there might be "moral blind alleys" in which real dilemmas do exist.
    See also Bernard Williams, "Politics and Moral Character," in Stuart Hampshire (ed.), Public and Private Morality, op. cit., pp. 55-73, esp. pp. 62-64.

and of reason...."[9] We compromise because we would
rather be gentle than hostile, because we prefer reason
(or at least peace) to force.

But compromise should also lead beyond itself
to a solution of underlying conflict. This need not
commit us to a consensus model of human society; conflict
is often useful and inevitable. But it does mean that
human problems, particularly the sorts of problems
confronted in politics, may be soluble or modifiable. Compromise is a technique devoted not merely to solving
existing differences but also to exploring the opportunities
for redefining underlying issues of social policy. This
is Charles Lindblom's point in praising the "reconstructive
leader" who can alter preferences rather than merely
react to them:

> ...compromise of existing preferences or
> interests is often dangerous....What every
> modern political system requires is moving
> compromise--specifically, a never-ending
> sequence of compromises, each successive
> one responding to a new alignment of preferences
> or interests.[10]

But should such a criterion be applied to compromise? Pruitt and Lewis have contrasted compromise with
integrative bargaining: the former involves a process
"by which bargainers concede along some obvious dimensions
to a point part way between their initial preferences,"
whereas the latter involves a search for a solution
providing joint benefit to both sides:

---

[9]Hampshire, "Morality and Pessimism," in his Public
and Private Morality, p. 22.
[10]Lindblom, The Policy-Making Process, op. cit., p. 106. See
also John Morley, On Compromise, op. cit., pp. 174-
178; T. V. Smith, The Ethics of Compromise and the
Art of Containment, op. cit., pp. 64-80.

> We admit that compromise can sometimes lead
> to the best available agreement, but we argue
> that more integrative solutions are usually
> available if bargainers will only seek them. In-
> deed, we suspect that the search for an acceptable
> compromise, with all its overtones of fairness
> and equitability, is sometimes responsible
> for failure to discover more integrative
> options.[11]

If we combine Lindblom's point with this last
observation, we may discover a useful criterion for
compromise outcomes. It is true that any particular
compromise solution may not be integrative, but we
can still expect it to be moving or progressive. A
compromise is a good resolution if it opens up the
possibility and opportunity for future integrative
solutions, or at least for later compromises which
may be in the best interests of all concerned. A compromise
which creates increased resentment is illegitimate,
not merely because resentment is a bad thing but because
it may undercut future negotiations and problem-solving
opportunities.

I am not suggesting that a good compromise is
one which papers over a dispute, or that any compromise
which lessens tension is therefore good. If a social
conflict is structural, then it must be faced eventually.[12]
But compromise may be an important method for leading

---

[11]Dean G. Pruitt and Steven A. Lewis, "The Psychology
of Integrative Bargaining," in Daniel Druckman (ed.),
Negotiations: Social-Psychological Perspectives (California: Sage Publications, 1977), p. 162. For a fuller
and more recent treatment, see Pruitt, Negotiation
Behavior (N.Y.: Academic Press, 1981), esp. pp. 137ff..
     Joseph Carens develops a similar criterion for
the political compromise process in his article, "Compromises in Politics," op. cit., pp. 126-129.
[12]We might wonder whether, from this perspective, the
various compromises between 1820 and 1854 to preserve
the Union were legitimate compromises.

decision makers from symptom to solution, from appearance
to structure. To use our windfall profits tax bill
here, this criterion would ask whether the tax created
a climate of conservation and production consonant
with the needs of the 1980s, rather than merely whether
it managed to satisfy (or, at least, not alienate)
the various parties to the dispute.

There is another element to this criterion. One
factor which may make a compromise a progressive one
is whether it is clearly understood as a compromise. When
significant amounts of value are sacrificed, it is
important for one's opponent to be aware of it, and
to be pressured to continue to deal with the problem
in the future. Openness and honesty are crucial at
the end of the compromise, as well as during the negotiation
process. John Morley made this point over one hundred
years ago:

> It is legitimate compromise to say:-- "I
> do not expect you to execute this improvement,
> or surrender that prejudice, in my time. But
> at any rate it shall not be my fault if the
> improvement remains unknown or rejected. There
> shall be one man at least who has surrendered
> the prejudice, and who does not hide the
> fact." It is illegitimate compromise to say:
> "I cannot persuade you to accept my truth,
> therefore I will pretend to accept your falsehood."[13]

We can expect compromises to lead beyond themselves
only if the compromisers recognize and admit that they
are essentially dissatisfied with the present resolution. The compromise may be the best I can get today,
but it need not be the best I will fight for tomorrow.

---

[13]Morley, On Compromise, p. 160.

IV. In cases where moral or political principles
are violated by compromise, the compromise
is illegitimate.

As chapter 6 has indicated, this criterion is
likely to be appealed to far more often than is appropriate. However, there are two different ways in which
principles may help limit or define the appropriateness
of political compromise, by functioning either as limits
or as guidelines. Let us examine these two functions
in some detail.14

A. Principles as limits. Moral or political principles
may serve as outer limits for our action, setting border-
lines beyond which we must not go. In T. D. Weldon's
term, political principles can function as "stop signs."15
However absolutist such a claim may appear to be, I
would not want to exclude entirely the possibility
of such situations arising in political life. There
may be certain rights which must always be protected,
certain promises which must always be kept, certain
procedures which must always be respected.16 Let us
look at a few hypothetical examples.

14David Gauthier makes a similar distinction, although
he applies it differently. See his Practical Reasoning,
op. cit., chapter 7.
15Weldon, "Political Principles," in Peter Laslett (ed.),
Philosophy, Politics, and Society (Oxford: Basil Blackwell,
1956), pp. 22-34.
16Note that the defense of such principles need not be
on strictly non-consequentialist grounds, as the rule
utilitarian tradition of ethics has amply demonstrated.
There may be effects of not always following such principles
which would convince us to follow them even in situations
where we might prefer to be freer to disregard their
authority. One can therefore be an "absolutist" for
purely consequentialist reasons.

First, our elected representatives have taken an oath to uphold the United States Constitution. If a policy decision directly threatened to contravene a provision of that document, we would expect the politician to refuse to go along. If a compromise were then proposed which still violated the provision but in a less harsh form, would such a compromise be legitimate? Occasionally, members of Congress use such arguments to support their views. For example, in the debate concerning Senator Danforth's proposal to tax the profits states make from oil on their land, the following statements were made:

> Senator Cranston: ...The principles of federalism do not permit a Federal tax on these revenues of State and local governments used for public purposes....[17]

> Senator Bentsen: ...there is a fundamental question of principle involved. The imposition of a Federal tax on a State nonbusiness property would be poor public policy. It would be in direct conflict with basic principles of Federal-State relations.[18]

As we saw in chapter 5, such appeals are largely rhetorical. But merely to react in that way is to miss the significance of such speeches: if a bill did contradict the Constitution, then senators would be obliged to oppose it. Senator Danforth's bill was not a very clear example for most senators, and regional factors make it difficult to determine the motives of these oil-producing-state members. But it would be illegitimate merely to water down a clearly unconstitutional provision of a bill, if the resulting compromise remained unconstitutional.

---

[17] Congressional Record, December 14, 1979, S18579.
[18] Congressional Record, December 15, 1979, S18657.

Of course, stating the problem in this way reveals how unlikely such a situation is. The Constitution is extremely vague on most policy matters, and the substance of the document is changed by legislative and executive actions which are then judged to be in accord with its basic intent. To believe that the oath to uphold the Constitution actually imposes many limits to compromise on policy decisions is to hold a highly idealized view of the American Constitutional process.

Similarly, there may be certain substantive principles or ideals of morality which may not be compromised. Benditt provides a useful hypothetical example: "...however earnest someone is about the propriety of genocide as a means of solving pressing social and economic problems, no one should accept an unforced compromise that merely waters down the genocidal policy."[19] The nature of the example again reveals how unlikely such principled decisions are. Perhaps the most recent case which some senators have seen in this light involved federal funding for abortion. For a senator who believes that abortion is simply a subset of murder, any federal funding must seem reprehensible. Whatever the reader may feel about Senator Helms' motives or political leanings, his refusal to compromise seems justifiable if he was serious about his stated beliefs. Even those opposed may grudgingly have to admit that his refusal to compromise was appropriate.

Finally, there may be certain procedural requirements which are not compromisable. Policies which deprive groups of due process of law, or which institute punishment

---

[19]Benditt, "Compromising Interests and Principles," in Pennock and Chapman (eds.), Compromise in Ethics, Law, and Politics, op. cit., pp. 36-37.

retroactively, might be objected to on moral as well
as political grounds. Indeed, there are those who argue
that purely procedural or formal criteria are the only
moral principles to which we can consistently and reasonably
appeal.[20] Although such situations arise infrequently,
they are probably much more common than threats to
Constitutional or substantive principles. Arthur Kuflik
has argued that these absolute procedural norms are
the very foundation of political compromise, and therefore
must not themselves be amenable to compromise:

> ...the democratic process has no special
> claim upon us to participate in it or to
> abide by its results unless there is prior
> assurance of some sort that certain matters
> are not subject to rule by democratic consensus.[21]

In the Senate, perhaps the care with which the
right to filibuster is protected is a sign of the importance
of such procedural rights. Democratic decision making
is not simply majority rule; it also consists of respect
for the minority, and that respect must be acted upon. Thus
there seem to be certain procedural rights which are
uncompromisable in American political institutions.

B. Principles as guidelines. Alternatively, moral
or political principles can function as guideposts,
as directors, as definers of what is right and wrong. This

---

[20]The strongest recent proponent of this position is
probably R. M. Hare. See esp. his Freedom and Reason
(London: Oxford University Press, 1972 [1963]). Note
that Hare's position would not disallow violation of
due process or retroactive punishment as long as the
actor were willing to universalize such violations,
meaning that they would have to apply to the actor
as well.
[21]Kuflik, "Morality and Compromise," in Pennock and Chapman
(eds.), Compromise in Ethics, Law, and Politics, op. cit.,
p. 43.

is the more usual usage of principles in political
life, although it is not the one admitted to when persons
claim to be appealing to principle. Our principles
are useful; they can be identified, fostered, cherished,
and realized. Without them, we are totally adrift in
a world of arbitrary action, as Wayne Leys pointed
out:

> ...the slogan of pragmatism becomes a cloak
> for blind hunch and a confused wallowing
> in unclassified cases, if situational problem-
> solving is not enlightened by some standards
> that enable us to recognize a problem when
> we see it. We need some idea of what is meant
> by the solution to a problem, other than
> that the thing has ceased to kick us in the
> teeth.[22]

We may not always act on our principles, and they are
notoriously difficult to apply to policy decisions. But
they remain relevant to such decisions, and our failure
to implement them must involve a recognition that they
do remain relevant.[23]

What are these principles, and how can we discover
them? This is the dominant question in political philosophy,
and I can merely point to a few fundamental insights

---

[22]Leys, Ethics for Policy Decisions: The Art of Asking
Deliberative Questions, op. cit., pp. 384-385. See
also: Charles Anderson, "The Place of Principles in
Policy Analysis," op. cit.; James Fishkin, "Moral Principles
and Public Policy," Daedalus 108 (Fall 1979), pp. 55-
67; Gauthier, Practical Reasoning, esp. ch. 7; Ronald
Dworkin, "Liberalism," in Stuart Hampshire (ed.), Public
and Private Morality, op. cit., pp. 113-143; Daniel
C. Maguire, The Moral Choice (Garden City: Doubleday
and Co., 1978), esp. ch. 7; and Williams, "Politics
and Moral Character," op. cit..
[23]See, for example, D. Z. Phillips, "Do Moral Considerations
Override Others?" Philosophical Quarterly 29 (July
1979), pp. 247-254.

which might be useful for judging political compromise. For the sake of focusing the argument, let me make a few comments about the principle of social justice.

<u>Social Justice</u>. David Miller has identified three different understandings of the principle of social justice.[24] They provide alternative ways of deciding upon the central issue of social justice: namely, what is due to each person? A <u>rights</u> perspective asks what each person is entitled to, primarily in terms of position in society or underlying qualities as a human being. A <u>desert</u> perspective asks what the person has earned, by virtue of productive efforts, virtue, or any other criterion. Finally, a <u>needs</u> perspective identifies the person's needs in relation to the resource being distributed, and argues that a just distribution occurs when those with greater need have those needs satisfied.[25]

Political philosophers have given different answers to this question of what is a just social policy. Many theories attempt to combine these different meanings,

---

[24]Miller defines social justice as follows:

Social justice...concerns the distribution of benefits and burdens throughout a society, as it results from the major social institutions--property systems, public organizations, etc. It deals with such matters as the regulation of wages and (where they exist) profits, the protection of persons' rights through the legal system, the allocation of housing, medicine, welfare benefits, etc.

(Miller, <u>Social Justice</u> [Oxford: Clarendon Press, 1976], p. 22.)

Miller's book is a particularly careful and important treatment of many of the crucial issues, and I shall use it extensively here. Note, in addition, that this category of social justice is one well suited to the sorts of decisions made by legislative organizations in American politics.

[25]Miller, <u>Social Justice</u>, pp. 24-31.

placing the emphasis on one or another of the meanings. Recently, Robert Nozick has developed the most persuasive argument for a combination of rights and desert, arguing essentially that questions of redistribution are secondary to the question of whether the person has a right to those resources already possessed. One gains such a right primarily on the basis of historical entitlement, such as having fairly earned or inherited property or position. In such a theory, there is a clear presumption of inequality, for persons begin with different amounts of these resources.[26] On the other pole, John Rawls has developed an elaborate procedure for deriving principles of justice which focus upon both rights such as liberty and strong consideration of need. Once basic rights are guaranteed, a just distribution must pay particular

---

[26]Nozick, Anarchy, State, and Utopia (N. Y.: Basic Books, 1974). Nozick's argument is much more complex, of course; it is also elegant, beautifully expressed, and compelling.

attention to the needs of the least advantaged members
of society.[27]

How do we choose between different conceptions
of justice? I suspect that the answer involves a combination
of intuition, social influences, and reason.[28] For
the purposes of our discussion, let me indicate my
commitment to a needs-based model of social justice. It
may be hard to prove that a hungry person is entitled

---

[27]Rawls, A Theory of Justice (Harvard University Press,
1971). Rawls' position is also extremely complex, and
I cannot go into more detail here. I should note, however,
that Rawls is apparently least comfortable with that
part of his theory (the so-called "difference principle")
upon which I am focusing. See, for example, his article,
"The Justification of Civil Disobedience," where he
argues that the difference principle is harder to apply
and provides less justification for acts of civil disobedience than the other two parts of his principles
of justice. (In Hugo Bedau [ed.], Civil Disobedience: Theory
and Practice [Indianapolis: Pegasus, 1969], pp. 240-255.)
    I should also note that I am interpreting Rawls
somewhat more narrowly than does Miller, who stresses
Rawls' efforts to derive a more fundamental principle
of justice lying behind the notions of rights, desert,
or need. For my purposes, it is more useful to emphasize
the difference principle as Rawls' major contribution
to the policy debate concerning the meaning of the
standard of social justice.
    For a fascinating effort to link Rawls' underlying
theory of justice with an understanding of political
compromise, see Arthur Kuflik, "Morality and Compromise,"
op. cit., esp. pp. 55-62.

[28]One of Miller's most interesting points concerns the
connection between the social system and the principle
of justice adopted by that society. Indeed, he argues
that there is no way to select one or another of the
three meanings of social justice except by reference
to the particular social and economic context. While
I am in basic agreement with him here, we can give
reasons for siding with the poor or oppressed, even
though we may have to admit that such reasons are not
ultimately convincing to everyone. See his Social Justice,
esp. ch. 8.

to food, but a social system which is unconcerned about
that hunger is unjust. I would make such statements
in particular about the basic needs of existence such
as food, shelter, and the opportunities to attain them. Concern for needs should be more important in questions
of distribution than concern for historical entitlement. Justice requires attention both to certain rights and
to the resources necessary to use them; the right to
liberty is not merely the right to be left alone but
also the right to have the opportunities to live one's
life fully. In public policy decisions, this suggests
that a just policy must consider particularly those
who are most in need of essential resources. "Who is
being hurt?" and "Are the poorest and most oppressed
members of society being helped?" are key questions
the principle of justice addresses to social policy.[29]

Of course, we may be required to adopt policies
which violate a principle of social justice for the
sake of protecting other basic rights. Indeed, justice
itself may require the protection of rights more basic
than what is demanded by a particular principle of
redistribution. Few of us would advocate redistributing
wealth by murdering all the millionaires, even if that
were the only way to achieve the goal. But we can try

---

[29]To defend these assertions would require a separate
book, of course. I can do no more here than indicate
that this emphasis stems from broad religious commitments
in my case, but it can be argued on non-religious grounds
as well.
    The attempt to lay out one's fundamental ethical
framework is fraught with risks. To fail to do so,
however, is to abdicate a major responsibility of citizen-
ship, especially if we want to be able to evaluate
the actions of our elected representatives. It would
be more convenient if such fundamental questions were
unrelated to political judgment, but such is not the
case.

to tax the wealthy, even though they may complain that
their rights are being violated. Although social justice
is one of the central principles, it is not the only
one, and it is always extremely difficult to say clearly
when a policy is just.

We may find cases, however, where we can apply
such a criterion. For example, there may be certain
minimum standards of justice, especially as they relate
to the distribution of crucial human resources. As
I indicated above, the more primary and essential any
resource is to human life and well-being, the more
important is the demand to distribute the moral minimum
to all.[30] Legislators may thus be allowed (or expected)
to establish lower acceptable levels of fair distribution,
and a compromise which threatens to transfer money
from a welfare program into tax credits for corporations
might then violate the principle of justice. It is
notoriously difficult to identify such transfers, of
course, and politicians are extremely adept at hiding
or denying them when they do occur. But the observer
can try to make such judgments, using the demands of
justice to determine whether the interests of the neediest
are being considered and protected.

An example may be helpful. We have seen the dilemma
a liberal Senator confronted over the food stamps bill. Does
he vote for a compromise lowering the benefits to poor
families, in order to assure that some food stamp program

---

[30]I am indebted especially to Chuck Powers for the notion
of the moral minimum. (See John Simon, Charles Powers,
and Jon Gunnemann, The Ethical Investor [Yale University
Press, 1972], esp. pp. 15-26.) The authors restrict
the concept to situations of negative duties, but I
would argue that elected officials have more positive
duties which should be guided by this criterion as
well.

will continue? We can say two things here. The transfer
of money away from such a program can be justified
only in terms of long-range benefits to the poor themselves. Furthermore, there is a minimum level of support
without which the program is completely undermined. If
families cannot survive, then one may as well refuse
to compromise at all.

Another aspect of a principle of justice arises
when we consider the issue of equality. Justice is
often linked up closely with equality, and a just social
policy is one which does not treat persons differently
unless there is a morally relevant reason for doing
so.[31] Once again, we have a significant difference
between the liberal view (which requires justification
of unequal treatment) and the more conservative one
(which either does not require such a justification
in all cases, or which assumes that some such relevant
difference is always present). Again, I would begin
from the more liberal end here, arguing that a social
policy which cannot justify unequal treatment in this
way is unjust.

---

[31]I believe David Miller is quite correct when he links
up the needs-based understanding of social justice
with the concept of equality:

> ...the logical extension of the principle
> of need is the principle of equality, interpreted
> as the claim that every man should enjoy
> an equal level of well-being. Equality is
> achieved by giving first priority to the
> satisfaction of needs, and then by satisfying
> as large a proportion of each person's further
> desires as resources will allow--it being
> assumed that resources are not sufficiently
> abundant to gratify every wish.

(Miller, Social Justice, pp. 143-144.)
There is a large body of recent philosophical
literature on the connection between justice and equality.

We saw the difficulty the Senate faced in trying to decide upon a fair distribution of tax policies and credits in the energy area. Senators from northern states insisted that they needed help because of the colder weather and fewer energy resources of their region; senators from southern states claimed that they needed help because of the warmer weather and because of the costs of development and production of energy resources. Should the southern states be penalized for their good fortune? Is it penalizing them at all to force them to help support the consumers of the north?

The resulting compromise can be evaluated in terms of whether the persons most immediately in need benefitted from the policy. If one examines the progress of that legislation, key attention was in fact given to this question. There was widespread agreement in the fall of 1979 that the most pressing question was to assure adequate energy resources at an affordable price to poorer persons in the northern states. The compromise assured such guarantees--perhaps not as fully as many would have liked, but in a way which recognized the factor of need as primary.

Finally, I would use the value of compassion as a central criterion of a just social policy. This may derive from religious sources, but it need not do so. The ability to "stand in the other's shoes" or to look at the situation through another's eyes is central to a needs-based view of social justice, especially in the political realm. The centrality of reciprocity, of respect for the other's views, of not calling the opponent's motives into question--all these organizational features of Senate life reveal and underscore the shared moral sense without which political action returns

to the Hobbesian war of each against each. A central
element in any evaluation of compromise is to ask whether
compassion has been enacted in the result. This may
be a counsel of perfection, but it is an important
counsel nevertheless.

This understanding of justice creates an additional
expectation: the powerful may be required to sacrifice
more than the weak. Of course, we cannot establish
such a rule for all cases, but concern for equality
and compassion will exert pressure <u>unequally</u> on the
parties to a dispute. Burke seemed to use such a criterion
in his famous <u>Speech on Conciliation with America</u> in
1775:

> I mean to give peace. Peace implies recon-
> ciliation, and, where there has been a material
> dispute, reconciliation does in a manner
> always imply concession on the one part or
> on the other. In this state of things I make
> no difficulty in affirming that the proposal
> ought to originate from us [Great Britain]. Great
> and acknowledged force is not impaired, either
> in effect or in opinion, by an unwillingness
> to exert itself. The superior power may offer
> peace with honor and with safety. Such an
> offer from such a power will be attributed
> to magnanimity. But the concessions of the
> weak are the concessions of fear.[32]

---

[32]Burke, <u>Speech on Conciliation with America</u> (N. Y.: Charles
E. Merrill Co., 1911 [1775]), p. 26.

Applications

Let us now consider some of the examples and types of compromise discussed above. I will consider three categories here as illustrative: the middle ground compromises, the lesser evil compromises, and trading-off compromises. I hope merely to indicate the sorts of questions we must ask to decide whether compromises are indeed legitimate.

There is an inevitable problem in evaluating such action. There is no Archimedean point from which to assess these actions. My concerns are to understand how political decisions are made, and to provide some further incentive for both observers and participants to improve their sensitivity concerning complex and important moral questions. The more willing we are to risk appearing arrogant by engaging in such evaluation, the more accountable our representatives must be, and the more reflective they may become in making decisions which affect us all.

(1) Arriving at the middle ground

Under what circumstances are different methods of finding the middle ground appropriate? As we saw in chapter 4, one has a range of alternatives here: splitting the difference, finding another central point, or blending the two extremes in some other way. Perhaps the most significant normative question concerns the choice between splitting the difference and all the other options. If we are concerned with social justice, are we committed to approving only of solutions in which each party receives equal concessions from the other?

There are some obvious problems with such a conclusion. First, one's starting demand determines how far

one is willing to go. If I know that an even split
is the likely outcome, I will make an unreasonably
high starting demand, and you are likely to do the
same. Obviously, if we adopt such a solution, we need
to believe that the starting demands are somehow determined
by actual needs rather than purely as bargaining strategies. But is there any way to determine this?

One way is to have a third party review the opening
bids and judge whether or not they are reasonable. In
organizations such as the Senate, there is no third
party. Alternatively, one could try to constrain the
negotiators to limit their opening bids in some other
way, perhaps by legislative fiat. Such a solution is
even more unlikely. We must simply accept the large
degree of freedom senators have in negotiating with
one another. Indeed, if we take seriously our earlier
discussion of the pressures of Senate life, we will
quickly recognize that senators are under constraints
to make higher opening demands rather than lower ones,
if only to convince their many observers (lobbyists,
constituents, etc.) of their commitment.

Thus, we are faced with the fact that, unless
both parties are equally unreasonable, the less reasonable
opener will gain an advantage under the splitting the
difference solution. In terms of the outcome of the
compromise, this seems unfair, both by standards of
justice and by the criterion of representing broader
public interests. There is therefore a strong prima
facie argument against such even split solutions.

On the other hand, we have some sound reasons
to prefer this option. If we assume that both parties
deserve respect and consideration, and if we acknowledge
that they must work out a solution for themselves,
then we may decide that the only fair way is to split

the difference--or else to toss a coin, and give everything to the winner. Such methods remove the effects of relative power or advantages gained by bargaining tactics or experience. But we have also thereby removed any reasons which explain why one side may in fact <u>deserve</u> or <u>need</u> more than an even split.

In a helpful discussion, Brian Barry has pointed out that a compromise solution can function as a substitute for either bargaining or discussion on the merits. Bargaining is defined here narrowly as discussion which does not consider the merits of the case at hand. Barry argues that we might in fact choose to accept an even split, not only as an alternative to a bargaining conflict, but also as a short-cut to considering the merits. I may believe that you deserve to receive as much as I do, or that the eventual outcome of our discussion will probably lead us to arrive at an even split eventually anyway.[33]

This is indeed the strength of such a solution, and the reason why it is chosen so frequently in the Senate. We must return once more to the structural feature of the egalitarian nature of the organization; power is spread too evenly to expect to win many concessions from a colleague. We saw, for example, that the Senate-House conference on the windfall profits tax bill simply agreed at the beginning of negotiations to split the difference on a two hundred billion dollar bill. But is this a legitimate compromise? We can certainly understand the necessity of passing a bill, and the difficulties the two chambers would experience in arriving at a compromise in any other way. But I believe that, on

---

[33]Barry, <u>Political Argument</u> (London: Routledge and Kegan Paul, 1965), pp. 302-303, fn. I.

balance, this was an inappropriate compromise approach for this sort of legislation. Let me indicate several reasons for this conclusion.

First, the very complexity of the legislation is a strong reason against arriving at such a point at the beginning of the negotiation process. By agreeing to such a figure at the outset, the members constrain themselves to piece the final bill together within this figure. But the total figures of the House and Senate versions were not carefully-thought-out figures. Because of the nature of the debate and amendment process, the final figures were basically the sum of the various pieces of special interest legislation which composed the bills. The one hundred billion dollar difference between the two versions did not reflect a considered view that the bill should be a certain size; instead, the difference reflected primarily the different details which, when added together, resulted in very different totals. Therefore, it seems inappropriate to treat the two figures as if they were representative of the basic positions which each chamber "deserved" to have considered. It is more appropriate to take the two bills apart, and attempt to find compromises on the separate components.

Second, by splitting the difference on the total figure, each chamber in effect asserts that the other side has used appropriately good judgment in passing the bill. But clearly they did not believe this, and the disagreements between the two sides revealed quite different assessments of the needs of the public. The problem was summed up in Senator Dole's complaint that "this bill started out as an energy bill but unfortunately has now degenerated into a revenue bill. I think it is the obligation of this Committee to reverse the

trend."[34] Dole originally opposed the bill, and was
now concerned that Congress was using the legislation
to raise money rather than to conserve and produce
more energy. But his point has a deeper force: once
a bill is viewed primarily in terms of revenue, it
becomes amenable to purely numerical negotiation, and
the most obvious way to settle such disputes is to
split the difference. This is the danger of beginning
with such a decision, since the substantive issues
of the bill (issues about which each chamber felt very
strongly for reasons it considered valid) are then
forced to "get in line" behind the rather arbitrary
dollar figure.

Third, the fact that the bill affects so many
people in such important ways mitigates against adopting
an even split, at least at the outset. There is no
guarantee that the different interests will balance
off in such a way that the actual needs of different
groups will be met within the final dollar figure. But
by arriving at the final figure as the first step,
Congress forces itself to make such concessions. If
the dollar figure were dictated by some clearer constraint
(such as the budget or the immediate availability of
funds), then perhaps we would be more inclined to accept
this "cart before the horse" strategy. But to recognize
the degree of arbitrariness in the totals is to be
highly skeptical about the legitimacy of this compromise
strategy.

Finally, such an even split does not give equal
amounts to each side; rather, each side is called upon
to make equal concessions. Thus, under the guise of
applying a principle of equal treatment, what occurs

[34]House-Senate Conference on HR3919, December 19, 1979.

is in fact extremely unequal. For instance, we may be concerned that different groups receive resources of equal value; in the windfall profits tax bill, we might want to insist that persons in each region receive comparable tax revenues. Or, we may want to distribute resources in terms of need; a person needing heating oil in the north should therefore receive more resources than someone planning to use the oil for recreational purposes. Consideration of the primacy of the resources, coupled with a strong commitment to need as the crucial criterion for distribution, lead us again to question a compromise which treats concessions as the basis of equality.

Consider the way the Senate Finance Committee arrived at its degree day formula on the same bill. We saw that the even split solution was not adopted here; instead, long wrangling occurred over the appropriate amount of money to give social security recipients in different states, and what percentage of this figure should be determined by the heating bills of each state. Is it a fair compromise if all persons receive the same amount of money, regardless of region? It might seem that this is the democratic way to achieve equality, but even the southern senators did not push such a proposal very strongly. How, then, might we look at the final formula and decide whether it was a good compromise? In particular, how much weight should be given to how much each side has actually conceded from its original demands?

I would suggest, once again, that in the case of a bill which so directly affects personal well-being, the central criterion should be how fairly the neediest groups are being treated, rather than how far the representatives of each side have conceded. It is true that, without any concessions, one would not have a compromise; indeed, one would not have a bill. But the fairness of the legislation must be judged primarily by weighing the benefits and costs to different groups, in light of their ability to forego benefits or to bear costs. Particular consideration was finally given to those in greatest need, although not as much as many northern senators would have liked.

We must then ask whether the compromise could ever be seen as legitimate by the northerners, unless it gave poorer persons virtually all of the available aid. Here, we must allow room in our evaluation for the obvious political realities. The northern sponsors were aware that, if the bill gave too much obvious preference to the colder states, the southern members would either filibuster or block the bill entirely. Such opposition would be costly to the south, due to the President's threat to withdraw decontrol of gasoline prices. But there was a perceived limit to the south's tolerance. As a result, the process of arriving at a compromise formula had to assume that the neediest (from the standpoint of the northern senators) would not receive as much as they "really deserved or needed." We might then wonder whether such a compromise could ever be judged as fair.

I think it is evident that, if our standards of judgment are so stringent that we demand a purely "Rawlsian" outcome in all such cases, then we will simply be disgusted with the outcome of every legislative fight. A certain amount of judgment and finesse is required to determine how much can be given away, and how much retained, in such a complex compromise. Because attention was given here to the different heating (and cooling) needs of the regions, and because the final formula clearly met the moral minimum required by the poorest users in the colder states, this particular compromise outcome seems to be both the best possible outcome which could have passed the Congress, and one which met the basic standards of justice.

I would not, however, want to equate the "best possible outcome" with an outcome meeting "the basic standards of justice" in all cases. We might be confronted with situations where all outcomes seem blatantly unfair; although politicians often remind us that "life is unfair," the observer need not be satisfied with every such compromise. It is to this problem that we now turn: can we ever say that a compromise between two evils is an illegitimate compromise in the world of politics? When we choose the lesser evil, are we always doing something good?

(2) Compromise between two evils

From our earlier discussion, we recognize that, however frustrating and unfortunate it may be, politicians must sometimes choose between two evils, and that such choices are not therefore illegitimate by definition. If we insist that the representative attend primarily to consequences for others, then we must allow room for decisions made between relative degrees of harm and cost. To have more regard generally for others' interests than for one's own moral purity is to be willing to choose a lesser evil.

Our typical case here might be the one involving the liberal Senator voting on the food stamps bill. As he saw the situation, he had only two alternatives: vote for the compromise proposal, which would cut benefits to the poor; or vote against the proposal, which would end the program. If his assessment was correct, did he make the correct choice in voting for the bill? I believe he did, primarily because he was convinced that sufficient aid would remain in the bill to benefit a large number of persons. But such a conclusion does not commit us to approve of all such compromises. Let me suggest several conditions which must be met in order to approve of such decisions.

First, the decision must be made only after attempts to find a more integrative solution have been exhausted. If we are called upon to choose between two evils, we should be able to point to efforts to redefine the situation. In our case, time factors were significant; if the conference committee did not act quickly, benefits would be affected by default. Although we can blame politicians for allowing such last minute crises to develop, once they have developed we may have to accept the decision to choose the lesser evil.

Second, the compromise proposal must be one which represents an actual improvement in the situation compared with what will occur if no bill is passed. In other words, we cannot compare purely "symbolic" effects here; we may find ourselves convinced that the world actually will be better if no bill is passed.[35] I believe it is to this possibility that Joseph Tussman was referring in his attack on the role of compromise in American politics. Let me quote him at length, because he raises the major attack on such compromises:

> The case for compromise is that it is better than warfare and that it holds a group to-gether. No one gets everything he wants but everyone gets something and, getting something, is content to go along. This is, after all,

---

[35]I am not suggesting that symbols are unimportant. But we must be able to identify their impact in such cases, if we are to use them as justifications for our action.

what the bargaining transaction involves; each gives up something and each gets something. But how does cohesiveness thus purchased leave the external problem? Has the bargain solved it? The answer, unfortunately, is that it has not. The result of the pulling and hauling, the gains and the concessions, is all too often the elimination of just those elements of clarity, simplicity, imagination, and daring which are needed. We never describe an improvement in a plan as a compromise. Nor is a compromise the 'best that is possible.' Everyone involved thinks that it is worse than something else, and most are probably right. The only consolation is that it could be worse; it is a lesser evil as it is also a lesser good. But, as Pascal pointed out, if the lesser evil is a kind of good it is also true that a lesser good is a kind of evil.[36]

Since such compromises are evils (at least from the standpoint of each party to the decision), it is necessary to justify them by comparison to the alternative evil. How certain are we that the alternative really is the greater evil? Is there a distinction between short term and long term evils? Perhaps the actual effects of not passing a bill will create a climate of opinion which will lead eventually to the passage of better legislation.

In another example we have already discussed, a moderate Senator who favored less restrictive abortion legislation was confronted with a compromise bill on federal funding. The two versions of the bill were both extremely restrictive in his opinion; one allowed funding for approximately six hundred cases, the other for twelve hundred. His decision to vote for the more stringent proposal was a statement that there was so little difference between the two versions that his

---

[36]Tussman, Obligation and the Body Politic (N.Y.: Oxford University Press, 1960), pp. 116-117.

goal of making abortions more available would be furthered by passing the more restrictive (and apparently the greater evil) version.

Such occurrences are more common than we might think. After all, politicians deal with issues of pressure and public opinion, and they may think of the possibility of creating more public outcry in favor of their positions by making the situation worse. Such temptations are always present when we are confronted with two apparently evil alternatives. Thus, to choose the greater evil by refusing to accept the lesser evil compromise, the actor must see an actual benefit in the long run. Our representatives cannot be allowed the luxury of purely symbolic votes against such compromises. Such voting may be difficult and uncomfortable, but that is what they have been elected to do.

This leads to a third observation. The degree and type of predictable harm caused to persons by the greater evil is a crucial factor. Indeed, this was the major distinguishing feature between the two cases we have been considering. In the food stamps case, the Senator believed that there were many people who needed the benefits, who would be deprived of them immediately if the lesser evil compromise were not passed, and who would then have no other alternative. Even if the defeat of the legislation would have led to the eventual passage of a stronger bill, the immediate suffering to so many people outweighed the possible longer term benefits. But, in our abortion case, the difference between six hundred and twelve hundred persons being able to receive federal funding was seen as too small. The fact that six hundred additional women would not receive the funding seemed less significant, perhaps because they might be able to receive abortions without

the aid, or because the number was so small compared
with the number of abortions already prohibited, or
because the Senator was a man.

We cannot set clear cut-off points concerning
how many persons must be harmed in what ways, or how
direct the harm must be, or how likely the harm is
to follow from the greater evil. But these questions
must be weighed in such a decision. I am uncomfortable
with the decision made by our Senator in the abortion
case, partly because I disagree with his political
assessment that any less restrictive abortion policy
would result, and also because I believe that the decision
to deprive six hundred women of the funding causes
sufficient immediate harm to mitigate against the rejection
of the lesser evil compromise.[37]

This suggests a fourth point. One might refuse
to compromise if a basic right is being denied, as
we discussed earlier in this chapter. But does this
mean that, if there is a right to federal funding for
abortions, then one should vote against any compromise
which would deprive any woman of that right? If our
earlier point about genocide is taken as the appropriate
analogy here, then the Senator did indeed act correctly
(from his standpoint) in adopting an "all-or-nothing"
strategy.

But the analogy is not a good one, for two closely
related reasons. First, the genocide example takes
its force from the assumption that our society does
not presently commit genocide. Thus, to adopt a watered-
down genocidal policy would be to alter radically our

[37]The discussion assumes agreement with the Senator's
underlying position on abortion, of course. The analysis
could proceed equally well by considering a senator
on the opposite side of this question.

perception of American society and American justice. But abortions are performed here, and federal funding is denied in certain cases. The debate is thus in the grey area of how much funding, under what conditions, who should pay for them, etc. We do not ask similar questions about genocide. As a result, the abortion issue calls for a radically different approach, and it is subsequently harder to justify a total refusal to compromise.

In addition, the analogy breaks down because of the nature of the right under consideration. I would suggest that genocide is perceived as an absolute evil in a very "underivative" manner. To kill an entire group of persons because of their membership in that group is seen as a clear violation of a number of basic values widely shared by our society. It is harder (at least for some of us) to see the right to federal funding in as direct a manner. The reasoning in favor of such a right must begin with a claim about the status of the fetus and rights of privacy and control of the woman, and move to a set of assertions about both equal treatment and the consequences of not providing federal funding. One cannot justify an absolute refusal to compromise as easily when the right under question is more distant and more debatable in the society.[38]

Another way to make this point is to ask ourselves the following question: Are we willing to live in a society which accepts either the lesser or the greater evil? I think this is the force of the genocide example; persons in our society seldom speak about committing a little bit of genocide, or about degrees of harm perpetrated by genocidal policies. But many do speak about degrees in the case of restricting federal funding for abortions. If we are confronted with policies which undercut the very basis of moral and social life, then the lesser evil becomes much harder, if not impossible, to choose.[39] Alan Donagan argues this point forcefully when he suggests that, in the case of a community asked to hand over an innocent member to an enemy in order to preserve itself, common morality rejects the choice of the apparently lesser evil:

---

[38]Of course, if one begins with the view that the fetus' personhood and consequent rights are precisely as self-evident, and as Constitutionally protected, as those of any adult human being, then the distinction drawn in the text between abortion and genocide may be unsupportable.

My own position is that the consequentialist argument is perhaps the most important one here. It is the virtually certain knowledge that many young, poor women will die from illegal abortions that makes the denial of federal funding so unfair. If these consequences were less chilling or less certain, I am not sure I would support the use of federal funds to support a practice which so many Americans find so morally abhorrent.

[39]I would not suggest that the abortion issue be decided simply by polling citizens to decide whether they considered it to be tantamount to genocide. But I do believe that the sort of disagreement existing in this society on the abortion issue (and which does not exist on the genocide issue) reflects a basic difference between the two questions. Of course, I recognize that others could argue that the perception of a difference simply reflects moral blindness.

> Common morality is outraged by the conse-
> quentialist position that, as long as human
> beings can remain alive, the lesser of two
> evils is always to be chosen. Its defenders
> maintain, on the contrary, that there are
> minimum conditions for a life worthy of a
> human being, and that nobody may purchase
> anything--not even the lives of a whole com-
> munity--by sacrificing those conditions. A
> community that surrenders its members at
> the whims of tyrants ceases to be anything
> properly called by that name; and individuals
> willing to accept benefits at the price of
> crimes committed upon other individuals degrade
> their humanity. Common morality allows a
> certain room for compliance with tyrannical
> external force, when resistance has become
> impossible; but there is a line that must
> be drawn beyond which compliance is excluded...[40]

Such choices are thankfully rare in American politics. If
they do occur, we should not insist that our representatives
choose the lesser evil simply to prove to us (or to
themselves) that they are appropriately pragmatic or
tough. But neither should we want them to use such
arguments in cases where the lesser evil really is
the lesser one, where no such fundamental rights or
horrors are involved, or where the resulting human
suffering of the greater evil is both real and direct.

(3) Trading-off for future benefits

Finally, we briefly consider another related form
of compromise. How can we determine whether a compromise
made for the sake of some future benefit is justified? The
sheer variety of future benefits again makes it impossible
to give a simple answer.

The most obvious point is that one must gain more
than is lost. Such a statement is less banal than it

---

[40]Donagan, The Theory of Morality (University of Chicago
Press, 1977), p. 183.

appears, if it forces us to consider who the "one" is. If the politician is both the judge and the recipient of the gains and losses, then certain factors will be considered very strongly. How much should senators sacrifice for the sake of re-election, for example? Quite a bit, they would reply; after all, how will they be able to do all the wonderful things they want to do in office if they are defeated? There may be some truth here, but it does lead to an important condition for such compromises. An elected official should be able to see and describe those particular goods which only she is able to bring to fruition, and those goods must be directly related to the constituents' basic interests. Otherwise, such reasoning opens the door to any compromise required to win re-election.

Perhaps the only recent example which might meet this criterion occurred in the case of Senator Fulbright of Arkansas, whose opposition to civil rights legislation was justified by his need to win re-election to continue in his role as Chairman of the Senate Foreign Relations Committee. If we believe that he personally favored civil rights legislation, if we recognize his pivotal role in countering the escalation of the Vietnam War, and if we agree that his support for civil rights legislation might have cost him the election, then we might consider approving of such a decision.

Note, however, that such a case forces us to consider the range of interests represented by this Senator. Opposition to the interests of black Americans might be justified by appealing to the interests of "the American people" in avoiding a hopeless and immoral war, or to the interests of the Vietnamese people. In either case, our first criterion may lead in the direction of compromising support for civil rights legislation.[41] But such situations are rare indeed, and the arguments are extremely hard to make. We must remind ourselves that the benefits to be gained must be as broadly based as possible. It is one thing to compromise on a bill to guarantee passage of a clean air bill; it is quite another to compromise to guarantee the funding for a new airport in one's state.

Consider our example of Senator Tsongas' support for a portion of a conservation bill. The amendment (offered by the Chairman, a southern Democrat) would directly help the southern state, and Tsongas had reason to object. Yet he agreed to support it, and explicitly demanded concessions for his interests in environmental matters. In this sort of situation, the willingness to vote for a "bad" amendment is traded off against the concern for environmental issues. In Tsongas' view, the two issues were significantly different. Of course, from the viewpoint of the environmentalist, environmental issues are not special interests at all, but simply "public interest" concerns. If a case can be made for this view, then Tsongas was trying to trade off some relatively minor evils for the sake of some eventual gains in a broader policy area.

It is never easy to make such determinations, and one person's special interest is another's public interest. But there are some general criteria upon which we may be able to agree, and the key question

---

[41]It is difficult to assess this case today, partly because Fulbright's support was not finally needed to pass the major civil rights bills. In addition, because so many young blacks died in Vietnam, the two sets of interests seem to overlap rather than conflict.

remains the comparison we noted earlier between the
narrower and broader interests being traded.

Conclusions

We have suggested several criteria for evaluating
the appropriateness of political compromise, and have
seen how they may be applied in specific cases. In
conclusion, let us take a broader perspective on the
issue of the ethical nature of compromise in American
politics.

In chapter 1, we saw that compromise could be
seen as a conflict either between two ideals or between
an ideal and the "real world." Our criteria are similarly
understandable in these two ways. They are ethical
values, but they are also elements of the world as
we confront it. No matter how skeptical a politician
may be of the doctrine of collective goods or the principle
of social justice, she is confronted with persons who
support their demands with such concepts, and she is
likely to use such appeals on occasion herself.

We could respond by trying to eliminate such language
from our political discourse wherever possible. As
I tried to indicate in chapter 6, certain appeals to
principle should be treated in this way. But such an
approach simply will not work in all cases, for some
ethical criteria seem essential in political decision
making. To choose to ignore considerations of social
justice or the collective good is to choose to use
some other value (such as efficiency) in their place.

It is more reasonable to recognize that most of
these ideals are appealed to because of the very nature
of political action. Whether there "really is" a norm
of justice or any collective good, the political world

is charged with deciding about the protection of certain resources which are defined by such terms. Problems of distribution of scarce resources, or of the protection of common ones, cannot be sidestepped, and their ethical dimensions seem to follow us step by step. We demand just distributions not merely because we may gain by doing so, but because the distributional questions seem to raise notions of justice and the collective good by their very nature.[42] We should probably expect our representatives to use such ethical standards, and to struggle with the ambiguities presented by (and present in) such criteria.

But which values or standards "win out"? How do we know which action is in fact the more reasonable, or the more just?   The complexity of the moral conflicts in politics may make us unwilling to impose our own solutions on elected officials.   This situation is reinforced by the fact that one form of power possessed by our representatives is their ability to help define "reality" for us, not merely by voting for certain bills but also by speaking about what the options are. As observers, we must learn to ask, not only why the politician has chosen one evil over another, but also what other (potentially hidden) interests may be at stake in such a choice.[43]

In addition, the criteria I have suggested are equally applicable to situations where the politician has <u>not</u> compromised. Serious regard for consequences

---

[42]For a related point concerning the nature of justice, see Hannah Pitkin, <u>Wittgenstein and Justice.</u>
[43]The field of the sociology of knowledge is perhaps the most helpful training for such questioning. Whether one can take such an approach seriously and avoid a paralyzing cynicism about all human action is a more difficult question.

will lead toward compromise perhaps as often as away from it. Perhaps if we lived in a world of politicians who consistently refused to compromise to secure our interests, we would be less concerned about finding limits to compromise than about finding arguments for it. The criteria already suggested would work equally well in both worlds, however.

This raises the interesting question of whether, in the political world, the expectation to compromise is itself the political principle par excellence. Perhaps politicians are in fact following highest principle when they compromise; this is the force of the quotation by Shaw (quoted on p. 239), and of much of the literature defining politics as the art of compromise. Our examination of life in one American political institution has revealed the centrality of compromise, and the ways in which progress and action depend upon it.

Yet I would resist drawing the conclusion that compromise should be seen as the key principle of political life. Compromise is a tool, a method of conflict resolution, a style of negotiation; to define it as a principle is to mistake the means for the end. In addition, to see compromise as intrinsically principled action is to undercut the call for an explanation. As I have insisted throughout the book, we should not accept the mere definition of an action as a compromise, as if that justified the action. Two questions are always relevant: (1) Was it truly a compromise at all? (2) Was it the right compromise in the situation? The first question asks whether something of value was in fact gained by the decision. The second question asks whether the higher value was protected. However difficult it may be to weigh such values, and however ignorant we often are of the details of the decisions, such questions are important. If we begin by accepting the view that compromises are simply principled actions, then our initiative to demand explanations is destroyed.

In a much broader sense, distrust of political compromise reflects an increasing disenchantment with the pluralistic and pragmatic orientation of American life. Several recent observers have called for a more substantive consensus out of which to confront political problems. Seeing the liberal tradition as bankrupt, they decry a purely interest-group approach to problem solving, and call into question the long-standing reliance upon compromise. Consider the following quotation from Bernard Barber, who sees American history as a series of compromises from the outset:

> With the land settled, the wealth squandered, the self-sufficiency traded away for luxury, and the endless abundance quite abruptly rendered finite, the peculiar compromises between republican ideals and American conditions that have been the genius of American politics have lost their legitimacy. Open spaces, empty jobs, and unmade fortunes are the conditions that made inequality tolerable to the least advantaged in America's compromised republic; with hope gone, the compromise is itself compromised, and inequality becomes a permanent, oppressive, intolerable burden. Diversity and private interest were the necessary conditions of capitalist expansion in America; but now, in the late stages of capitalist development, in which speculation and entrepreneurship are no longer virtues and in which pointless consumption becomes more salient than expanding production, privatism nourishes alienation and despair, feeding only that scourge faction--the dark side of pluralism so dreaded by the founders.[44]

---

[44]Barber, "The Compromised Republic," op. cit., p. 31. For a similar diagnosis, see William M. Sullivan, Reconstructing Public Philosophy (University of California Press, 1982).

Such writers are asking whether our long-standing commitment to political compromise can work in an age of scarcity, radical pluralism, and mass society.

What responses are appropriate following from this study? If we distrust the compromise mentality, with what shall we replace it? Compromise is less necessary when value consensus exists. If the American people are in fact a "people" in any meaningful sense, then the core value may be little more than an often-grudging willingness to put up with people who are different, strange, and often even threatening. If we had more of a true value consensus on specific issues, then compromise might be unnecessary but the country might also be unrecognizable. In spite of one's evaluation of the pluralist process, there is a convincing case to be made for the existence of conflicting interest groups vying for scarce resources. If we examine the struggles over energy policy or food stamps or abortion funding, the absence of agreement on such distributional questions is evident. For better or worse, our politicians will have to compromise in order to arrive at policy decisions at all.

Yet, this answer need not lead to an easy acceptance of the status quo. We can push for more clarification (and perhaps, eventually, for more agreement) concerning the public values upon which such compromises should be built. Our criterion of progressive compromising should lead us in this direction. By introducing considerations of justice, we may find ourselves able on occasion to arrive at compromises which are more than the lowest common denominator of public preferences. By insisting on consideration of broader interests, the opportunities may emerge for creating a broader national policy, rather than settling for a maze of overlapping bills.

We should not expect too much here, however. The society remains extremely diverse, and political decision making will only become more complex. Our national political institutions are unlikely to alter either the temptations or the opportunities for making bad compromises, nor are they moving toward a more ordered set of procedures for making public policy. Because the problems do not stem from evil individuals, we will continue to live with the ambiguities of political compromise, struggling to clarify them when they occur and to improve the connection between the compromises and the ends toward which they are designed.

Yet, we should not treat pluralism as the curse of American society. Diversity has its costs, but also its benefits. The desire to find more common ground upon which to build an American value consensus is often motivated by a distaste for the pluralistic culture which makes compromise so essential. For those of us who prize this diversity, and who no longer expect to find many substantive areas of agreement among different groups, the task is to develop norms to control the compromises which will (and should) remain central to American politics.

We return therefore to the place where we began: namely, the connection between American democracy and compromise. We need not sing hymns of praise to the genius of American politics, but we can recognize that, if anything resembling a democratic form of government is going to govern our pluralistic society, compromise in its many manifestations will continue to be important.[45]

In the midst of a compromising world, it remains noteworthy that the idea of refusing to compromise for reasons of higher principle still strikes a chord in our hearts. However aware we may be of the reasons for, and however resigned we may be to the inevitability of, compromise, most of us still long for a world in which such compromises might not be required. Indeed, examples of principled political action may provide us with models of strength and courage. Persons who "take a stand on principle" stand somewhere, even if it is not where we want them to stand. We want to agree with Burke's observation that "none will barter away the immediate jewel of his soul."[46] This appeal may have little to do with the content of the particular principles or values, or whether we share them. What is not compromised, we seem to want to believe, is personal integrity, the self standing alone against all odds, engaging the elements in all their fury. Our most moving discussions of political action and moral heroism--A Man for All Seasons, The Deputy, Profiles in Courage, All the King's Men, Becket--all praise the person who stands somewhere. Perhaps we are afraid that our political life, so "smirched with compromise, rotted with opportunism, mildewed by expediency" (in

---

[45]Among the most interesting discussions of this point are the following: Joseph Carens, "Compromises in Politics," op. cit.; Carl Cohen, Democracy (University of Georgia Press, 1971); and the works of T. V. Smith, cited above.
This issue is complex and difficult, and I have merely touched upon it in this book. In one sense, however, the entire project rests upon a particular understanding of the nature of American democracy and the positive evaluation of a pluralistic culture.
[46]Burke, Speech on Conciliation with America, p. 95.

Shaw's words), will not provide us with such opportunities for heroism; as a result, we all too eagerly are potential dupes for such claims. Because we possess no objective standard to identify when integrity is truly at stake, our gullibility may let us settle for too little, while our skepticism may make us demand too much.

APPENDIX

The major research for this book was conducted in Washington, D.C., from September 1979 to June 1980. During that period, I was the Aspen Institute Fellow for Ethics and Governance at the Aspen Institute's Washington office. My responsibilities were not defined precisely, except that I had been brought to the city primarily to help a United States Senator who was trying to write a book about political ethics.

After a brief period, it became apparent that the Senator did not have the time to continue his research, and I developed some ideas for conducting a study of my own. The major part of the study design was a series of interviews with members of the Senate and their staff aides. The interviews with the senators themselves will be described first, followed by those with staff. I will then comment briefly on the other aspects of the research.

Interviews with Senators

The goal of the interview study was to understand the range of compromises engaged in by members of the Senate, and to identify the ways in which they viewed the compromise process. I was particularly interested in three questions:

1. What do senators mean by the term "compromise"?
2. Are there limits to the compromise process?
3. How do senators see their roles, especially regarding their obligation to follow the views of their constituents?

These questions constituted the core of the interview. I decided upon a relatively unstructured, open-ended interview for several reasons. I was interested in hearing the ways the members spoke about compromise, so I wanted to let them use their own words and their own examples. Furthermore, the interviews were limited in time, and I wanted to identify the central features of compromise quickly. I also wanted to take advantage of the informality of the setting to increase the likelihood that the members would sit back and think about their responses.

The time factor was frustrating. Interviews were set up for thirty minutes; most lasted between thirty and forty minutes, with three or four being shorter and three being much longer. The research is therefore constrained by the inability to speak in more depth to these persons (although re-interviewing did occur with two members, at their invitation). This limitation comes with the territory; an outsider is fortunate indeed to be granted thirty minutes with these figures. As is the case in much research, one takes what one can get.

I wanted to interview a range of senators to make sure that the sample was fairly representative. I originally had several long conversations with my contact Senator about the nature of compromise, and the sorts of questions I wanted to ask. Together, we identified seven or eight other members who would be expected to vary on their approach to this issue; the interviews were conducted (in the late fall and early winter), after which I presented some of my findings to the Senator. He then asked whether I wanted to interview anyone else; taking a deep breath, I indicated that, if possible, I would like to arrange interviews with another ten members, at which point he asked, "Why only ten?" I quickly rushed into the breach, and said that I would prefer to interview roughly one-third of the members. He agreed, and I drew a sample of an additional twenty-five Senators.

The final sample thus is made up of thirty-four members of the Senate. Seldom is one able to interview one-third of one's population, and issues of representativeness are therefore minimal. However, to make sure that the sample was not skewed, I drew the sample to try to assure a representative distribution along major dimensions which might be expected to affect one's view toward compromise: seniority, political orientation (liberal/moderate/conservative), region, party, and several other related factors. The following tables indicate the distribution of the sample on some of these dimensions, comparing them to the full complement of one hundred Senators:

	1979-1980 Senate	Sample
First Term:		
Yes	47	17
No	53	17
Region:		
North	46	15
South	26	10
West	28	9
Size of State:		
Smallest	20	7
Moderate	60	23
Largest	20	4
Party:		
Republican	47	22
Democratic	53	12
Ideological		
Liberal	35	10
Moderate	36	11
Conservative	29	13

The sample is slightly over-representative of conservatives and Republicans, due partly to the recommendations made by my contact Senator. I was not troubled by this discrepancy, primarily because my own political leanings ran in the opposite direction. (Indeed, in retrospect, it is somewhat reassuring to recognize that the composition of my sample reflects the 1984 Senate even more closely.)[1]

The interviews were all conducted in the offices of the senators, with three exceptions. (Two were conducted in a small room near the Senate chamber, because the members were unable to leave; one was conducted on an informal walk around the Capital grounds.) The offices are plush and relaxing (the interviewer may have to fight off the temptation to get _too_ comfortable, in fact), and provided an appropriate atmosphere for reflection.

However, I wanted to distinguish this interview from the myriad other interviews given to constituents, press or lobbyists in the course of a working day. Several techniques were used here:

(1) No tape recorder was used. This was a difficult decision to make, and one which I often regretted in the course of the analysis. I still believe, however, that the information gained was more honest and rich than it would have been with a tape recorder present. The

------

[1]The ideological stances were determined using ratings of the senators' voting records by major liberal and conservative groups. In several cases of new members, observation of their recent voting records was used as a substitute.

reason is not so much that the recorder itself is so distracting (from other interview experience, I recognized that people usually forget about the recorder after a few minutes); rather, I wanted to establish the context of an "informal chat" between an interested observer and a participant, instead of an atmosphere of testing out what the senator might have to say. I believed (and still do believe) that the absence of a recorder helped to create this environment.

(2) I dressed in an informal manner, wearing a sports jacket, a plain shirt, and either Levis or cotton pants. This decision was not a difficult one, since that is the way I always dressed anyway. But I resisted the temptation to wear a tie or a suit, partly because I wanted to appear more as a "student" than as a "professional", and partly because I was more comfortable dressing in my usual way. To appear in this way as an outsider was important, and it worked to undercut any impression that I was a staff member working for the contact senator. (My dress was commented on only once, by a secretary who looked at me for a moment and asked, in her best non-threatening manner, "Are you going to go in to see the Senator like that?" My response was to indicate that I didn't see any reason not to, and she quickly backed off. Whether other senators experienced surprise, dismay, or relief at the way I was dressed, I can only guess.)

(3) I conducted the interview as informally as possible. My interview style is quite "interactive" normally, and I made no effort to turn this off. I tried to treat the conversation as just that: a <u>conversation</u> between an insider and an outsider. After some initial

probings in several of the interviews, the strategy
seemed to work quite well, as members usually were
able and willing to sit back and reflect on their exper-
iences. Many times during the interviews, when I would
ask for an example or would request some elaboration
of a point, the senator would rock back in the chair,
look up at the ceiling, and start searching for the
right phrase or example out loud. (Once again, the
absence of a tape recorder was an important factor
here, I think.) Comments were heard such as "I don't
really feel good about what I'm about to say, but...,"
"I have to admit that...," and "I guess, to be honest
about it, I'd have to say...."

It is impossible to prove to the reader that the
interviews were honest, relaxed, or genuine. I am not
sure whether they all were, either; I was acutely aware
throughout the interview process that these were persons
who spoke for a living, who were always "on stage,"
and who were not about to jeopardize their political
futures in front of someone they had never met before.
However, I believe that the context of the interviews,
coupled with the fact that a colleague had arranged
the interviews (often with a personal request made
directly to the Senator), maximized the opportunity
for them to experience the interviews as an interlude
from the usual studied and controlled atmosphere of
questions and answers. I can only report that, in most
cases, I felt that they were being as honest and open
as one could expect someone to be with a total stranger.

I took some notes during the interview, jotting
down key phrases and occasional sentences. Immediately
after each interview, I sat down (often in the hallway

outside of the office, or on the bus ride home) and wrote out detailed notes of what was said. In this way, I was able to garner some sentence-long direct quotations from the interviews, as well as summaries of other comments.

The analysis consisted mainly of content analysis examination of the interviews. I read over the notes many times, abstracted themes and categorized responses, compared the categories to those found in the literature in similar studies, and tried to order the data in different ways. Most of the distinctions discussed in the book came out of this analysis and reanalysis process.

Interviews with Staff

Twenty staff members were interviewed, several of them more than once. These interviews were much more informal, and were held in offices, coffee shops, the Senate cafeteria, and on well-manicured lawns. I was not as interested in the representativeness of the staff members as I was in their functioning as informants; as a result, I simply followed the recommendations of either senators or other staff members. As is usually the case, three or four of these persons turned out to be extremely helpful and illuminating, and were re-interviewed repeatedly.

Many of the comments made about the Senatorial interviews also apply here. Time was limited in most cases; the average interview lasted about forty-five minutes, with the shortest about thirty minutes and the longest about two hours. Staff members were particularly helpful in providing insider perceptions of the differences

between Senatorial styles of compromise; the members
themselves were occasionally reticent to say anything
negative about one of their colleagues, and one or
two senators even directed me to their staff as a way
of indirectly helping me get the "inside" story. (This
is a most interesting phenomenon in its own right,
revealing the use of a subordinate as a source of information to a third party.)

The most interesting aspect of the staff interviews
was the willingness of some persons to admit to extremely
negative feelings about their own bosses. The relationship
between senator and staff member is extremely strong,
and staff members are legally treated in many respects
as extensions of the senators themselves. Loyalty is
expected and demanded; a staffer who publically criticizes
his own senator is likely to be looking for a new job. In
some respects, therefore, the interviews provided these
people with a chance to "unload" some of their feelings
and resentments.

A final comment should be made concerning the
confidentiality of both sets of interviews. The assumption
of total anonymity was present in all interviews, and
I underscored that at the beginning of the interviews. Few
senators seemed very interested in this limitation,
and two even objected to it, saying that they preferred
to be cited directly if they said anything. One cost
of such a guarantee, of course, is that one's writing
is studded with references to "a Senator" or "one Senator,"
rather than being able to reveal the "inside dope"
about which members said what. For my purposes, this
was not a serious problem, since I was more interested
in looking at the Senate itself than in providing a

detailed look at the individual members.

Observation

Much of the information gathered for this book came from informal observation of the Senate institution. Many hours were spent attending hearings and markup sessions, watching the Senate floor proceedings, chatting informally with staff members, and just "soaking up" the environment. Overheard phone conversations, waiting room arguments, and hallway discussions all provided invaluable insight into the workings of this organization. I attempted to test out many of the comments made in the interviews by observing the practices of the members.

Such observation is easy to do in most situations in the Senate, if only because there are likely to be so many other observers present. However, this has its costs as well. In particular, it is exceedingly difficult to observe the bargains struck behind closed doors (although, if one is lucky, one may overhear some of them while seated in an interview). The more observers who are present (or allowed to be present), the less spontaneous the interaction among the participants is likely to be. Nevertheless, such informal observation is a crucial component of such research, and it proved extremely useful in sorting out the myriad dimensions of organizational structure and interaction.

Transcripts and Other Literature

American government is a virtual treasure-chest of documentation. The observer can usually gain access to an enormous wealth of written material on any subject. I found three sources particularly helpful in this research.

(1) Transcripts of committee hearings and markup sessions were easily available. Unless one wishes to sit through endless hours of such meetings, transcripts are the best source of the interaction and bargaining which occur in markup sessions. I sat through enough sessions to make sure that the transcripts were accurate reflections of the process; since they are verbatim, typed, and complete, they allowed me to piece together the process of compromise in many instances. It was also interesting to find that, in the many hours I spent reading through these documents, no one else was using them as well.

(2) The Library of Congress Congressional Research Service writes an enormous number of reports and background papers on virtually every topic coming before Congress. In addition, they have studied various aspects of Senate life. I was fortunate to have access to most of these materials through my quasi-insider status; many of these documents were very helpful, both for my own information and for gaining a better understanding of the sort of information the senators and staff aides are provided with on such issues.

(3) Finally, the Library of Congress itself is, of course, a rich resource of books and articles on American politics. Any researcher spending time in Washington should take full advantage of the Library, even if one is not a bibliophile.

A final note may not be out of place. Empirical research is always hard work, and there are moments when one wishes for the quiet of the library stacks. But I found a degree of exhiliration in this research which made me wonder whether I was becoming coopted by the institution. This was not due to the kindness of the senators and staff (although most were exceedingly kind), nor to the ease of access to the information. I think it was due largely to the heady sense one receives by being in close proximity with wielders of enormous power, or at least with persons who are used to being viewed as such. The capacity to retain an outsider's stance, therefore, is in some ways one of the hardest aspects of this research. It was far too easy to be taken for another staff member, and I often had to struggle to maintain a separate identity. Such political institutional settings are seductive, which helps explain both why senators are so desparate to stay in office and why staffers continue to put up with such awful working conditions and demands for deference.

To write about compromise in such a setting is particularly difficult. To question one of the central norms of Senate life is to maintain one's stance as an outsider, for who else would even dare to ask why compromises do occur or whether they should occur? The willingness to appear naive and challenging is a necessary part of such research.

BIBLIOGRAPHY

Anderson, Charles. "The Place of Principles in Policy Analysis." American Political Science Review 73 (September 1979): 711-723.

Anderson, John B. (ed.). Congress and Conscience. Philadelphia: L. P. Lippincott, 1970.

Arendt, Hannah. The Human Condition. University of Chicago Press, 1958.

_____. "Truth and Politics." In her Between Past and Future. N. Y.: Penguin, 1954.

Asbell, Bernard. The Senate Nobody Knows. N.Y.: Doubleday and Co., 1978.

Association of the Bar of the City of New York, Special Committee on Congressional Ethics. Congress and the Public Trust. N.Y.: Atheneum, 1971.

Bailey, Stephen K. Ethics and the Politician. California: Center for the Study of Democratic Institutions, 1960.

Baker, Ross. Friend and Foe in the U. S. Senate. N.Y.: The Free Press, 1980.

Barber, Benjamin R. "The Compromised Republic: Public Purposelessness in America." In Horwitz, Robert H. (ed.), The Moral Foundations of the American Republic.

Barker, Ernest. "Burke and His Bristol Constituency, 1774-1780." In his Essays in Government. N. J.: Oxford University Press, 1945.

Barry, Brian. Political Argument. London: Routledge and Kegan Paul, 1965.

_____. "The Public Interest." In King, J. Charles, and McGilvray, James A. (eds.), Political and Social Philosophy.

Beard, Charles, and Lewis, John. "Representative Government in Evolution." American Political Science Review 26 (April 1932): 223-240 (reprinted in Riemer, Neal [ed.], The Representative).

Beard, Edmund, and Horn, Stephen. Congressional Ethics: The View from the House. Washington: Brookings Institution, 1975.

Bedau, Hugo (ed.). Civil Disobedience: Theory and Practice. Indianopolis: Pegasus, 1969.

Benditt, Theodore M. "Compromising Interests and Principles." In Pennock, J. Roland, and Chapman, John W., Compromise in Ethics, Law, and Politics.

Bentham, Jeremy. The Handbook of Political Fallacies. N.Y.: Harper, 1952 (1788).

Berger, Peter L. Invitation to Sociology. N.Y.: Doubleday and Co., 1963.

_____. The Precarious Vision. N.Y.: Doubleday and Co., 1961.

_____. Pyramids of Sacrifice: Political Ethics and Social Change. N.Y.: Doubleday, 1974.

_____. The Sacred Canopy. N. Y.: Doubleday
    and Co., 1967.
Berki, R. N. "The Distinction Between Moderation and
    Extremism." In Parekh, Bhikhu, and Berki, R. N.
    (eds.), The Morality of Politics.
_____. "Machiavellianism: A Philosophical Defense."
    Ethics 81 (January 1971): 107-127.
Bierman, A. K. "On the Relation Between Politics and
    Morals." Journal of Social Philosophy 3 (April 1972):
    8-11.
Blanshard, Brand. "Morality and Politics." In DeGeorge,
    Richard T. (ed.), Ethics and Society.
Bowie, Norman E. (ed.). Ethical Issues in Government.
    Philadelphia: Temple University Press, 1981.
Brandt, Richard. Ethical Theory. N. J.: Prentice-Hall,
    1959.
_____ (ed.). Social Justice. N. J.: Prentice-
    Hall, 1962.
Braybrooke, David, and Lindblom, C. A Strategy of Decision.
    N.Y.: Free Press of Glencoe, 1963.
Bredvold, Louis I., and Ross, Ralph G. (eds.). The
    Philosophy of Edmund Burke. University of Michigan
    Press, 1977.
Buchanan, James M., and Tullock, Gordon. The Calculus
    of Consent: Logical Foundations of Constitutional
    Democracy. University of Michigan Press, 1962.
Burke, Edmund. Speech on Conciliation with America. N.Y.:
    Charles E. Merrill Co., 1911 (1775).
_____. The Works of the Right Honourable Edmund
    Burke, 4th edition. Boston: Little, Brown, and
    Company, 1871.
Burke, Richard J. "Politics as Rhetoric." Ethics 93
    (October 1982): 45-55.
Calabresi, Guido, and Bobbitt, Philip. Tragic Choices.
    N.Y.: W. W. Norton and Co., 1978.
Carens, Joseph H. "Compromise in Politics." In Pennock,
    J. Roland, and Chapman, John W., Compromise in
    Ethics, Law, and Politics.
Cohen, Carl. Democracy. University of Georgia Press,
    1971.
Cohen, Marshall; Nagel, T.; and Scanlon, T. (eds.). War
    and Moral Responsibility. Princeton University
    Press, 1974.
Commission on the Operation of the Senate. Senators:
    Offices, Ethics, and Pressures. Washington: Government
    Printing Office, 1977.
Committee on Rules and Administration, U. S. Senate.
    Standing Rules for Conducting Business in the
    United States Senate. Washington: Government Printing
    Office, 1979.

Congresional Quarterly. Guide to Congress, 2nd edition.
   Washington: Congressional Quarterly, 1976.
Connolly, William. Appearance and Reality in Politics.
   Cambridge University Press, 1981.
Cranston, Maurice. Politics and Ethics. London: Weidenfeld
   and Nicolson, 1972.
Cuddihy, John Murray. No Offense: Civil Religion and
   Protestant Taste. N.Y.: The Seabury Pres, 1978.
Davidson, Roger. The Role of the Congressman. N. Y.: Pegasus
   Press, 1969.
DeGeorge, Richard T. (ed.). Ethics and Society. N.Y.: Anchor
   Books, 1966.
Dewar, Helen. "Liberals Lose Four Skirmishes in Budget
   War." The Washington Post, May 1, 1980.
Dexter, Lewis. "The Representative and His District."
   Human Organization 16 (Spring 1957): 2-13.
_____. The Sociology and Politics of Congress.
   Chicago: Rand McNally and Co., 1969.
Donagan, Alan. The Theory of Morality. University of
   Chicago Press, 1977.
Douglas, Paul. Ethics in Government. Harvard University
   Press, 1952.
_____. "Improvement of Ethical Standards in
   the Federal Government: Problems and Proposals."
   The Annals of the American Academy of Political
   and Social Science 280 (March 1952): 149-157.
Druckman, Daniel (ed.). Negotiations: Social-Psychological
   Perspectives. California: Sage Publications, 1977.
Dworkin, Ronald. "Liberalism." In Hampshire, Stuart
   (ed.), Public and Private Morality.
Edelman, Murray. Political Language. N.Y.: Academic
   Press, 1977.
_____. The Symbolic Uses of Politics. University
   of Illinois Press, 1964.
Edwards, George C. III, and Sharkansky, Ira. The Policy
   Predicament. San Francisco: W. H. Freeman and
   Co., 1978.
Ellsberg, Daniel. "The Theory and Practice of Blackmail."
   Rand Corporation Paper P-3883 (July 1968 [1959]).
Etzioni, Amitai. The Active Society. N.Y.: The Free
   Press, 1968.
Eulau, Heinz. "Changing Views of Representation." In
   Pool, Ithiel de Sola (ed.), Contemporary Political
   Science.
Eulau, Heinz; Wahlke, J.C.; Buchanan, W.; and Ferguson, L.
   "The Role of the Representative: Some Empirical
   Observations on the Theory of Edmund Burke." American
   Political Science Review 53 (September 1959): 742-756.
Fishkin, James. "Moral Principles and Public Policy."
   Daedalus 108 (Fall 1979): 55-67.

Flathman, Richard. The Public Interest: An Essay Concerning the Normative Discourse of Politics. N.Y.: John Wiley and Sons, 1966.

Flynn, James R. "The Realm of the Moral." American Philosophical Quarterly 13 (October 1976): 273-286.

Foley, Michael. The New Senate: Liberal Influences on a Conservative Institution, 1959-1972. Yale University Press, 1980.

Foot, Phillipa. "When is a Principle a Moral Principle?" A Symposium. The Aristotelian Society, Supplementary Volume 28 (1954): 95-110.

Fox, Harrison W. Jr., and Hammond, Susan Webb. Congressional Staffs: The Invisible Force in American Lawmaking. N.Y.: Free Press, 1977.

Franck, Thomas M., and Weisband, Edward. "Congress and the Concept of Ethical Autonomy." In Jones, Donald G. (ed.), Private and Public Ethics.

French, Peter. Ethics in Government. N. J.: Prentice-Hall, 1983.

Friedrich, Carl J. (ed.). The Public Interest. N.Y.: Atherton Press, 1962.

Froman, Lewis A. Jr., and Cohen, Michael D. "Compromise and Logrolling: Comparing the Efficiency of Two Bargaining Processes." Behavioral Science 15 (1970): 180-183.

Gauthier, David. Practical Reasoning. Oxford University Press, 1963.

Gerth, H. H., and Mills, C. Wright (eds.), From Max Weber. N. Y.: Oxford University Press, 1946.

Getz, Robert S. Congressional Ethics: The Conflict of Interest Issue. Princeton: D. Van Nostrand Co., 1966.

Gilbert, Joseph. "Features of Morality." The Personalist 51 (Autumn 1970): 470-476.

Golding, Martin P. "The Nature of Compromise: A Preliminary Inquiry." In Pennock, J. Roland, and Chapman, John W., Compromise in Ethics, Law, and Politics.

Goldman, Alan H. The Moral Foundations of Professional Ethics. N. J.: Rowman and Littlefield, 1980.

Goodin, Robert E. Political Theory and Public Policy. University of Chicago Press, 1982.

Gordis, Robert. Politics and Ethics. California: Center for the Study of Democratic Institutions, 1961.

Graham, George A. Morality in American Politics. N.Y.: Random House, 1952.

Hampshire, Stuart (ed.). Public and Private Morality. Cambridge University Press, 1978.

Hare, R. M. Freedom and Reason. London: Oxford University
     Press, 1972 (1963).
_____. "Principles." Proceedings of The Aristotelian
     Society 73 (1972-1973): 1-18.
Harrison, Jonathon. "When is a Principle a Moral Principle?"
     A Symposium. The Aristotelian Society, Supplementary
     Volume 28 (1954): 111-134.
Hatfield, Mark. Between a Rock and a Hard Place. Waco:
     Word Books, 1976.
Haughey, John C. (ed.). Personal Values in Public Policy.
     N. Y.: Paulist Press, 1979.
Haynes, George H. The Senate of the United States: Its
     History and Practice. Boston: Houghton Mifflin
     Co., 1938.
Herberg, Will. Protestant, Catholic, Jew. N.Y.: Anchor
     Books, 1960.
Herz, John H. Political Realism and Political Idealism: A
     Study in Theories and Realities. University of
     Chicago Press, 1951.
Horn, Stephen. Unused Power: The Work of the Senate
     Committee on Appropriations. Washington: The Brookings
     Institution, 1970.
Horwitz, Robert H. (ed.). The Moral Foundations of
     the American Republic, 2nd edition. University
     of Virginia Press, 1979.
James, Edward W. "A Reasoned Ethical Incoherence?"
     Ethics 89 (April 1979): 240-253.
_____. "Working in and Working to Principles."
     Ethics 83 (October 1972): 51-57.
Jones, Donald (ed.). Private and Public Ethics. N. Y.: Edwin
     Mellen Press, 1978.
Jones, Rochelle, and Woll, Peter. The Private World
     of Congress. N.Y.: The Free Press, 1979.
Kennedy, John F. Profiles in Courage. N.Y.: Harper
     and Row, 1964 (1955).
King, J. Charles, and Mcgilvray, James A. (eds.). Political
     and Social Philosophy. N.Y.: McGraw-Hill, 1973
     (1964).
Kirkpatrick, Samuel A., and Pettit, Lawrence K. Legislative
     Role Structures, Power Bases and Behavior Patterns: An
     Empirical Examination of the U. S. Senate. Legislative
     Research Series Monograph Number 6, Bureau of
     Government Research, University of Oklahoma, 1973.
Kuflik, Arthur. "Morality and Compromise." In Pennock,
     J. Roland, and Chapman, John W. (eds.), Compromise
     in Ethics, Law, and Politics.
Laslett, Peter (ed.). Philosophy, Politics, and Society.
     Oxford: Basil Blackwell, 1956.
Lerner, Max. "Introduction" to Machiavelli, Niccolo,
     The Prince and The Discourses.

Leys, Wayne. Ethics for Policy Decisions: The Art of Asking Deliberative Questions. N.Y.: Greenwood Press, 1968 (1952).

Lieber, Francis. Manual of Political Ethics, 2nd edition, revised. Philadelphia: J. B. Lippincott and Co., 1875.

Lindblom, Charles. The Policy-Making Process. N.J.: Prentice-Hall, 1968.

Lippmann, Walter. A Preface to Politics. University of Michigan Press, 1962 (1914).

Little, David. "Duties of Station vs. Duties of Conscience: Are there Two Moralities?" In Jones, Donald G. (ed.), Private and Public Ethics.

Long, Edward Leroy Jr. Conscience and Compromise: An Approach to Protestant Casuistry. Philadelphia: Westminster Press, 1954.

_____. "The Social Roles of the Moral Self." In Jones, Donald G. (ed.), Private and Public Ethics.

Machiavelli, Niccolo. The Prince and The Discourses. N.Y.: Modern Library, 1950 (1510-1520).

MacIver, R. M. (ed.). Integrity and Compromise. New York: Harper and Brothers, 1957.

Maguire, Daniel C. The Moral Choice. Garden City: Doubleday and Co., 1978.

Matthews, Donald. U. S. Senators and Their World. University of North Carolina Press, 1960.

McCarthy, Eugene. "Political Reflections on the American Character." Christianity and Crisis (May 27, 1963): 91-94.

McDonald, Lee C. "Three Forms of Political Ethics." The Western Political Quarterly 31 (March 1978): 7-18.

Miller, David. Social Justice. Oxford: Clarendon Press, 1976.

Miller, William Lee. Piety Along the Potomac: Notes on Politics and Morals in the Fifties. Boston: Houghton Mifflin Co., 1964.

_____. "Politics and Ethics." In Hastings Center Report--Special Supplement: The Teaching of Ethics (December 1977): 13-14.

Mills, C. Wright. "Situated Actions and Vocabularies of Motive." American Sociological Review 5 (December, 1940): 904-913.

Morison, Elting E. (ed.). The American Style. New York: Harper and Brothers, 1958.

Morley, John. On Compromise. London: Chapman and Hall, 1874.

Mowat, R. B. Public and Private Morality. Great Britain: Arrowsmith, 1933.

Muehl, William. Politics for Christians. N.Y.: Association
    Press, 1956.
Musgrave, Richard A., and Musgrave, Peggy B. Public
    Finance in Theory and Practice, 3rd edition. N.Y.:
    McGraw-Hill, 1980.
Nagel, Thomas. "War and Massacre." In Cohen, Marshall;
    Nagel, T.; and Scanlon, T. (eds.), War and Moral
    Responsibility.
Nichols, R. L., and White, D. M. "Politics Proper: On
    Action and Prudence." Ethics 89 (July 1979): 372-384.
Niebuhr, Reinhold. Moral Man and Immoral Society. N. Y.:
    Charles Scribner's Sons, 1932.
Nozick, Robert. Anarchy, State, and Utopia. N.Y.: Basic
    Books, 1974.
Orwell, George. "Politics and the English Language."
    In his A Collection of Essays by George Orwell. N.Y.:
    Harcourt, Brace, Jovanovich, 1946.
Parekh, Bhikhu, and Berki, R. N. (eds.). The Morality
    of Politics. London: George Allen and Unwin, 1972.
Pennock, J. Roland, and Chapman, John W. (eds.). Compromise
    in Ethics, Law, and Politics. New York University
    Press, 1979.
_____. Represen-
    tation. N. Y.: Atherton Press, 1968.
Phillips, D. Z. "Do Moral Considerations Override Others?"
    Philosophical Quarterly 29 (July 1979): 247-254.
Pitkin, Hanna. The Concept of Representation. University
    of California Press, 1967.
_____ (ed.). Representation. N.Y.: Atherton
    Press, 1969.
_____. Wittgenstein and Justice. University
    of California Press, 1972.
Pool, Ithiel de Sola (ed.). Contemporary Political
    Science. N.Y.: McGraw-Hill, 1967.
Preston, Nathaniel Stone (ed.). The Senate Institution.
    N.Y.: Van Nostrand Reinhold Co., 1969.
Pruitt, Dean G. Negotiation Behavior. N.Y.: Academic
    Press, 1981.
Pruitt, Dean G., and Lewis, Steven A. "The Psychology
    of Integrative Bargaining." In Druckman, Daniel
    (ed.), Negotiations: Social-Psychological Perspectives.
Ramsey, Paul. Basic Christian Ethics. N. Y.: Charles
    Scribner's Sons, 1950.
Rawls, John. "The Justification of Civil Disobedience."
    In Bedau, Hugo (ed.), Civil Disobedience: Theory
    and Practice.
_____. A Theory of Justice. Harvard University
    Press, 1971.
Redman, Eric. The Dance of Legislation. N.Y.: Simon
    and Schuster, 1973.

Riemer, Neil (ed.). The Representative. Boston: D.C. Heath
    and Co., 1967.
Rienow, Robert, and Rienow, Leona Train. Of Snuff,
    Sin and the Senate. Chicago: Follett Publishing
    Co., 1965.
Ripley, Randall. Power in the Senate. N.Y.: St. Martin's
    Press, 1969.
Rostow, W. W. "The National Style." In Morison, Elting
    E. (ed.), The American Style.
Sartre, Jean-Paul. Being and Nothingness (translated
    by Hazel Barnes). N.Y.: Simon and Schuster, 1966
    (1943).
Schelling, Thomas C. The Strategy of Conflict. N.Y.: Oxford
    University Press, 1963.
Schubert, Glendon. The Public Interest: A Critique
    of the Theory of a Political Concept. Illinois: Free
    Press of Glencoe, 1960.
Shienbaum, Kim Ezra. "Ideology vs. Rhetoric in American
    Politics." The Midwest Quarterly 21 (Autumn 1979): 21-
    32.
Simon, Herbert. Administrative Behavior, 2nd edition. N.Y.:
    The Free Press, 1957.
Simon, John; Powers, Charles; and Gunnemann, Jon. The
    Ethical Investor. Yale University Press, 1972.
Singer, Peter. Democracy and Disobedience. Oxford: Clarendon
    Press, 1973.
Smith, T. V. The Ethics of Compromise and the Art of
    Containment. Boston: Starr King Press, 1956.
_____. The Promise of American Politics, 2nd
    edition. University of Chicago Press, 1936.
Solomon, William David. "Moral Reasons." American Philoso-
    phical Quarterly 12 (October 1975): 331-339.
Strauss, Anselm. Negotiations. San Francisco: Jossey-Bass,
    1978.
Subcommittee of the Committee on Labor and Public Welfare,
    United States Senate. Ethical Standards in Government.
    Washington: Government Printing Office, 1951.
Sullivan, William M. Reconstructing Public Philosophy.
    University of California Press, 1982.
Thielicke, Helmut. Theological Ethics (edited by William
    H. Lazareth). London: Adam and Charles Black,
    1968 (1951).
Thompson, Dennis. "Moral Responsibility of Public Of-
    ficials: The Problem of Many Hands." American
    Political Science Review 74 (December 1980): 905-916.
Thompson, Kenneth. Christian Ethics and the Dilemmas
    of Foreign Policy. Duke University Press, 1959.
_____. The Moral Issue in Statecraft. Louisiana
    State University Press, 1966.

Tullock, Gordon. Toward a Mathematics of Politics. University of Michigan Press, 1967.
Tussman, Joseph. Obligation and the Body Politic. N.Y.: Oxford University Press, 1960.
U. S. Commission on the Operation of the Senate. Toward a Modern Senate. Washington: Government Printing Office, 1976.
Walzer, Michael. Obligations. N. Y.: Simon and Schuster, 1971.
_____. "Political Action: The Problem of Dirty Hands." Philosophy and Public Affairs (Winter 1973) (reprinted in Donald Jones [ed.], Private and Public Ethics).
Weber, Max. "Politics as a Vocation." In Gerth, H. H., and Mills, C. Wright (eds.), From Max Weber.
Weldon, T. D. "Political Principles." In Laslett, Peter (ed.), Philosophy, Politics, and Society.
White, William S. Citadel: The Story of the U. S. Senate. N.Y.: Harper and Brothers, 1956.
Wildavsky, Aaron. The Politics of the Budgetary Process. Boston: Little, Brown and Co., 1964.
Williams, Bernard. "Politics and Moral Character." In Hampshire, Stuart (ed.), Public and Private Morality.
Wills, Garry. The Confessions of a Conservative. N. Y.: Doubleday and Co., 1979.
Wolin, Sheldon. Politics and Vision. Boston: Little, Brown and Co., 1960.

INDEX